Governing the Excluded

Rural Livelihoods Beyond Coca in Colombia's Peace Laboratory

ALEX DIAMOND

The University of Chicago Press
Chicago and London

The University of Chicago Press, Chicago 60637
The University of Chicago Press, Ltd., London
© 2026 by The University of Chicago
Published 2026
Printed in the United States of America

35 34 33 32 31 30 29 28 27 26   1 2 3 4 5

ISBN-13: 978-0-226-84618-7 (cloth)
ISBN-13: 978-0-226-84620-0 (paper)
ISBN-13: 978-0-226-84619-4 (ebook)
DOI: https://doi.org/10.7208/chicago/9780226846194.001.0001

Library of Congress Cataloging-in-Publication Data

Names: Diamond, Alex (Sociologist) author
Title: Governing the excluded : rural livelihoods beyond coca in Colombia's peace laboratory / Alex Diamond.
Other titles: Rural livelihoods beyond coca in Colombia's peace laboratory
    Description: Chicago ; London : The University of Chicago Press, 2026. |
    Includes bibliographical references and index.
Identifiers: LCCN 2025025209 | ISBN 9780226846187 cloth | ISBN 9780226846200
    paperback | ISBN 9780226846194 ebook
Subjects: LCSH: Fuerzas Armadas Revolucionarias de Colombia | Rural poor—
    Colombia—Briceño (Antioquia)—Social conditions | Rural poor—Colombia—
    Briceño (Antioquia) | Rural conditions | Coca industry—Colombia—Briceño
    (Antioquia) | Agriculture and state—Colombia | Social change—Colombia—
    Briceño (Antioquia) | Reconciliation—Colombia | Briceño (Antioquia, Colombia)—
    Economic conditions—21st century | Colombia—Politics and government—
    21st century
Classification: LCC HC200.P6 D53 2026 | DDC 362.509861/26—dc23/eng/20250805
LC record available at https://lccn.loc.gov/2025025209

♾ This paper meets the requirements of ANSI/NISO Z39.48-1992
(Permanence of Paper).

Authorized Representative for EU General Product Safety Regulation (GPSR)
queries: **Easy Access System Europe**—Mustamäe tee 50, 10621 Tallinn, Estonia,
gpsr.requests@easproject.com
Any other queries: https://press.uchicago.edu/press/contact.html

Contents

Introduction

The four-inch cylindrical shell casing is covered with dirt and cool to the touch, a reminder of an era of violence that Eduardo hopes his northern Colombian village of Briceño has left behind for good. "That was in 2013," he tells me as he takes the casing back from my outstretched hand, "when the army helicopters came to support the paramilitaries and drive out the guerrillas." It's just past dawn on Eduardo's farm. Sunlight creeps down the verdant valley walls and the chatter of birdsong punctuates his speech. On such a tranquil morning, it's hard to imagine the chaotic scenes he describes: paramilitaries running helter-skelter through bursts of fire that clip the leaves of the plantain trees; a hailstorm of shells from the army helicopters that pepper the guerrilla positions below; and Eduardo hiding with his wife and three kids, praying that no stray bullets pierce the packed dirt walls of their small home.

"I lived in war for twenty years, where I had to see children mutilated by land mines and mourn friends who were shot," Eduardo tells me as he loads dirt into plastic bags for coffee seedlings. "So however much money I made with coca, or however much the state *nos incumple* [fails to live up to its agreement with us], I don't want to go back to that time."

The agreement he refers to is the landmark 2016 peace accord with the Revolutionary Armed Forces of Colombia (FARC) that promised to end a half-century-long civil war. Eduardo is no guerrilla. Nevertheless, one of the agreement's six central points targeted people like him; it was a coca substitution program to help campesinos replace the illicit crop that provides the raw material for cocaine and has long funded Colombia's conflict.[1] Briceño played host to the pilot substitution program, making Eduardo and other area campesinos the first in the nation to voluntarily pull out their coca through the peace process. Briceño was thrust into the national spotlight as the "peace laboratory," stoking local hopes for a new era in which unprecedented state investment would bring peace and prosperity.

The region has indeed been transformed, with relative tranquility, fields free of coca, new roads and schools, and Colombia's largest hydroelectric dam. Nevertheless, peace in Briceño has not lived up to its promise. The local economy has collapsed because of the disappearance of coca, the dam's destruction of traditional economies like gold panning, and agricultural policy that exposes farmers to competition from industrially produced and imported crops that drive prices perilously low. Eduardo and his neighbors depend on state resources to meet their everyday needs, a situation that reflects both the shifting role of the state in their lives and the newfound precarity of their changing livelihoods. Others pursue their livelihoods through an alternative authority: a FARC guerrilla group has rearmed in the region, and it encourages disgruntled locals to plant coca again. Its ranks swell with youth who previously worked in the coca economy. Eduardo worries that Briceño's violent past is, like the buried shell casing, all too close to the surface.

*   *   *

Underlying Briceño's imperfect transformation are questions that have long preoccupied both policymakers and social theorists. Why do peace processes succeed or fail? How is the authority of the state (or of alternative governors) established? Why do people participate in drug economies and join armed groups?

Throughout this book, I use the case study of Briceño to address these questions through investigation of the fraught relationship between peace, state formation, and economic development. In drawing these connections, I zoom out to describe phenomena like global agrarian transformations, national political struggles around a controversial peace agreement, and international drug economies and the US-led War on Drugs that seeks to dismantle them. However, my analysis is firmly rooted in the lives of people like Eduardo. Their experiences are critical to understanding the outcomes of policy decisions made in Bogotá and Washington; global flows of cocaine, coffee, corn, and capital; and broader transformations in how people make a living and resolve the collective problems of everyday life.

This book's central argument is that poor people's exclusion from legal markets is changing authority relations across the Global South, with the potential to either establish state authority or drive violence and criminal governance. Unable to find stable wage labor or compete with industrially produced food crops, the poor cast a wide net as they struggle to subsist and build a better future for their families. As part of these struggles, they engage state and alternative authorities who provide needed resources and services to generate loyalty, wealth, and power. These engagements, rooted in needs left unmet by legal markets, provide the basis for poor people's relationships to those who would govern them—and alongside it, the chances for subduing or intensifying internal conflict.

Zooming in on the case of Briceño shows how economic and political shifts combine to reconfigure community relations with different claimants to authority. When economic liberalization sank the price of coffee, Briceño's campesinos began cultivating coca, not to get rich, but as part of a broader transformation in which corporate food production has increasingly priced small-scale farmers out of legal agricultural economies. With prices protected by its illegality, coca allowed them to avoid the fate of poor farmers across the Global South: migration to urban slums, which have themselves become sites of economic exclusion in the face of increasing deindustrialization. But cultivating coca also pushed them to authorize the governance practices of the guerrilla and paramilitary groups that regulated the coca economy, helping establish the authority of those groups at the expense of a state that sought to destroy their crops.

If coca once impelled armed groups' control of the village, its disappearance in a context of ongoing exclusion has created a foothold for state authority. In their efforts to develop new livelihoods, villagers participate strenuously in local elections in the hope of securing access to municipal resources. They call repeatedly on the mayor and other local officials for help with their roads and dwellings, and complain when the state fails to live up to their expectations. Their motivation is material need. However, these behaviors get under the skin of those who engage in them, reconfiguring attitudes toward the state by publicly demonstrating consent to state power and developing collective habits through which local people treat state officials and institutions as "the state."[2] And just as critical to state governance are the relationships local communities develop with state officials to access resources under their control. Officials draw on these relationships to enlist help in executing state projects and understanding complex social and property relations that would otherwise be illegible.

Yet even as state authority takes hold in Briceño, a rearmed guerrilla group has resumed many of the governance practices it carried out for decades, solving problems—such as the enforcement of collective labor—that the state does not, and absorbing the excluded labor of young men (and some women) who take up arms in the absence of alternative sources of income and dignity. Local struggles over authority—who has the right and ability to rule—rest on locals' decisions to turn to the state or armed groups to pursue

their livelihoods and resolve the pressing problems of everyday life. Monopolizing this problem-solving—an ongoing and incomplete project—is the key
to supplanting armed group authority, replacing drug economies, and establishing a lasting peace.

While the lives of Eduardo and his neighbors, one-time coca farmers
caught between opposing authority figures, may seem very distant from most
people's daily realities, in at least one way they are not. The most critical structural element behind their experience is a global economic production system, transformed through trade liberalization and a variety of technological
advances, that has little place for much of humanity. Across the Global South,
poor people pursue livelihoods that they do not find in legal markets through
distinct authority figures. They enroll in state welfare programs, pledge loyalty to politicians or criminal bosses in exchange for jobs, and cultivate or
sell drugs for criminal organizations. Economic exclusion, in short, brings
them to the state—or to groups that challenge its authority. Their decisions of
where to turn for help determine who governs the excluded.

Eduardo, Act One

Eduardo—a short man with an infectious laugh, an affable manner that inspires confidence, and the dark skin and muscular forearms of a lifetime of
outdoor physical labor—was born in 1979 in the city of Medellín. He refers
to himself as both an orphan and a gift. When he was one month old, his
drug-addicted mother gave him away to another woman. When he was nine,
that woman gifted him to a confirmed bachelor in Briceño. From that time
on, Eduardo was responsible for himself, moving from family to family in the
isolated hamlet (*vereda*) where he still lives. "I kept my clothes in a cardboard
box," he says, "and when I wanted to go, I grabbed the box." Wherever he arrived, he picked coffee, cut sugarcane, and milked cows in exchange for food
and a place to sleep. Along with other community members, he also panned
for gold on the banks of the Cauca River (fig. I.1), sleeping on the beach under
improvised plastic tents and eating freshly caught fish.

Coca's arrival in the late 1990s marked a turning point in Briceño's history,
when men who had picked the crop in a nearby village brought the seeds,
along with tales of the profits they had generated. Within a couple of years,
nearly all people in the area abandoned their coffee and other crops for coca.

"Why did it spread so quickly?" I ask Eduardo. His wife Flor, having
served us a savory meat stew, bustles around, clearing our dirty dishes. Fixed
gender roles, with men working in the fields and women performing domestic labor, are strongly entrenched.

FIGURE I.1. Panning for gold in a local stream.

"Traditional crops have really low prices," Eduardo says. "Also, you can put a kilo of coca paste in a backpack and take off walking. To get that same amount of money from coffee, you need to transport and sell around four hundred kilos." (At the time of our conversation, the community had not yet built the steep and precarious dirt road that now leads to the hamlet. Getting goods to market is still a problem, but back then it involved a full-day excursion with mules.)

What Eduardo doesn't mention is that in the late 1990s the price of coffee plummeted below the cost of production, victim to the disappearance of an international quota system that had protected prices. Coffee farmers couldn't afford the labor they needed to harvest their beans, especially when young men like Eduardo were making more money picking coca. With coca's arrival, the going rate for a daily wage doubled from two US dollars to four, and by 2015, able coca pickers were making as much as forty dollars a day, a staggering sum.[3] Most local farmers, excluded from further production for global coffee markets, replaced their coffee with coca.

Unlike coffee's yearly harvest, coca's leaves grow back after two to three months, providing consistent work. "If someone didn't have coca ready for harvest," Eduardo says, "one of their neighbors would." Coca also allowed for upward mobility. High prices and quick harvests permitted a land tenure system in which landless campesinos planted coca on another person's property, paying 10 percent of the earnings as rent. In 2005, Eduardo began planting on rented land. By 2008 he had saved enough money to buy his own farm.

But the coca economy brought violence. While the FARC had been in Briceño since roughly 1981, the arrival of coca attracted right-wing drug-trafficking paramilitaries who violently disputed the FARC's territorial control. Pitched fighting gradually made way for shifting and invisible borders. The more isolated regions, including Eduardo's hamlet, stayed mostly under guerrilla dominion. The paramilitaries controlled the village center and surrounding areas. Here the police and military were present, but they openly collaborated with paramilitaries, referring to them as their cousins. Police even stood guard as paramilitaries unloaded bundles of cash and loaded coca paste onto helicopters that landed on the soccer field.

At the same time, coca eradication programs—carried out by the Colombian military but funded by the US government in the context of the War on Drugs—destroyed farmers' crops. In 2011, four hundred army soldiers worked their way across the municipality with coca eradicators who pulled out all the coca by hand. "I lost seventy thousand plants," Eduardo says. "But by the time eradicators got to that side of the hamlet," he says, indicating it with an index finger, "we had already begun replanting here." With neither the resources to plant legal crops nor a way to sell them at a fair price, campesinos went back to the crop that would guarantee their families' livelihoods. Within seven months, they were again harvesting coca leaves.

In Eduardo's hamlet, the FARC fulfilled governance functions usually associated with the formal state, maintaining law and order, resolving disputes, and setting the rules of daily life. They mediated their control through the local community action board (*junta de acción comunal*). The guerrillas ensured that people attended the monthly meetings and participated in *convites* (days of communal work) that were mostly organized to maintain local mule paths. If people fought or spread false rumors, they would be forced to do community service or fined, with proceeds turned over to the community action board. The FARC also policed more serious crimes like theft; the "real" police never left the village center. Offenders were subject to a three-strikes policy: fined for a first offense, made to leave for a second, and killed for a third.

For years, Eduardo had traveled to the Cauca River to pan for gold whenever there was a lull in coca production. Around 2008 he heard rumors of a new hydroelectric dam, later named Hidroituango, that would flood the beaches where he had long worked. Public Enterprises of Medellín (EPM), the public-private partnership that was building the dam, was legally responsible for compensating those whose livelihoods would be affected. It performed an unannounced census to identify beneficiaries, a full day's journey from Eduardo's hamlet. No one from his community was included.

By 2011, with dam construction underway, the military began forcibly removing gold panners from the riverbanks. Eduardo participated in three different road blockages (*paros*) to demand compensation. The final one lasted a full two months, with locals camping out on the road to prevent construction materials from getting through. Finally, Colombia's notorious riot police arrived with black body armor, nightsticks, tear gas canisters, and rubber bullets. The campesinos fled. Eduardo, now excluded from the global trade in gold, hasn't returned to the river since.

The dam project, however, also affected Briceño in an entirely unexpected way. In 2015, the FARC and government collaborated for the first time on a land mine removal program intended to build the legitimacy of a peace agreement that was still under negotiation. Briceño's hamlet of El Orejón, on the valley walls above the dam, was chosen to host the program. Both government officials and FARC representatives who participated in the peace negotiations have privately confirmed to me what locals like Eduardo assumed from the start: Briceño's selection was based on the need to pacify the region that was home to Colombia's largest hydroelectric dam.

But land mine removal was only the beginning. FARC guerrillas visited the community action board meeting in Eduardo's hamlet to warn of a bigger impending change: Briceño would also host the pilot for a coca substitution program. The guerrillas said that coca farmers would receive resources totaling eleven thousand dollars each in goods and cash in exchange for uprooting their coca plants. The FARC negotiated a role for itself to ensure, along with the United Nations, that the state lived up to the agreement. Those farmers who refused to join would have their coca forcibly eradicated and would receive nothing.

Eduardo recalls that many farmers were skeptical of the agreement, reluctant to trust either a state with little history of community investment or legal agricultural economies with notoriously thin profit margins. But locals were tired of living with the ever-present specter of violence. And besides, coca's profits had dipped, due to agricultural blights and the rising prices of the chemicals used to grow and process it. They also had little choice. The FARC announced that it would be ceding control of the area to the formal state, and that campesinos had better figure out how to make a living from legal crops.

The coca substitution program was launched to great fanfare with the visit of Colombian President Juan Manuel Santos to Briceño in 2017. Every two months for a year, Eduardo and other beneficiaries each received a subsidy payment of seven hundred dollars to cover basic family expenses. After the first payment, Eduardo uprooted his coca plants by hand. After the second, he was supposed to receive goods to help him transition to licit agriculture.

Program officials told him there was a slight delay in contracting the program operator, but that in two more months, the goods would arrive. They did not.

"And what do they tell you now?" I ask.

Eduardo laughs. "To wait two more months."

Eduardo, a deeply religious man who does not even drink alcohol, feels much better farming coffee than coca. But while coca previously earned him enough money to buy his own farm, the legal stimulant is more of a struggle. Coffee's global market price is subject to wild swings, largely determined by competition from massive industrialized farms in places like Brazil. Sometimes the price even dips below production costs, as it did when coca first spread through the municipality. Now Eduardo has founded his own brand of coffee and a growers' association, in the hope of guaranteeing high prices by selling directly to foreign distributors. Breaking into overseas markets, however, has proven difficult.

Campesinos across Briceño have turned to a variety of livelihood strategies in their struggle to provide their families with a comfortable life in the wake of coca's disappearance. Aside from razor-thin profit margins, what these strategies share is a newfound dependence on state resources. Coca substitution is the largest in a range of agricultural programs that provide farmers with goods, machinery, and technical assistance. Campesinos draw on other state programs for help with their homes, whether to fix a leaky roof, put in a cement floor, or install an indoor bathroom. Municipal jobs are also essentially the only work available that pays even the minimum wage.

With coca money having disappeared from the municipality and campesinos excluded from most legal agricultural markets, access to these goods, programs, and jobs has become essential to locals' efforts to meet daily needs and even improve their standard of living. Nearly all these resources are distributed at the mayor's discretion, used to reward political supporters. As a result, mayoral elections have become a high-stakes affair as locals seek to trade their political support for access to sorely needed material goods. It is a system that excludes many, but which also brings rewards. Eduardo, for example, was able to leverage his campaign support for Danilo Agudelo—Briceño's mayor from 2016 to 2019, known locally by his nickname, Cenizo—into an addition to his home: a new room, paid for with municipal funds.

Perhaps most consequential to campesino livelihoods, however, are the roads needed to transport legal agricultural goods. Most of Briceño's surface area occupies a triangular wedge between the Cauca and Espiritu Santo Rivers, which meet in the village's northeastern corner. Of the municipality's 155 square miles, none are flat; steep valley walls between the two rivers rise from roughly

FIGURE I.2. Corn meets coffee on a hillside farm.

300 meters above sea level to a high of 2,600 meters. Roughly 2,500 people live in the village center, twenty-eight kilometers of mostly unpaved road from the national highway that connects Medellín to the Caribbean coast. Another 5,500 people live in the village's rural areas, split between thirty-five hamlets (*veredas*), dispersed population centers of twenty to three hundred people each. Though some hamlets lie along the entrance road, most are reachable from newer and more rudimentary roads that cut across the village's mountains from the village center, crossing dozens of mountain streams and subject to periodic landslides. The municipality still has pockets of jungle, but most of its surface area has been taken over by cultivation, primarily cow pasture interspersed with smaller plots of coffee, sugarcane, and cacao and subsistence crops like corn, beans, plantains, and yuca (fig. I.2). Though their habitat is disappearing, the village is still home to a variety of wild monkeys, ocelots, and colorful birds like toucans, tanagers, and hummingbirds.

On my first visit to Eduardo's farm, an hour from the village center, I fall from my motorcycle, the bike sliding out from under me on a perilous descent. As I recount my misadventure later, Eduardo laughingly tells me that the road, opened a scant two years ago, is nearly as inexperienced with motorcycles as I am. "Before that," he says, "if you wanted to bring something in or out, it had to be on a mule's back."

"I imagine people really wanted a road," I say.

"Before, we didn't," he replies. "The road only arrived to [the hamlet above]. We were hidden away. If the soldiers were coming, someone would call and tell us, so we would know what to do. If I had gasoline [used in the chemical transformation of coca] or coca paste, I had to go hide it."

"Because they would take it?"

"They would take it, or more likely they would say, 'We need two, three thousand dollars.' The road left us more exposed to extortion."

It was only when the FARC guerrillas called a community meeting to inform them that the substitution program would put an end to coca that Eduardo's community realized they would need a road to get heavier legal products to market. Suddenly, they needed the state. They reached out to the mayor, offering some money that the community had raised and asking him to cover the rest and provide the use of the municipal excavator. The mayor agreed. However, it was locals themselves who directed the roadbuilding. The finished road is often blocked by landslides. Fortunately, Eduardo, by now the community president, has an in with the mayor. "I supported Cenizo when he was campaigning," he tells me, "and when we need the machine [to fix the road], he sends it."

Thus, the role of the state in community life has flipped: rather than trying to keep the state away, locals now depend on it. This transformation is also evident in local landscapes, with fields free of coca, new roads and schools, and Colombia's largest hydroelectric dam.

However, the mayor is not the only local authority with whom Eduardo must maintain a relationship. Less than a year after demobilizing, a small number of the local FARC guerrillas rearmed, citing their own frustrations with the state's failure to live up to the peace agreement. They resumed governance roles they had fulfilled for decades: enforcing law and order, resolving disputes between community members, and organizing collective labor. Participation in communal work groups known as *convites* to maintain the road and local paths had flagged after FARC disarmament; with the guerrillas back in the picture, the community again fell in line.

The biggest problem with the rearmed guerrillas, as Eduardo describes it, is that young men have begun to join them in alarming numbers: five from his hamlet and another five from the neighboring community, all between fifteen and eighteen years old. They previously made a living picking coca, but were left unemployed by its disappearance.

Guerrillas notwithstanding, the peace process has brought a new era of tranquility to Briceño, as the paramilitaries who fought the FARC for decades have mostly stayed away.[4] Still, the promised economic benefits of peace have been missing. When the peace agreement was signed in 2016, national government officials spoke of the peace dividends that would result—primarily from newfound access to a range of natural resources that the conflict had long prevented the nation from exploiting. Briceño, where a proposed multinational gold mine had long been prevented by guerrilla control, seemed the perfect example. Immediately after the FARC disarmed, the Canadian company that owned mining concessions in Briceño entered the territory to perform soil tests and to quell opposition by farmers who feared the mine would endanger their water sources. Upon rearming, however, the guerrillas violently interceded, murdering three mine employees and stopping the project in its tracks. Still, the ongoing potential for the mine threatens future pollution and violence.

Although campesinos have for now dodged the threat of the mine, the economic benefits of peace also seem to have passed them by. The substitution program has kept local farmers waiting more than five years for most of the promised resources for development of legal crops. For the crops they do grow, they receive a pittance, with prices squeezed by competition from corporate agriculture. Panning for gold along the silty banks of the Cauca River once offered a supplemental income for local farmers—but then they were displaced by dam construction, with the reservoir flooding the beaches where they used to work.

In the face of local economic collapse, more than half of Eduardo's community has left Briceño, many to cities like Medellín. There they engage in a variety of informal hustles, and have access to improved education for their children, but are largely excluded from formal wage employment. Even worse, without land on which to grow their own food, they face the specter of hunger. Those who stay depend on state resources controlled by local politicians—resources they can only access by establishing the right relationships with the right local politicians. Through helping out with roads, agricultural resources, and jobs, the state has established unprecedented local authority. However, the rearmed FARC guerrillas make authority claims of their own, and a growing number of farmers consider replanting coca or even taking up arms. The future of Briceño hangs in the balance.

Situating Briceño

All ethnographers face the question of generalizability: how far does their fine-grained description of social life travel outside the people and places they study? Put differently, is this book relevant only to understanding the experiences of rural Colombia, or can it help us understand other settings characterized by violence, drug cultivation, capitalist development, and struggles between competing authority figures? The following section, a carefully tailored history of the post–World War II Global South around this book's central themes of economic exclusion, state formation, and conflict and drug economies, is meant to set the bounds of my analysis. I will show that the calamity that befell Briceño's farmers when coffee's prices dropped after being exposed to unfettered global market forces is exemplary of the economic exclusion faced by masses of rural and urban poor across the Global South who find themselves unable to meet basic needs through either wage labor or agricultural production for globalized markets. I will show that these farmers join billions of excluded poor in turning to the state for help in filling these gaps, and that this help has become the central means through which Global South states extend their power. However, I will also show that in places like Briceño, where other organizations challenge state authority, economic exclusion can push the poor to alternative governors and can prolong conflict and criminality. In short, the basic dilemma faced by farmers like Eduardo—whether to pursue their livelihoods through the state or through alternative authorities—confronts poor people across the Global South.

ECONOMIC EXCLUSION: FROM RURAL FARMERS TO URBAN OUTCASTS

For most of recorded history, humankind has been dominated by small-scale rural farmers like Eduardo. As recently as 1900 only one in six people lived in cities, while by 1950 more than 70 percent of the world's population was still rural (Klein Goldewijk, Beusen, and Janssen 2010). It was only in 2007 that city dwellers came to constitute half the world's population; as farmers' inexorable march to cities has continued, that number is now 57 percent.

Intimately related to the most extensive migration in human history are fundamental changes in how we feed ourselves. As growing cities filled with hungry mouths, farmers began producing for the market in addition to their own sustenance. Technological innovations—fertilizers, irrigation systems, genetically engineered seeds, and chemical herbicides and insecticides, among others—have greatly increased the number of calories produced by a given plot of land subject to a given amount of human labor. On a global scale, the liberalization of trade has only increased this "efficiency," as Brazilian soy and coffee plantations and Midwestern US corn and wheat fields send massive low-cost harvests all over the world. As recently as 1950, two-thirds of the world's labor went to agriculture. Now it's less than a quarter, and yet humans produce more food than ever—2,800 calories per person, a number that only highlights the profound inequalities in distribution that leave 12 percent of the world severely undernourished (FAO et al. 2022; Federico 2010).

In one framing, these advances in food production represent both triumph and an enabling of human progress, as all this extra nutrition has liberated human energy and industry. It has also, however, produced profound dislocations as smallholding farmers struggle to compete with falling prices and the landless rural poor find their labor increasingly unnecessary to wealthy landowners. And even as people like Eduardo see their crops excluded from global and national markets, their land and its resources, like Briceño's water and gold, are highly sought after. As part of a phenomenon scholars call the global land grab, smallholding farmers across the world are increasingly displaced to make way for mines, hydroelectric dams, petroleum fields, or agro-industry (Borras et al. 2012). Classical theories of modernization see their dispossession as a necessary evil: Why, after all, should a few thousand inefficient farmers stand in the way of a dam that will provide energy for a nation?

For those who are pushed or priced out, the alternative is often urban slums, where they find that without subsistence crops, they need cash to feed their families (Davis 2006). While both modernization theory and classical Marxist doctrine predict that their labor will be absorbed into the urban industrial workforce, the simple fact is that for unskilled workers in places like Colombia, jobs are few and far between. Medellín, the city that absorbs most of Briceño's migration, was once home to a thriving and labor-intensive textile industry. In the 1980s, however, the industry was sunk by competition from foreign manufacturers, and the few surviving companies replaced their workers with machines (Tubb 2020). On a global level, just as technological advances and trade liberalization have torpedoed small-scale agricultural production, manufacturing jobs have been slashed by increasing automation and cheap imported goods from countries like China.

The result is a massive increase in the Global South workforce (20 percent annual growth in the 1980s and 1990s) at the same time as the jobs available to it are shrinking (Krohn-Hansen 2022; Munck 2013). In most Global South countries, more than half the population labors in the informal economy, eking out a living by selling gum on buses, chasing an elusive day of work cleaning a home or picking a harvest, or engaging in a variety of other precarious enterprises that economists optimistically call microentrepreneurship. Scholars have coined many terms for these people with no clear place in the global economy: surplus or redundant populations, disposable people, wasted lives, castaways of development, and the precariat (Bauman 2003; Ferguson 2015; Latouche 1993; Li 2010; Munck 2013).

Critics of this intellectual current point out that these populations are not necessarily superfluous to processes of capital accumulation. Their bodies and labor produce profit for others when they take out extortionate short-term loans, distribute consumer goods through small-scale commerce, and even sort through garbage at the dump for a $200 billion global trade in discarded materials (Breman 2013; Cowan, Campbell, and Kalb 2023; Kasmir and Carbonella 2014; Krohn-Hansen 2022; Millar 2014). But even if they sometimes contribute to circuits of global capital, their exclusion is manifest in the fact that their labor and inconsistent earnings are still insufficient for basic social reproduction, including food, shelter, and the resources they need to bring up new generations. Their desperate attempts to make up for these shortfalls, as I argue here, are critical to local dynamics of violence and structures of authority.

What is new about this predicament? Zygmunt Bauman (2003) argues that modernization has always produced outcasts, people whose outdated ways of life do not fit within newly established social orders and economic systems. When modernization was mostly limited to Europe, Western powers sent those who had no place in rapidly industrializing societies to colonize the rest of the world, clearing the way with superior military might and disease that wiped out as much as 80 percent of native populations. But now that postcolonial nations in these same territories are undergoing their own processes of modernization, they have no "new world" to absorb their outcasts. Ironically, this predicament has reversed colonial migration patterns: the West now faces a refugee crisis driven by Global South residents fleeing poverty and violence. But modernization has also brought political transformation, most notably the growth and democratization of states in ways that establish opportunities for the majority of the excluded who stay within national boundaries.

BUILDING AND DEMOCRATIZING STATES

The counterpart to the economic *exclusion* of many residents of the Global South has been some measure of political *inclusion* in democratizing states. Even as the bargaining power offered to the poor by their labor wanes, their political leverage has increased through the power of their vote and a growing moral imperative for states to provide for the most destitute members of society. Thus, through a diversity of mechanisms and with varying degrees of effectiveness, states across the Global South help citizens with needs they cannot meet through the market. These expanded functions have fundamentally changed how poor people experience the state, and how states extend their power and supplant challengers to their authority.

But before expanding on the state's increasing importance to the livelihoods of the poor, a quick word on state formation, which from an ethnographic perspective may be understood as "the embedding of ideas and practices of 'state' in the everyday life of the state's subjects" (Stepputat 1999, 213): Given the extent to which states have come to dominate social and political life, it is easy to forget that until five hundred years ago most of humanity lived outside state power—and that even today, their authority cannot be taken for granted in places like Briceño. Historical analysis of how state power spreads is based primarily on the experiences of Europe, where state formation was driven by war. Bloody struggles between regional powerholders incentivized fledgling states to extend their influence across their territory to extract both taxes and military conscripts from subject populations. Those who did so effectively conquered and absorbed other states, as Europe passed from five hundred distinct sovereigns in 1500 to fewer than fifty today (Lachmann 2010; Tilly 1990). Over time, and in negotiation with subjects who resisted war-motivated extraction, Western states assumed growing roles within their citizens' lives, including dispute resolution, provision of services like education and health care, and regulation of the economy (Tilly 1990).

The trajectory of Global South states is markedly different, rooted in a history of colonial domination that is still responsible for many of the conditions behind internal conflict. While European states were built from the inside out, with their borders drawn and redrawn through warfare with external enemies, the independence movements in Asia, Africa, and Latin America that ousted their colonial masters inherited large territories they did not necessarily control in any meaningful sense (Centeno 2002). Large swaths of countries like Colombia continue to be far removed from central state power, hidden behind mountain ranges and impassable jungle and home to violent actors whom states struggle to bring under heel.

In this context, Thomas Hobbes's seventeeth-century depiction of a state leviathan able to pacify daily life throughout a given territory continues to dominate the peacebuilding industry. If those who live outside state power experience "nasty, brutish, and short" existences, in which they live with "continual fear and danger of violent death" (Hobbes 1998 [1651], 84), peacebuilders see state formation as the solution to violence (Lemay-Hébert 2014). But as Joel Migdal (1988) has pointed out, these areas with limited state penetration are usually characterized less by an absence of governance than by the existence of alternative authorities like local strongmen, tribes, clans, religions, paramilitaries, and guerrilla groups. Would-be governors often fight over territorial control but, as I explain throughout this book, just as important is the combination of rewards and sanctions they employ to enlist community support.

This focus on local support highlights the fact that state formation is as much a symbolic as a material achievement. In places usually considered to have "strong states," we may struggle to conceive of alternatives to state power, a recognition that grants state institutions the legitimacy they need to penetrate deeper into our lives. Scholars describe the historical development of this symbolic power (again, primarily in the European context) as a cultural revolution through which subject populations gradually came to take state authority for granted (Bourdieu 2014; Corrigan and Sayer 1985). This recognition explains why we take driving tests, stop at red lights, and register our births, marriages, and property acquisitions. It turns what would otherwise be a kidnapping into a legitimate "police arrest" and extortion into "taxes." However, for people like Eduardo, who have long experienced the FARC guerrillas as local governors and state actors as a threat, the symbolic recognition of "the state" as ultimate authority cannot be taken for granted. Arrests may be stymied, and laws may be flaunted. Alternative claimants to authority may win out or coexist with the formal state. What ultimately matters in these local power struggles is where local communities turn to establish order, resolve disputes, and meet collective needs.

The capacity of Global South states to be recognized by their subjects is hampered by their unequal position in a world economic system in which wealth continues flowing to the prosperous West. Consider that coffee and coca growers alike receive only 1 percent of the final retail price of the cup of coffee or line of cocaine eagerly consumed in Western nations. But following the devastation of World War II, Western nations concerned with forestalling another global conflict established the World Bank and the International Monetary Fund (IMF) as central institutions in an international development apparatus with a stated mission of combating poverty across the world. Billions of dollars were invested in development programs based on the idea that catching up to the West meant imitating the industrializing path it had taken to prosperity (Escobar 2011; Rostow 1971). These programs often failed in their stated goals of poverty reduction, but expanded the influence and reach of both Global South states and a slew of Western experts and organizations that claimed to hold the key to modernizing the "underdeveloped" world (Escobar 2011; Ferguson 1990).

In the 1980s, technical prescriptions for combating poverty consolidated around the "Washington Consensus," a cookie-cutter model for economic modernization imposed as a condition of IMF and World Bank loans. Subject to varying degrees of coercion, Global South states adopted a host of "structural adjustments" that (1) lifted restrictions on foreign investment and the importation of goods, (2) eliminated state subsidies and economic regulation, and (3) reduced and privatized state services (Robinson 1999). These policies were critical to the economic exclusion described above. Farmers and national industries alike were exposed to competition from imported goods just as austerity measures eliminated many state subsidies. Rural communities were dispossessed of land and traditional economies when foreign direct investment in extractive industries like mining, petroleum, and timber skyrocketed as states removed barriers to foreign capital.

But accounts of these reforms as the "hollowing out of the state" missed a concurrent transformation: a wave of democratization that saw the percentage of autocratic states dip from 62 percent in 1977 to only a quarter by 1995 and 13 percent by 2017 (DeSilver 2019; Huntington 1993). These democratizing states across the world often fail to live up to normative ideals of working for the common good or ensuring the effective participation of all. But just as Eduardo and his neighbors seek to trade their votes for state resources, populations denied the full rights of citizenship engage in what Partha Chatterjee (2004) describes as the politics of the governed, making claims to shelter, nutrition, and water and electrical infrastructures through "temporary, contextual and unstable arrangements arrived at through direct political negotiations" (Chatterjee 2008, 57). Karl Marx influentially argued that the development of early capitalism depended on a process of dispossession that left a newly established industrial working class with only its labor power to sell for its survival. In contrast, this moment of global capitalism has produced a massive would-be workforce, excluded from the possibility of stable wage labor, that has only its vote and the discomfiting image of its destitution to barter for its survival.

Thus, a curious predicament has arisen across much of the Global South, in which democratic states that are complicit in the economic dispossession of their most vulnerable citizens simultaneously take an active role in ensuring their survival. Like the social welfare programs that offer monthly payments to poor families with children in Briceño, cash transfers to mothers, the elderly, or the infirm may provide most of the money that circulates in marginalized communities (Ferguson 2015). Politicians distribute food and resources to court voters, and do so even outside elections. They also install party representatives to establish political loyalty by channeling state resources to help the poor buy medicine and fill empty stomachs (Auyero 2001; Phillips 2018). Impoverished communities may also organize as a voting bloc to secure housing, road paving, drinking water, or electrification (Álvarez-Rivadulla 2017; Anand 2017; Gay 1994).

Kalyan Sanyal (2007), one of the few thinkers who has theorized the links between economic exclusion and democratization, argues that postcolonial states participate in a tenuous balancing act by establishing the conditions for capitalist expansion while simultaneously legitimizing their rule by guaranteeing the survival of those who are dispossessed as a result (see also Fox 1993). The Colombian version of this seesaw came about through simultaneous economic and political reforms: the so-called *apertura* (opening) that removed trade barriers to expose both campesinos and national industry to competition from imported goods beginning in 1990 (see chapter 1); and a democratic deepening that instituted competitive mayoral elections (before 1988, mayors were appointed by governors, themselves appointed by the president) while transferring significant funds to local government to provide services like health and education (see chapter 6). This situation brings desperate people to the state, setting terms of engagement that center around their struggles to meet basic needs.

My ethnographic description extends this work on Global South states in three ways. First, I show that on the margins of state power, local experiences of the state are primarily determined by personal relationships with state officials that are established through ongoing negotiations in which communities seek to meet material needs and officials pursue political support. Second, I show that state formation is carried out through these relationships in both material and symbolic ways: officials harness these relationships to execute state projects that would otherwise be impossible, and communities that make a collective habit of turning to state officials for assistance provide public evidence of consent to state power and establish a taken-for-granted understanding of the state as ultimate political authority. And finally, I argue that state aid and the relationships established through it have become the primary means through which Global South states extend their power and supplant challengers to their authority. If state formation in the European model historically hinged on the *extraction* of taxes and military conscripts from subject populations, modern-day Global South states are just as likely to increase their power and influence through resource *distribution*. But it is not only opposing politicians who compete for the loyalty of the excluded poor.

ALTERNATIVE GOVERNORS: DRUGS, CONFLICT, AND TURNING AWAY FROM THE STATE

Poor people's struggles to eke out a living not only push them to the state; they can also bring them to alternative authorities that challenge state authority. As it does for the state, the resulting support allows a variety of insurgencies and armed groups to both govern and mobilize the funds and troops that allow their continued existence. Thus, while economic exclusion often enables state formation, in many areas of the Global South it is also behind conflict and illegal economies, none bigger than drugs.

Many of the world's major areas of drug cultivation have emerged in response to the same kind of exclusionary global market forces that pushed Briceño's farmers to replace their coffee with coca. Afghan farmers planted poppies for opium and heroin when the price of wheat cratered, Mexican farmers turned to marijuana and poppies when cheap imported corn destroyed traditional agriculture, and in Myanmar it was farmers priced out of globalizing tea and garlic markets who started growing poppies (Bradford 2019; Maldonado Aranda 2013; Meehan 2021; Morris 2020). In the United States, marijuana growers proliferated in Oregon and Northern California when the timber industry collapsed, and poor urban youth dealt drugs when deindustrialization decimated factory jobs (Bourgois 2003; Polson 2013). In most cases the marginalized have stayed poor, as the drug trade's considerable profits concentrate in the hands of powerful criminal organizations and armed groups. Nevertheless, drug economies may give farmers like Eduardo their best shot at a dignified living, the only way to avoid precarious urban futures and to continue living on and from the land.

While illegality protects crops like coca from the competition of corporate agriculture, it sets farmers' livelihoods directly against the US-led international drug control regime. This regime justifies intervention in drug-cultivating countries by casting drug production and trafficking as a global "public bad" that emerges from state weakness (Mansfield 2016, 17). With certain states unable to stop their drugs from flooding world markets, the logic goes, countries like the United States must step in to protect their citizens. In practice, these interventions—whether in Colombia, Peru, Mexico, Afghanistan, or elsewhere—have mostly displaced drug production and trafficking to other areas while generating terrible violence. However, fighting the international War on Drugs also creates political and economic opportunities: for the United States to extend its power and influence, for elites from Global South producer countries to attract military aid and trade deals, and for both to pacify territories that are home to valuable natural resources (Bradford 2019; Mercille 2011; Paley 2014). Ironically, the "opportunities" created by drug repression generally concentrate profits in elite hands while intensifying economic exclusion and producing even more potential drug cultivators, traffickers, dealers, and addicts.

The illegality of drugs also pushes the regulation of drug economies outside the purview of states, leaving a lucrative void for extralegal actors. Drug profits sustain a dizzying array of violent groups across the world: cartels, urban gangs, warlords, insurgents, paramilitaries, guerrillas, international drug-trafficking organizations, and even corrupt militaries. These groups and the illegal economies that sustain them play an increasingly consequential role in ongoing conflict. Since the end of World War II, warfare has moved internal, with low-intensity civil wars replacing massive interstate conflicts (Goldstein 2012). These civil wars, economists have found, are increasingly motivated and sustained by greed rather than, or in addition to, ideological or political grievances (Collier and Hoeffler 2004). Diamonds in Africa, oil fields in the Middle East, and drug economies in Colombia, Afghanistan, and Myanmar can motivate groups to rebel, help finance insurgencies once they've started, and even remove incentives to end civil wars that prove good for business (Keen 2000; Richani 2013).

Potential material rewards notwithstanding, joining an armed group is a risky commitment rarely made by people with better options. Economists have found that few things predict civil war better than a ready-made supply of unemployed young men, and that creating jobs for unskilled men is the best way to ensure the success of a peace process (Collier 2008, 2009). Economic exclusion does not guarantee conflict, but few if any internal conflicts would sustain themselves if their potential troops could access a dignified stable income through legal markets. Understood in this way, the puzzle of Briceño—that eliminating a coca economy usually identified as a major driver of conflict actually promoted the growth of the rearmed guerrillas— becomes less surprising. The guerrillas' new recruits are not enthusiastic about violence or ideologically committed to revolution. They are poor rural youth who have only signed up for a highly risky "job" after other opportunities like legal agriculture, formal employment, gold panning, and, most recently, picking coca have been closed to them.

Widespread economic exclusion is also a necessary if not sufficient condition for internal conflict along lines of ethnic hatred. For example, the 1994 genocide of eight hundred thousand Tutsi at the hands of the Hutu majority in Rwanda is usually explained as a consequence of long-standing ethnic enmity rooted in a system of colonial control in which the Belgians mediated their violent domination through the Tutsi minority. But just as critical to the massacre was the same 1990s drop in coffee's global price that had driven the rise of coca and violence in Briceño. Rwanda's coffee economy, which accounted for 70 percent of the country's total exports, was central to the livelihoods of the rural poor (Chakravarty 2015). When the coffee sector collapsed just as structural conditions imposed by a World Bank loan slashed state social services and the country experienced a drought, famine swept through the countryside (Kamola 2008). Hutu political elites mobilized ethnic tension to redirect popular anger against their Tutsi neighbors, and recruited economically destitute former coffee farmers into the militias that would carry out the horrific genocide (Kamola 2008).

But employment as drug cultivators or troops is not the only way armed groups support and depend on communities in areas they seek to control. As Mao Zedong famously observed, without the backing of the people, guerrillas (and other would-be governors) are like fish out of water; they cannot survive. Similar to early European states-in-formation, armed groups minimally impose a system of social control but often perform a range of governance functions in their efforts to control territory, elicit civilian cooperation, and raise funds: they resolve disputes, establish security, and provide services like health and education and goods like roads, electricity, and sewage systems (Arjona 2016; Tilly 1990). They behave, in short, much like the formal state. And when they are challenged, by either the state itself or a different organization, the outcome often rests on the collective behavior of the people who occupy the disputed territory. Whose system of social control do they follow, and to whom do they turn as the guarantor of order and provider of the public good?

WHO GOVERNS THE EXCLUDED?

It is in answering this question that ethnography becomes indispensable. Ethnography, as Kristin Phillips (2018, xii) writes, invites "new characters and unanticipated plots to enter the story . . . demonstrating relationships between and among processes social scientists often separate." Throughout this book, a sustained engagement with the lives of rural farmers leads to provocative and perhaps surprising findings: that advances in humanity's ability to efficiently feed the world sustain drug economies and conflict; that antidrug initiatives may threaten rather than establish state authority; that the disappearance of drug economies can bolster state power while simultaneously producing new recruits for armed groups; and that extractive megaprojects presented as the "dividends of peace" may instead drive a return to violence.

We can only understand the real impact of broader political and economic shifts by looking to how communities like Briceño engage with them. As Mezzadra and Neilson (2019, 3) have written, while it is useful to identify common rationalities and operations of global forces like capitalism, their ultimate consequences for real people and places depend on specific "spatial, social, legal, and political formations with which capital must grapple as it becomes enmeshed in dense constellations of flesh and earth." A deep examination of local lives as lived in these contexts, as I undertake here, necessarily moves between levels of analysis: from economic policy and the flows of global capital to the decisions made by farmers to pursue different livelihood strategies; from how these decisions configure relations with distinct claimants to authority to the outcomes of state projects like the peace process; from the often contradictory pressures of international peacebuilders, multinational mining companies, and the War on Drugs to national political struggles that play out on the ground in villages like Briceño. Broader trends like economic exclusion, internal conflict, state formation, the global land grab, and the proliferation of drug economies all play out in local contexts, with their own flesh-and-blood people entangled in intersecting webs of culture, history, ecology, and economy.

Alongside providing a window into understanding historical shifts, these people are also history makers, though rarely in circumstances of their own choosing. The actions taken by the Eduardos of the world as they confront changing opportunity structures in the context of economic and political transformation are decisive for peacebuilding, drug economies, and state power. Put concretely, if somewhat simplistically, Briceño's future depends largely on how its inhabitants seek to build their futures: whether through coca, local politics, urban migration, joining the guerrillas, legal agriculture, or some combination of the above. In the early 2000s, the collective decision to plant coca allowed farmers to preserve valued rural lifestyles, but also unleashed a bloody conflict. More recently, local decisions to join the substitution program have enabled a new era of relative peace and increased state authority, but also an economic downturn that occasions a new set of difficult choices. The way communities around Colombia resolve these issues—and the authority figures they turn to as they do so—will be critical to the future of Colombia's embattled peace process.

If this is a local story that illuminates global forces, it is also a contemporary account deeply rooted in history. As a peace laboratory,[5] Briceño is central to the hopes and frustrations of a nation that must come to terms with both a controversial peace process and the decades of violence it seeks to end. This history not only gives weight to the stories within these pages, but has influenced the village's experiences of conflict and, more recently, an uncomfortable peace.

Colombia's Seventy-Five-Year Quest for Peace

If truth is the first casualty of war, efforts to revive it are critical to peace, as establishing what has happened and why is central to peace processes across the world. These are particularly thorny questions for Colombia's conflict, one of the longest the world has ever seen. In 2014, as the FARC and the Colombian government advanced in their peace negotiations in Havana, they established a historical commission, tasking twelve academics with explaining the root causes of the conflict, why it persisted, and with what effects. However, the experts were unable to agree on much of anything, ultimately publishing twelve separate accounts (Burnyeat 2022). Indeed, the idea that if we only dig deep enough we can access an objective "truth" that lies behind conflict overlooks how narratives—to make sense of violence or of anything else—represent a contingent act of cultural production that both reflects and creates political interests (Nordstrom 1997; Polletta 2006).

Has the country been victim to an impenetrable topography that prevented state power from monopolizing violence throughout the territory? Does the fault lie, rather, with the destabilizing effects of cocaine profits and how they have incentivized criminality and drawn the country into the US-driven War on Drugs? Is the real answer to be found in patterns of dispossession that have long driven rural inequality? Each explanation for Colombia's long-standing conflict, among others that have been advanced by both academics and politicians, implies and legitimizes distinct peacemaking interventions.

The discerning reader has no doubt gathered that I believe any explanation must include an account of the economic exclusion that has left thousands of young people without better alternatives to armed groups. More than thirteen thousand FARC fighters demobilized through the 2016 peace agreement, a number that seems large until it's compared with the sixty-seven thousand other members of all armed groups who demobilized individually or collectively between 2001 and 2021, the ninety thousand combatants who lost their lives from 1985 to 2018, and those (including an estimated seventeen thousand in the twenty-seven distinct armed groups currently active in Colombia) who have never been registered with state databases (Agencia para la Reincorporación y la Normalización 2022; CEVCR 2022; Redacción Cambio 2023). Membership in Colombia's armed groups has long been a revolving door characterized by young recruits who eventually age or die out. In this context, Colombia has carried out many peace agreements, consigning multiple armed groups to the dustbin of history but never completely eliminating violent challengers to state authority.

The FARC itself has gone through several iterations, but it began as a self-defense measure in response to a failed peace process. From 1948 to 1958, Colombia suffered from "La Violencia," a period of intense violence between supporters of the rival Liberal and Conservative parties that claimed an estimated twenty thousand lives. In this context, groups of communist-sympathizing campesino self-defense groups who had established autonomous communities participated in peace negotiations that promised political pardons, agrarian loans, access to health care, and rural infrastructural development—concessions not dissimilar to those negotiated in the FARC's peace agreement nearly sixty years later (Karl 2017). National political struggles sank the agreement, however, and Cold War–era US military advisors still smarting from the 1959 communist revolution in Cuba pushed the Colombian military to attack the small communist communities. In 1964, sixteen thousand Colombian troops descended on one of those autonomous villages, known as the Republic of Marquetalia, where forty-eight armed men defended a population of a thousand (Brittain 2010). Its inhabitants scattered, reuniting in the jungle to found the FARC.

For roughly its first fifteen years, the FARC never exceeded six hundred members and posed no real threat to central state power (Gutiérrez Sanín 2004). Instead, it defended rural campesinos from the depredations of Colombia's economic modernization plan, known as Accelerated Economic Development. The plan was the brainchild of Lauchlin Currie, a Canadian economist who rose to prominence as White House chief economic adviser during World War II before being facing accusations of being a Soviet spy. He moved to Colombia and for decades advised a string of its presidents on economic policy. He held that small-scale farming represented a "mal-use, misuse, and underuse of human resources" (Currie 1971, 887), and campesinos should instead be relocated to urban areas to provide an industrial workforce while their land was seized and consolidated into large estates, producing goods like meat and dairy for international export (Brittain 2005). A fact no doubt unrelated was that Currie owned the country's largest dairy farm. Many displaced campesinos only retreated further into the jungle. These newly colonized agricultural frontiers, far from central state power, made up the political and territorial base of the FARC. The guerrillas called for agrarian reform, articulated a communist alternative to capitalist expansion, and funded themselves by extorting wealthy landowners, but rarely fought state forces.

In their 1982 national conference, the FARC officially changed strategy by adopting offensive revolutionary military tactics designed to seize power, and by expanding to territories with valuable resources to fund its revolution (Brittain 2010). But this aggressive expansion was also enabled by the spread of coca cultivation through rural Colombia, beginning in the late 1970s—a development, as I describe in chapter 1, that was a direct result of US foreign policy which pushed attacks on traditional growers in Peru and Bolivia just as the American appetite for cocaine was growing. Coca would transform the Colombian conflict forever.

While the FARC initially prohibited coca in areas under its control, it began regulating and taxing the crop when they realized its potential profitability for both campesinos and their revolution (Brittain 2010). It is estimated that by the 1990s the FARC was making $200 million a year from coca (Richani 2013), and debates began about whether the group had sold out its revolutionary ideology for drug profits. The question of whether the FARC is best understood as a revolutionary movement or as a drug gang is complicated by the fact that its members were never one coherent entity. At its height, the FARC was made up of eighty different fronts, each with its own semi-autonomous commander. In some territories and time periods, they faced little military competition and established miniature revolutionary states that kept law and order, built roads and electrical infrastructures, and used well-worn Marxist texts to teach civilians and their own troops alike how to read and wage class struggle (Brittain 2010). In others, they faced bloody competition for territorial control and devoted their energies to warfare and raising the money they needed to defeat their opponents (Hough 2011). The eventual peace agreement, in which the FARC negotiated increased state investment and political participation for its rural base, shows that the guerrillas did not entirely abandon their ideological commitments. However, the experience of places like Briceño (see chapter 5) suggest that as time went on, many rural communities increasingly experienced the FARC as one among many armed groups competing for coca or other illicit profits.

However else it affected the guerrillas, coca money helped the FARC grow to pose a real threat to state power even as the collapse of the Soviet Union left many communist insurrections floundering. By the late Nineties, the FARC had roughly twenty thousand troops; was present in more than half the national territory; was launching massive offensives against Colombian military bases; and was, according to a US Defense Intelligence Agency report, potentially five years away from defeating the Colombian army (Leech 2011).

With FARC power growing in the 1980s, another armed actor entered the conflict: paramilitary groups founded by regional elites to counter guerrilla extortion, kidnappings, and violence, often with the support of the military. Many of these paramilitary groups also took on an active role in the cocaine trade, particularly as more traditional drug barons like Pablo Escobar were killed or imprisoned. The huge influx of resources allowed paramilitaries to become relatively autonomous standing armies (Tate 2015). Rural elites also used these private armies to violently clear out poor campesinos who stood in the way of expanded cattle farms and agro-industrial, mining, and energy projects like the Hidroituango dam in Briceño (Grajales 2021; Oslender 2008; Ramírez Cuellar 2005). At least 8.3 million hectares (roughly four Israels) have been seized or abandoned due to violence, mostly perpetrated by paramilitaries, in the Colombian conflict (CNMH 2013, 76). Nearly 8.5 million Colombians are registered as victims of forced displacement, including 8,864 in Briceño (CEVCR 2022; RUV 2023).

As violence began escalating, Belisario Betancur's presidential administration (1982–86) attempted to reach a peace agreement with the half-dozen guerrilla groups that had spread across the country (Hylton 2006). In 1984, the FARC signed a bilateral ceasefire with the government, and in the next year it formed a political party known as the Patriotic Union (UP) as a prelude to laying down arms. However, their move from the bullet to the ballot had a tragic end; five thousand UP members, including more than one hundred elected politicians and successive presidential candidates, were assassinated by the military and paramilitaries, and peace talks broke down, though four other guerrilla groups did disarm.

In this context—as in Briceño, where the FARC and paramilitaries coexisted for nearly two decades—violence was ever present but never escalated to a point that would put a definitive end to conflict. Nazih Richani (2013) argues that the Colombian conflict settled into a comfortable impasse: the guerrillas and paramilitaries profited from coca and other illicit economies, the Colombian military received unprecedented US aid to combat the drug trade, and none of the groups were incentivized to escalate the conflict enough to vanquish their opponents.

The Andrés Pastrana administration (1998–2002) made the next attempt at an agreement with the FARC, even officially ceding them control of a Switzerland-sized portion of Colombia as part of a ceasefire. These discussions also collapsed, however, as neither side seemed to be negotiating in good faith. The FARC carried out several high-profile attacks; paramilitary violence escalated, supported by the Colombian military; and Pastrana was simultaneously negotiating Plan Colombia, a counternarcotics military aid package from the US government that only promised to intensify conflict further (Segura and Mechoulan 2017).

And intensify it did, as Pastrana was succeeded in office by the hardliner Álvaro Uribe, who promised to use an iron-fisted approach to bring the guerrillas to heel. After being elected, he installed a "democratic security" policy regime that militarized Colombian society, seeking to spread state power to rectify "the historical inability of Colombian democracy to affirm the authority of its institutions over the entirety of the territory" (quoted in Fattal 2018, 10). He was openly supported by the United Self-Defense Forces of Colombia

(AUC), an umbrella organization founded in 1997 that joined together the country's many paramilitary groups. Even as its members made untold sums trafficking cocaine, the AUC cast itself as the advance troops of state formation, clearing out guerrillas for the state to take their place (Ballvé 2020). It also gained tremendous influence within the state, controlling local governments and even, as the paramilitary leader Salvatore Mancuso famously bragged, exercising influence over 35 percent of the members of the National Congress (Gutiérrez Sanín 2019a).

Democratic security found additional support from the US government, which repeatedly turned a blind eye to the Uribe administration's ties to drug-trafficking paramilitaries. The US-funded Plan Colombia provided $10 billion of mostly military aid from 2000 to 2015, enabling the Colombian armed forces to double in size and win significant military victories against the FARC (Ballvé 2020; Tate 2015). Despite flagrant human rights abuses, *Uribismo* became wildly popular on the basis of its seeming effectiveness at pacifying Colombian society. As I will describe in chapter 4, democratic security and US interests through Plan Colombia converged to help transform rural Colombia into an extractive powerhouse, attracting foreign capital and clearing out guerrillas and campesinos alike from territories that held valuable minerals, oil, and coal (Paley 2014; Sankey 2020).

As the military's capacity to fight the guerrillas grew and paramilitary abuse damaged the country's reputation, Uribe carried out a peace process with his paramilitary allies. From 2003 to 2006, more than thirty thousand paramilitary troops officially demobilized. The process, however, was widely criticized for allowing commanders to maintain their ill-gotten wealth, recruiting civilians off the street to pose as combatants, and, as happened in Briceño, leading to a reorganization rather than the elimination of paramilitary groups (Civico 2016; Sánchez-Moreno 2005).

When Uribe's defense minister and handpicked successor Juan Manuel Santos was elected president in 2010, Colombians expected a continuation of the militarized approach. However, in a move Uribe denounced as a betrayal, Santos began peace negotiations with the FARC, still the country's largest and most important armed group. Santos shared Uribe's economic goal of attracting foreign investment to intensify resource extraction across rural Colombia. Yet while Uribe had harnessed violence to pacify regions that held valuable natural resources, Santos sought to use a negotiated peace process to change the country's violent image and enable extraction in FARC-controlled territories.

When the FARC and government finally reached an agreement, it was championed by international observers as the most comprehensive peace accord in history, promising not only the group's disarmament but a broader transformation of rural Colombia that would bring development to jump-start legal agriculture and replace coca (Presidencia de la República de Colombia and FARC-EP 2016). This vision of rural Colombia as site of campesino production exists in direct contradiction to the vision of a pacified countryside dominated by extractive projects that tend to displace campesinos. As I will describe in chapter 4, the violence the rearmed guerrillas used to halt a proposed multinational gold mine in Briceño illuminates how this unresolved tension imperils the agreement's future. In presenting the agreement, however, the Santos administration sidestepped the contradiction by optimistically forecasting that intensified extraction would pay for the rest of the peace process.

The agreement awakened the hopes of many Colombians for a long-desired peace, and netted Santos the Nobel Peace Prize. However, a significant portion of Colombian society, primarily followers of the still powerful Álvaro Uribe, opposed the agreement. The Santos administration put the peace accords to a popular vote in October 2016, expecting the Colombian electorate to authorize a nascent peace process. This was a costly miscalculation; the agreement was shockingly defeated at the polls by a margin of 50.2 to 49.8 percent. The Santos administration scrambled to negotiate minor changes with the *Uribista* opposition and was able to get Congress to ratify the agreement the next month. Nevertheless, the unexpected electoral failure damaged the agreement's legitimacy. The 2018 victory of *Uribista* presidential candidate Iván Duque, who campaigned on a platform hostile to the peace process, reflected many Colombians' mistrust of the agreement and, as I will describe in chapter 2, disrupted the already delayed peace process implementation.

Thus, while this book illuminates broader political and economic shifts across the Global South, it also comes out of an ongoing national struggle to overcome decades of violence—a struggle in which Briceño, as a peace laboratory, has repeatedly been thrust to center stage. The experiences of campesinos like Eduardo have become a matter of great national interest, invoked by powerful actors across the political spectrum to advance competing political agendas. These narratives usually flatten or misrepresent a complex reality, but they highlight the point that Briceño has important lessons to offer—not because it is typical of rural Colombia, but because it is precisely Briceño's status as an extreme case that makes its experience so insightful.

Where better to understand the failures of successive attempts to build peace than the peace laboratory that gave rise to a rearmed guerrilla front? Where better to study the persistence of coca economies, if not the village

where the coca substitution program was launched? Where better to analyze the depredations of extractive megaprojects than the home of Colombia's
largest hydroelectric dam? In describing these phenomena, I will avoid being overly prescriptive. Ethnographers are poor policymakers, and are better
suited to showing why well-intentioned policies go awry. Nevertheless, one
of my central goals is to harness the story of Briceño to offer insights for a
country that has spent decades seeking an elusive peace.

An Ethnography of the Peace Laboratory

Perhaps a month into my first period of extended field work in Briceño, a
group of community members had a conversation speculating about me, the
gringo who asked indiscreet questions and wrote down everything they told
him. They knew my explanation for why I was there as a graduate student
conducting a research project on the community's experiences of the peace
process. But some wondered whether it was only a cover story. Was I really a
diplomat interested in tracking international investment in Colombia's peace
process? A US spy gathering intelligence on the growth of a rearmed guerrilla
group? Even worse, could I be working for the Canadian company that was
seeking to establish a massive gold mine in the community?

Four years passed before a friend laughingly described this conversation
to me. Over that time I had deepened my ties to the community and presumably allayed local concerns over my potentially clandestine motives. But more
than an account of the pitfalls of establishing trust and access in a field site,
this anecdote is indicative of the reciprocal processes of interpretation that
occur through ethnographic research. Just as we ethnographers seek to understand the people we study, so too do our interlocutors seek to make sense
of us. The ways in which they do so—largely a function of the relationships
we are able to build—are critical to the data we gather.

I first arrived in Briceño in January 2018 on the recommendation of Isabel
Peñaranda, a Colombian anthropologist who had spent time in the village
and graciously put me in contact with several local leaders. From these contacts came others, along with invitations to people's farms and to countless
meetings organized by government officials. On several occasions I realized
that people initially talked with me in the hopes of accessing resources, particularly when they associated me with the wealth of the US government or
the slew of national and international state and nonstate organizations that
had arrived in Briceño since it had become the peace laboratory. This experience, based on my own disruptive presence in the field (Levenson 2022; Stuart

2018), helped me understand how people had come to see distributive claims on those with access to institutional funds—or on those they misidentified as such—as critical elements of their livelihoods.

While I quickly clarified that I controlled no resources, I did seek to support local livelihood strategies and political struggles in other ways. A critical moment early in my fieldwork came as local leaders organized a demonstration against the military's killing of an innocent campesino (see chapter 5). I got permission to attend their meetings, offering up my laptop and assistance in writing a press release. When the demonstration occurred, organizers invited me to speak in front of the community—likely a strategic move based on the legitimacy a foreigner's endorsement could bring to their cause, but an honor nonetheless. Publicly denouncing a killing that had caused widespread outrage allowed me to position myself as a community advocate. After speaking at the rally, I published an online article in Spanish and English on the demonstration and its relationship to the state's failure to live up to the coca substitution program, another target of local indignation (Diamond 2018). This article, along with six others I published over the next few years that described community perspectives on the peace process, substitution program, and hydroelectric dam, was widely shared by villagers on social media. This exposure helped my local reputation and led local leaders to see me as a useful ally.

Participation in local political mobilization also created significant fieldwork dilemmas, particularly in relation to village electoral campaigns. As I will describe in chapter 6, Briceño split around the two candidates for the 2019 mayoral election, with each side seeking to demonstrate its strength. At different times, both campaigns sought to present me as part of their teams, whether by circulating pictures of me with their candidates, by asking me to speak at campaign rallies, or by referring to me publicly as part of their future administration's "international cooperation." I eventually decided to maintain an official position of neutrality. It was a decision calculated to avoid alienating important contacts on either side; but it also, I believe, offended at least one of the candidates.

All told, I spent more than three years total in Briceño between 2018 and 2024. The opportunity to do such long-term embedded fieldwork carries major advantages. Rather than offering a snapshot of the village's experience, I'm able to describe a dynamic process that has changed over time. It is one thing to say that the promised goods of the substitution program have been significantly delayed. It is quite another to observe interactions between beneficiaries and program officials over several years that repeatedly raised and then dashed local hopes for needed goods. I was able to observe the changes in people's relationships with the local politicians they hoped would help them access state resources, and a shift in local mobilizations against the dam from outright resistance to pushing the dam company to contribute to the community's development. I even shared in the collective benefits of ongoing state formation, as my motorcycle trips throughout the territory gradually became smoother and quicker due to improvements to the region's roads.

The spread of Covid-19 in the middle of my fieldwork brought both challenges and opportunities. For roughly five months at the start of the pandemic, I was fortunate to socially isolate with two families on their farms, an experience that deepened my understanding of rural lives and livelihoods. After leaving their farms, I had to rethink how to safely and ethically conduct ethnography in the era of Covid-19. I adopted a reduced research protocol designed to limit risk to my participants and myself, conducting interviews and observing meetings outdoors with the use of a face mask, and following virtual conversations about village politics through social media.

Digital ethnography through Facebook and WhatsApp was a critical element of my research. Living in a village like Briceño meant that research bled into other parts of my life. Visits to my butcher led to fascinating stories about the village's electrification. Basketball practice with the village team turned into gripe sessions about the lack of opportunities for local youth (at least two former teammates became guerrilla collaborators). The same came to be true of my use of social media. I would go on Facebook with no particular purpose and, after scrolling past a college friend's baby pictures, I would see a publication from the mayor's office with photos documenting road repairs, or, alternatively, a disgruntled community member complaining that their community was left stranded because the mayor had not sent the excavator to repair a landslide. My social media ethnography usually followed what Urbanik and Roks (2020) have referred to as the "one-way mirror approach," in which I observed without interacting.[6] While ethical and practical guidelines of how to conduct and disseminate social media research have not been well established, I follow other ethnographers in choosing to refer only to public posts, and in preserving posters' anonymity by ensuring that they cannot be found in online searches (Shams 2020; Urbanik et al. 2020).

Photography has also been central to my gathering and presentation of data. Cameras have practical advantages for ethnographers. Asking to take someone's photo is an easy way to strike up a conversation. Subsequently sending them the photo helps in building a relationship. And taking pictures is a good way to fill the awkward moments, common in my fieldwork, of hanging around with little obvious purpose. But as I began to publish my photos, I found that they served both a theoretical and a political purpose.

FIGURE I.3. Adrián, Suso, and the other protagonists of *An Uncomfortable Peace* have played an active role in determining the documentary's content.

Ariella Azoulay (2008) has characterized the relationships developed through the camera as a civil contract between the photographed, the photographer, and the spectator which, in portraying violence or social marginalization, demands that the spectator respond to injustice. While photography may "other" research subjects, it can also generate intimacy, recognition, and responsibility (Thomas 2019). I hope the reader will agree that far from misery porn, my photos depict a beautiful region and dignified ways of life. I do not want to romanticize the difficulties of campesino lifestyles, but I am convinced that their natural beauty is central to many people's attachment to rural living and ongoing struggle to establish a place for themselves in a transformed territory.

In addition to photography, my fieldwork has been shaped by my participation as codirector in a documentary film called *An Uncomfortable Peace* (fig. I.3). The project is a collaboration with one Chilean (Ricardo Venegas) and three Colombian filmmakers (Luis Gallego, Óscar Osorio, and Carlos Álvarez), in participation with the two families who are the film's protagonists. Much more than portraying research findings, the process of designing the film alongside its campesino protagonists has been critical to helping me understand Briceño's transformation through their eyes. As just one example, their insistence on portraying their struggles around their road helped me realize the centrality of roads to local experiences of the Colombian state. I have also drawn on hours of film footage of meetings, social mobilizations, and interviews to write this book.

Throughout this text I will focus on a cast of characters whose stories illuminate the linkages between the many elements that constitute Briceño's broader transformation. These people have experienced the peace process era in different ways: Eduardo, a former coca farmer trying to develop a coffee brand; Dideison, a young former coca picker caught between the authority of local politicians and the rearmed guerrillas; Suso and Eugenia, who, after years of fighting for rural development in Briceño, are in the process of leaving the town to seek a better future for their children; and Fabio and Angélica, a couple who share agroecological farming and anti-dam activism.[7] Particularly at the beginning of chapters, I will go into depth on their life stories, livelihood strategies, and political struggles. An understanding of how broader forces interrelate to shape people's everyday choices—which themselves affect conflict, local authority relations, and economic transformation—is inseparable from these lived experiences.

The Roadmap: Governing the Excluded

In the pages that follow, I will describe how the ongoing struggle between state and guerrilla authority for the right to govern Briceño has been configured by campesinos' responses to their exclusion from global systems of production. Chapter 1 chronicles and contextualizes Briceño's experiences with coca, arguing that rather than being a deviant act, coca cultivation represented a means for farmers to preserve valued rural lifestyles in the face of economic exclusion. I describe how farmers began planting coca in the context of plummeting agricultural prices caused by national trade liberalization that exposed them to unfettered market competition. I then analyze the consequences of coca's spread for local authority. Coca tied campesinos' livelihoods to the guerrilla and paramilitary groups that regulated the coca economy. At the same time, coca eradication campaigns driven by the US-sponsored War on Drugs turned state power into a repressive force farmers sought to avoid.

Chapter 2 analyzes the relationship between the peace process and the construction of state authority in Briceño, focusing on local experiences of coca substitution. I explain communities' decision to accept the substitution program and to turn to the state as an authority as being based on three factors: a local desire for the state as source of peace and prosperity, the disarmed guerrillas' authorization of the program, and a combination of ecological factors and state actions that submarined coca's profitability. I then describe collective claims-making on the state that has emerged from the failures of and the opportunities opened by the peace process. Even when these claims criticize state action, they help establish symbolically consequential understandings of the state's rightful role and responsibility. I end by describing how the state has outsourced the substitution program's execution to nonstate actors, which allows state officials to dodge responsibility for delays but also jeopardizes the development of the state's symbolic power.

Chapter 3 describes the patchwork livelihoods to which locals turn in a transformed territory. I focus on four strategies they use to access cash: developing their own brands to secure high coffee prices, deforesting hillsides to farm cattle, replanting coca, and migrating to cities or coca-producing regions. I show how these livelihood strategies are critical to the potential for peace but continue to be undermined by exclusion from legal markets.

Chapter 4 focuses on a different driver of exclusion: extractive megaprojects like a proposed multinational gold mine and a hydroelectric dam that has cut off campesino access to the river and eliminated gold panning economies that were previously critical to local livelihoods. A comparison of the two megaprojects illuminates an incomplete shift in the regimes of dispossession employed by Colombian elites to turn the country into an extractive powerhouse. In the 1990s and 2000s, paramilitary violence was used to enable megaprojects like the Hidroituango dam; but by the 2010s, the Santos administration sought to harness the peace process to "free" resources, such as Briceño's gold, that were hidden within guerrilla territory. However, the example of Briceño—where the rearmed guerrillas stepped in to violently forestall the establishment of a state-supported gold mine—suggests that these projects may only lead to more conflict and compromise state authority. I end by analyzing ongoing local mobilization around Hidroituango, showing how communities have shifted from resistance *against* the dam to a politics of contentious accommodation in which they push the dam company to help them establish a place *within* a transformed territory—another way in which they have begun to pursue their livelihoods through the state.

While the disarmament of the FARC through a landmark peace process promised to establish state authority in areas that were long controlled by the FARC, in Briceño this process has been compromised by the rearmed guerrillas. Chapter 5 describes FARC governance practices, rooting their present-day authority in the historical failures of the formal state to establish law and order in rural communities. While most literature on civil wars would expect the FARC to be locked with the state in a direct battle for local authority, I describe the surprising entanglements between state officials and guerrillas, showing how in many cases governance functions are shared between the two. I use the example of helmet use for motorcyclists—required by national law but prohibited by the FARC—to discuss how communities come to treat either the FARC or the state as authority figures in the face of distinct problems. Finally, in contrast to the spectacle of state rule, I describe the invisible presence of guerrilla authority, rooted in silence, unconfirmed threats, and motorcycles passing in the night.

While earlier chapters describe the disappearance of coca farming and gold panning, two economies mostly independent of the state, chapter 6 explains the political practices that have developed around the influx of state resources that have replaced these informal economies. My analysis centers on ethnographic description of the 2019 mayoral election campaigns. I show how elections have become a privileged time in which villagers across social classes seek to leverage their political support to get guaranteed access to needed state resources. I root these political practices in the economic exclusion that has left locals dependent on state funds, and I describe how their clientelist relationships with local politicians are critical to their experience of a state that has become increasingly consequential to their lives and livelihoods.

Chapter 7 shows how community members' efforts to make a living from heavy and perishable legal agriculture have pushed them to need roads—and, through these roads, the state. I describe how collective struggles around road construction and maintenance turn groups of neighbors into publics— political collectivities brought together around shared interests. This process enables state formation in two ways. The act of repeatedly turning to state officials for help spreads a commonsense belief in the state's rightful role and responsibility, and state officials draw on relationships with representatives of these publics to interface with communities and carry out a range of projects.

Finally, the conclusion to this book revisits Briceño to analyze how a new left-wing national government's attempts at reform have played out on the ground to affect peacebuilding and change livelihood strategies and authority relations. I end with the story of the tragic death of one of the book's protagonists, which illustrates the human stakes of the struggle to make a living in the face of economic exclusion.

Coca: Preserving Valued Rural Lifestyles in the Face of Economic Exclusion

Dideison, Act One

Like most young men from Briceño's rural areas, Dideison came of age through the coca economy. Born in 1999, just as coca was spreading through the village, Dideison was the product of a clandestine relationship between his mother and the man who employed her to cook and clean on his farm. The man, who refused to recognize Dideison as his son, was killed in central Colombia in a robbery when Dideison was only four. Dideison credits his stepfather, a coca farmer, for serving as father figure. As is common in rural Colombia, Dideison helped out on the family farm from the time he could walk. He spread fertilizer on coca plants, picked coca leaves, and served as a messenger to neighboring coca farms.

When Dideison was eight, his stepfather ran afoul of the paramilitary group that controlled the area.[1] Aside from buying the coca, the paramilitaries charged a tax of roughly 150 grams of coca paste a month. When the family's coca plants were infected with a fungus that greatly reduced production, Dideison's stepfather was unable to pay the tax. The paramilitaries accused him of "pirating," selling his crop to outside buyers who offered higher prices.

"They started to threaten us, saying that he was 'pirating,'" Dideison says. "My mother and stepfather were living with fear. Sometimes when we left and came back to the house, we found paramilitaries sleeping inside, or we found bullet shells on the ground. So we had to leave."

They moved to a house owned by one of Dideison's uncles on the urban margins of Medellín. In the city, Dideison says, he felt lost, missing the freedom, communion with nature, and beautiful landscapes of the countryside. He cites exposure to crime and violence as one of the major downsides to city living: "It was a complete change going from a farm to a city, which obviously has more dangers, in all the senses. It's not a secret to anyone that Medellín has a lot of drugs and vandals." It is illustrative of how much campesinos value rural lifestyles that even after suffering violent displacement from a war-torn rural region, Dideison still understands the countryside as a place of tranquility in comparison to urban landscapes.

The change to city living was equally difficult for his stepfather, who had spent a lifetime farming and was ill-suited to the few city jobs available. And if money was hard to come by, it was also newly essential to their subsistence: "Here you can grow plantain or other foods, but there, you have to buy everything," Dideison says. After one year, his mother sent Dideison (but not his younger brother and sister) back to live with his grandparents in Briceño. After another year, when a guerrilla offensive reclaimed territory from the paramilitaries, the whole family returned, with Dideison's grandfather giving them a piece of land on the family farm.

When Dideison finished fifth grade at the age of twelve, he dropped out of school to work full-time picking coca and contribute a needed income to his household. His uncles and cousins—many of whom had also left school—introduced him to the world of *raspachines*—literally, "scrapers," the word used to refer to coca pickers. *Raspachines* get their name from their picking technique: they bend over the coca plant, grip the bottom of a stem, and alternately draw each hand along the branch back toward their body in a quick scraping motion, taking the leaves while leaving the branch intact. They were paid by the *arroba*, twenty-five-pound sacks of leaves that they carried two at a time to nearby jungle laboratories. There, "chemists" would cut up the leaves with Weedwackers before soaking them in gasoline and cooking the liquid with a toxic brew of chemicals to extract coca's psychoactive alkaloids. The process produced coca paste, chalky rocks that are an intermediate stage in the production of cocaine. Farmers would sell their coca paste to whichever armed group controlled their territory: either paramilitaries or buyers organized by the FARC guerrillas.

Dideison began traveling through the territory, following coca harvests from farm to farm with his relatives and other *raspachines* he befriended along the way. Room and board were included in their pay. The biggest farms had bunk beds for as many as sixty laborers, and employed local women to cook and clean for the *raspachines*. These women, including Dideison's mother, were arguably the hardest workers in the coca economy. They would wake up before dawn to light the wood stove and make *los tragos* (the drinks), usually a pre-breakfast snack of crackers and hot chocolate that sent the *raspachines* into the coca fields. When the fields were far from the house, the women would prepare and pack dozens of breakfasts and lunches into plastic Tupperware containers that someone, usually the women's younger children, would carry to the workers. The women would clean and do laundry before preparing dinner for the workforce, facing a mountain of dishes to wash before they could go to sleep.

While some women did pick coca, the social world of the *raspachín* was dominated by young men. In the fields, Dideison says, they told exaggerated stories of their sexual exploits and bet their earnings on who could pick more coca faster. After a long day of picking, the nights turned into summer camp. Young men played cards, dominoes, and chess with each other, often betting portions of the following day's harvest. Some *raspachines* learned magic tricks and showed them off to great delight. They also played a game called *desquite* (revenge), in which they sparred with PVC pipes, no head shots allowed. The improvised duels left bruises but rarely hard feelings.

The grown men who worked as *raspachines* also joined in the fun, transmitting their practical knowledge to the youth. They worked together to build free weights to use for workouts, or even a swing set. "And there was one *señor* who picked and dried plantain leaves, and used them to make hats," Dideison says. "I learned, more or less, how to make a hat, though I never perfected it. But it was a way to entertain yourself. I learned how to sew, I learned how to cook helping the *señora* that made the food."

When they had stripped all the coca plants of their leaves, the *raspachines* moved on to the next farm. Normally, the next harvest wasn't hard to find—owners of coca fields communicated with each other when they needed workers. Sometimes Dideison and his friends had to cross the "invisible borders" that demarcated FARC and paramilitary territory. In these cases, the owners of the coca fields called local commanders on both sides for permission to let them pass. Dideison spent as long as two months moving between coca farms without returning home, carrying his clothes, toothbrush, and earnings in a backpack.

After weeks on isolated farms and with their pockets full of cash, many of the young men he worked with would travel to the village center, which, with the influx of coca money, became a bustling center of commerce and vice. Coca farmers, *raspachines*, and armed paramilitaries filled local bars. Business owners carried handheld scales to accept payment in coca paste; this setting of the currency used for commerce is just one example of a central state function that was displaced by the coca economy.

At times, Dideison indulged in the partying, but he says most of his earnings went to support his family, elevating their standard of living (fig. 1.1). When he returned from picking coca, he would give his mother all the money he had for safekeeping. "Until one time I asked her, and she told me that she had one thousand dollars. So I started buying things. I bought a television, I

FIGURE 1.1. Dideison helps his mother process coffee on the family farm.

bought her a rice cooker, which at that time was the new cool thing [*lo último en guaracha*], because we had cooked everything on a wood stove. After that, I bought her a new gas stove. I bought myself a cell phone, and I gave one to her as well. And I helped my stepfather with the groceries."

Nevertheless, his mother had never approved of his decision to drop out of school. When Dideison returned home from picking his coca, she pressured him to reenroll. Dideison was resistant: "I thought, 'If I study, how I will I make money? When here I am working, and I have a good income coming in. So why would I return to school?' And she would tell me, 'Look, this isn't forever. At some point [coca] is going to disappear, and without an education you'll be left with nothing.'" At the age of thirteen, after a year as a full-time *raspachín*, Dideison returned to school. When there were harvests nearby, he would pick coca in the afternoon after class, and during vacation periods he would still chase coca harvests around the territory with his friends and cousins. However, he also completed his high school degree, finishing as one of the top students in his class.

Shortly after Dideison returned to school, and five years before the state would launch a coca substitution program to incentivize farmers to voluntarily give up their coca, his community filled with nearly one thousand manual eradicators—soldiers tasked with destroying coca crops. The soldiers set up a massive camp not far from Dideison's family farm, and traveled from farm to farm, ripping out farmers' plants by hand. An air of tension took over. "There was a very tense coexistence," Dideison says, describing repeated confrontations between soldiers and the community members whose livelihoods they were destroying. "The army started seeing the community as an enemy, treating us poorly."

The eradication campaign and others that followed interrupted the regional economy, destroying several months of coca harvests. However, most local farmers replanted their coca as soon as manual eradicators left. Fumigation was even less effective, as farmers saved their plants by bathing them in home remedies or cutting off the tops before the poison could reach the roots.

Coca survived in the region until the farmers themselves put an end to it in 2017, joining a coca substitution program that promised them resources to develop legal crops. Dideison worked one final harvest just after the substitution program began, picking coca leaves even as other young men followed him, uprooting the plants for good. "They paid us double for that one," he says laughing. "But what's left for us now?"

In early 2018, with no work available in Briceño, Dideison moved to Medellín to work for an aunt who ran a small-scale clothing manufacturing business. He was nineteen. Six days a week, he woke at 3:15 a.m. to catch the public aerial cable car that connected his aunt's neighborhood, high up the walls of the Aburrá River valley, to the rest of Medellín. Two trains and one bus later, he had traversed the congested city to reach the workshop. After working at sewing machines from seven to four, the return trip was even worse. "Those long lines [for the train and cable car] made me want to cry," he says. He often did not arrive home until 9 p.m.

Urban living, Dideison says, makes him miserable. Like many campesino youth, he is more comfortable hearing birdsong rather than car horns, riding a mule or dirt bike rather than a crowded bus, and picking a plantain from a tree rather than from an aisle of a grocery store. But he knows that without coca, building a prosperous rural future is a challenge.

Introduction

From Hollywood movies to hip-hop songs to Netflix series, images of riches, glamour, and spectacular violence dominate popular representations of the cocaine trade. However, long before becoming the white powder that goes up noses around the world, funds ostentatious drug mansions, and bankrolls armed groups in Colombian jungles, cocaine begins as an unassuming light green coca plant tended by rural campesinos in places like Briceño. For these farmers, who see little more than 1 percent of cocaine's eventual profits (Mejía and Rico 2010), coca has a different meaning. For them, it is a crop they coax from the soil with the aid of sunshine, rainwater, a variety of agrochemicals, and their own labor. It is a crop, like coffee, corn, and beans before it, that they hope will provide them with enough income to feed their families, improve their future prospects, and maybe even squeeze some pleasure out of life along the way. It is a crop that enabled Dideison to buy his mother a rice cooker and Eduardo a farm to establish a family.

Coca, however, differs from traditional crops in one way that is highly consequential for rural farmers: it is illegal. This means, on the one hand, that the coca economy exists outside the purview of the Colombian state and is controlled by a variety of armed groups. When the state does participate, it is with eradication programs that treat coca farmers like criminals and seek to destroy their livelihoods. However, coca's illegality brings a significant advantage: it exists outside a global corporate food production regime that excludes them by driving the prices of legal crops untenably low. Unlike coffee, corn, and beans, coca is insulated from competition with cheap mass-produced goods controlled by giant agribusiness.

In this chapter I offer a multiscale political economy of coca that shows how international economic transformations and national policy changes combined to motivate and morally authorize local decisions to cultivate coca—decisions that altered local authority dynamics by creating material incentives for farmers to side with armed groups that organized the coca economy at the expense of a state that sought to destroy their livelihoods.

The first section of this chapter moves between local testimony and macro-economic analysis to situate coca cultivation in the context of transformations in global food production that have excluded smallholding farmers. In Briceño, the trigger was a major dip in coffee prices that were newly exposed to unfettered market forces. As prices fell below the local cost of production, farmers turned to coca as the only crop that offered a productive niche within the global economy.

Second, I explore the meaning of coca within the moral world of the village. While coca carries significant ethical ambiguity, it came to represent less a moral transgression than a way for campesinos to preserve morally valued rural lifestyles in the face of structural dispossession. Thus, even more than ensuring their survival, coca allowed campesinos to avoid the precarity and squalor of urban alternatives, and even improved their families' standard of living.

But in tying campesino livelihoods to the guerrillas and paramilitaries who organized the coca economy, coca also helped armed groups extend their governance practices and authority. In the third section, I show that while community members generally sought to maintain neutrality in the face of terrifying violence, coca cultivation pushed communities to turn to armed groups as the local authority.

At the same time, coca growers turned away from the state. The final section describes how local experiences with coca eradication campaigns established state power as something to be avoided. A 2020 eradication campaign in which the community, obliged by the rearmed FARC guerrillas, collectively mobilized to remove military eradicators reveals how coca repression turned communities *against* the state while aligning their interests *with* the guerrillas.

The Bonanza: Coca and the Preservation of Rural Lifestyles

In telling the story of coca's spread through Briceño in the late 1990s to early 2000s, I make a single overarching argument: In the face of forces that have assaulted rural lifestyles by excluding smallholders from participation in a globalized food production regime, coca granted Briceño's campesinos a productive niche within the global economy. At the same time as the prices of agricultural goods plummeted and urban slums the world over filled with dispossessed farmers, coca's very illegality insulated Briceño's campesinos from competition with massive agribusiness, allowing them to stay in the territory and preserve valued rural lifestyles. In this context, planting coca was a response to global forces that made legal goods untenable. However, it was more than an individual decision; coca spread through a fundamentally collective process that provided communal authorization which helped overcome the illegal crop's moral ambiguity.

Before coca took over, coffee was Briceño's major cash crop. Coffee's one yearly harvest, from roughly October to December, was critical to the temporal organization of economic life. During this time, coffee farmers depended on the labor of young men to pick the ripe beans by hand (fig. 1.2). For the rest of the year, paid labor was only occasionally available, on a small number of larger cattle or sugarcane haciendas owned by wealthy families. Many locals, men and women alike, also made money by both panning for gold and fishing along the Cauca River.

Most families, living on isolated farms up to a day's journey from the village center, fed themselves primarily with subsistence agriculture. They cultivated staple crops like plantains, yuca, rice, corn, and beans, while also maintaining vegetable gardens, chickens for eggs and meat, and, for the better-off, cows for milk. In addition to coffee, they would sell surplus crops of corn and beans after saving enough for their families' consumption. Some also raised cattle to sell for meat.

FIGURE 1.2. Adrián picks coffee. Before coca took over the municipality, coffee's yearly harvest provided paid labor for the village's young men.

People described this time—roughly the 1960s through the 1990s—in different ways. Emilio, for example, focused on the poverty: "The houses had no floors, the walls were made of mud. We had no milk and few eggs. Families slept on one bed, made from leaves. We wore torn shirts and walked through the jungle without shoes. It was absolute poverty. Many kids died of dysentery and gastroenteritis, and women died while giving birth." In contrast, Lina described her childhood in idyllic terms: "We all stayed in the same bed, four children. In the patio we would throw toads at each other for fun. The food was delicious. We got everything from nature. I remember that the only things we bought were salt, soap, and candles. And we lived content, happy. I had a tranquil childhood."

Coca cultivation, everyone agrees, made a significant dent in both the poverty and the tranquility of rural life. The crop came to different parts of the municipality at different times, brought by enterprising young men from Briceño who had worked as *raspachines* picking coca in the nearby municipality of Tarazá. But while the first accounts of coca in Briceño date back to the early 1990s, the crop did not spread through the municipality until around 2000.

Why then? Coffee's global price nosedived from the late 1990s to the early 2000s, dropping from a relative high of $1.79 a pound in 1997 to $1.29 a pound in 1998, $1.04 in 1999, $0.90 in 2000, $0.56 in 2001, and finally a low of $0.54 a pound in 2002 (Macrotrends 2024). In this context, coca emerged as a needed alternative. Like a boulder picking up pace as it rolled downhill, coca eliminated all other economies in its wake. Farmers distressed by plummeting coffee prices began following the lead of neighbors they saw profiting from the new crop. Even campesinos who wanted to continue growing coffee were left with little choice; the young men they had long depended on to pick their yearly harvest started picking coca, making twice as much. It hardly mattered, though. Coffee's plummeting prices dropped so low that even at the original wage, farmers would have had to pay pickers more than the beans fetched on the market. Ripe coffee beans rotted on their bushes, and each year, more farmers turned to coca.

THE ECONOMIC CONTEXT OF DRUG CULTIVATION: EXCLUSION THROUGH GLOBAL MARKET INTEGRATION

Coca spread through Briceño, therefore, as a direct result of what economists would call a negative price shock that decimated the coffee economy. This may seem like an inevitable feature of coffee prices, which are notorious for volatility based on environmental conditions like frosts and droughts and outbreaks of violence that periodically slash worldwide production. The fact that coffee takes two years to mature only intensifies these swings; farmers who react to high prices by planting more coffee often find that by the time their plants are maturing, global supply has overcorrected and driven prices back down. But underlying the dip in the price of coffee—and also explaining why coca rather than legal crops replaced it—are fundamental transformations in the organization of agricultural production and trade that have integrated smallholders within global markets before systematically excluding them through falling prices that give them little chance to compete.

Indeed, a description of the market factors behind coffee's price swings overlooks the fact that coffee has not always been subject to unfettered market forces. Following the 1959 Cuban Revolution, and with Cold War anti-communist fears dominating national politics, US President John F. Kennedy created the "Alliance for Progress" to weaken communist insurrections by stabilizing Latin American economies. Among its initiatives was the International Coffee Agreement (ICA), which established flexible worldwide production quotas, protecting coffee prices from 1963 to 1989 (Hough 2022; Kamola 2008). With the ICA in place, coffee prices increased sixfold by 1980 (Kamola 2008), bringing prosperity to farmers and altering dynamics of rural authority—just as coca would do decades later.

In this case, however, the entity that took on governance functions was not an armed group, but Colombia's National Coffee Federation (Fedecafé). Indeed, Fedecafé had long taxed Colombian coffee exports, using the money to develop the coffee sector. But coffee's rising profits allowed it to increase its influence in coffee-growing communities. Fedecafé issued ID cards that their members used to access benefits like technical assistance, subsidized credit and fertilizers, and purchase points with price floors which ensured that farmers would always be able to sell their coffee at a profit (Hough 2022). They set up municipal and departmental coffee committees with elected officers to serve as a bridge between the national organization and local farmers. They also built schools, hospitals, aqueducts, and electrical grids, turning core coffee regions into the most developed rural areas in the country (Hough 2022). Briceño was not as privileged as many coffee regions, but its local coffee committee did successfully petition Fedecafé for resources to help construct sewage systems, schools, and roads.

Phillip Hough (2022) argues that Fedecafé intervention changed campesino attitudes and cultivating practices in two ways, each of which primed them for the eventual transition to coca. First, it incentivized campesinos to devote more of their land and labor to coffee rather than subsistence crops, increasing their integration within, and dependence on, world markets. Second, Fedecafé technicians pushed campesinos to maximize production through costly inputs like fertilizers, herbicides, insecticides, and specially bred seeds. When prices were high, this meant more profits; but it also meant increased exposure to price dips.

When the Berlin Wall and the communist threat crumbled in 1989, the ICA collapsed along with them. No longer subject to the quota system, coffee from countries like Vietnam began flooding the market. Coffee prices cratered from 1989 to 1992 before recovering in 1994 due to drought and frost in Brazil (Hough 2022). Still, once Brazilian production recovered, coffee prices entered into a deeper and longer-lasting crisis. Fedecafé could no longer maintain national price floors, nor could it subsidize fertilizers and loans (Hough 2022). In this context, facing economic ruin, Briceño's farmers turned to coca.

Coca, of course, is not the only alternative to coffee. However, at the same time as the ICA's collapse eliminated protections for coffee growers, other legal crops in Colombia were similarly exposed to unfettered market competition through broader shifts in agricultural economies.

We pick up the story in the 1950s, when development policies began spreading Green Revolution technologies like high-yielding seeds, irrigation systems, and chemical fertilizers, herbicides, and insecticides to farmers across the world (Friedmann and McMichael 1989; Gupta 1998). At the same time, US producers started shipping massive quantities of state-subsidized surplus grain to the Global South, on the basis of the theory that access to cheap grain would drive industrial development and counter the communist threat by feeding a growing mass of rural farmers who would relocate to cities to work in factories (Araghi 2009; Friedmann and McMichael 1989). The result was a global division—and reduction—of agricultural labor. The Colombian market was flooded with cheap imported rice and wheat even as the state supported crops like corn, rice, and beans with both tariffs to protect prices and Green Revolution technologies to increase production (Brittain 2010; Machado C. 1986; Roa-Clavijo 2021).

Protections for and investment in smallholding farming, however, would not last long. On an international level, developmentalist approaches to agriculture were replaced in the 1970s by what McMichael (2005) refers to as the corporate food regime, which rests on the economic doctrine of comparative advantage: if a food product can be produced more efficiently by a particular region or group, then that region or group should produce more, and should export it to less efficient regions.

In Colombia the inflection point was 1990, when the administration of President César Gaviria began pushing a series of market-driven liberalizing policies known as the Opening (*Apertura*). These reforms dropped tariffs for agricultural goods from 31.5 percent to 15 percent, and from 1990 to 1997 agricultural imports grew at a staggering 23 percent yearly (Jaramillo 2001). Then, in 1999, the Colombian economy collapsed and the government took out a $2.7 billion loan from the IMF that included structural adjustment conditions requiring Colombia to privatize public services, eliminate agricultural subsidies, and open the economy even more to foreign investments and products (Leech 2011). In 2012, a free trade agreement with the United States took effect, further cutting tariffs that protected smallholder agriculture. By 2015, US food exports to Colombia had increased by a factor of five (including previously protected products like corn, beans, and milk), Colombia was importing 30 percent of its food, and agriculture's share of the GDP had dropped to 6.2 percent. In 1990, when the Opening began, the share had been 21.8 percent (Hylton and Tauss 2016). The prices that campesinos fetched for their crops plummeted.

It makes sense that Briceño's farmers, cultivating on steep hillsides without agricultural machinery or the capital to invest in fertilizers and other agricultural inputs, would be at a significant disadvantage in comparison to massive flatland Midwest US corn farms. However, their disadvantage was only deepened by the fact that, even as Global South states cut support, agricultural subsidies persisted in the Global North, driving prices artificially low. In 2002, the same year in which the global price of coffee hit an all-time low and coca completely took over Briceño's economy, heavily subsidized US agribusiness exports were priced at 43 percent below the cost of production for wheat, 25 percent below the cost for soybeans, 13 percent below it for corn, and 35 percent below it for rice (McMichael 2005). Smallholding farmers across the Global South have little hope of competing.

Thus, even as the corporate food regime has proven remarkably efficient at producing massive quantities of food, it has excluded large numbers of smallholding farmers from legal global agricultural markets. Millions have lost their land, congregating in urban slums where they find very limited opportunities for formal employment (Araghi 2009; Davis 2006; Li 2010; Mc-Michael 2009).

Alternatively, smallholding farmers may turn to illegal drug crops like coca, which need only one subsidy from the state: their continued illegality (Bourgois 2018). Coca's illegality guarantees it a place outside the competition of the corporate food regime—even if climate allowed, it's difficult to imagine an eight-hundred-acre coca farm in the flatlands of rural Iowa. Coca's illegality turns isolation and lack of roads into an advantage, affording some protection from eradicators, and granting smallholding rural farmers an increasingly elusive productive niche within global capitalist markets.

Indeed, the underlying economic forces that drove coca cultivation in Briceño—where smallholding farmers were drawn into production for markets, found themselves unable to compete with prices depressed by unfettered market competition, and turned to illicit crops—are present in many areas of drug cultivation. In the world center of opium production, Afghanistan's Helmand Province, development programs first drew subsistence farmers into cash economies before a 1970s downturn in global wheat and cotton prices pushed a shift to opium poppies (Bradford 2019). Poppy cultivation spread through Myanmar's Shan state in the late 1990s as integration into international markets sank the prices of crops like tea and garlic (Meehan 2021). In the 1980s, Mexican farmers began cultivating marijuana for the US market after cuts in state agricultural support and international dips in food prices (Maldonado Aranda 2013). The 1994 North American Free Trade Agreement (NAFTA) then cut tariffs on US food imports, driving down corn prices by 66 percent and destroying the livelihoods of more than a million Mexican farmers. Many of those farmers then planted marijuana or opium poppies to produce heroin for the growing US market (Dube et al. 2016; Morris 2020). Even Colombia's first drug boom, a marijuana bonanza that supplied as much as 70 percent of the weed smoked in the US in the 1970s, was led by growers and smugglers excluded from legal livelihoods after global economic recession hit Colombia's manufacturing and coffee economies (Britto 2020).

In all these cases, illicit crops have cushioned smallholders from capitalist market imperatives that would otherwise dispossess them (Thomson 2023). While millions of smallholders were excluded from global economic production and condemned to urban slums, Briceño and other coca-growing areas maintained a degree of prosperity, even attracting unemployed city dwellers (Richani 2013, 69). But also critical to coca's ability to protect rural lifestyles are a set of labor-intensive growing practices that distribute its profits widely.

COCA: AN INCLUSIVE AGRICULTURAL ECONOMY

As distinct from legal agricultural production that has used technological advances to become more capital- and less labor-intensive, coca is a highly inclusive economy that extends its economic benefits across class and gender lines. In Briceño, those who grew coca, whether on their own land or on rented plots in exchange for 10 percent of the profits, enjoyed four to five harvests a year. Landowners, of course, also profited greatly from these rental arrangements. For every harvest, farmers hired coca pickers like Dideison to pick the coca in exchange for a certain price per kilo of leaves. With roughly a ton of handpicked leaves going into making a kilo of coca paste, there was plenty of work to go around. For this process of transformation, many farmers also hired "chemists" who specialized in extracting coca's alkaloids.

In the context of gender roles in which men served as breadwinners and women performed unpaid domestic labor, coca also expanded the paid labor available to women in the village. Women were hired to cook and clean for the coca pickers who stayed on isolated farms during harvests. And even when farmers' wives did the cooking and cleaning for no pay, coca was lucrative enough that its dirty dishes provided them with some discretionary income. Women who washed the pans and utensils used to cook coca paste would apply water and acid to extract additional coca, cut it with ammonia, and then cook it to produce a small quantity of coca paste known as the *repela*. While this did not approach the earnings of male farmers, some women reported making as much as $250 from a single batch.

Coca offered a route to upward mobility through which poor men like Eduardo, as described in the introduction to this book, could acquire land and some measure of prosperity: pick coca for pay, save money to establish your own crop on rented land, and finally buy your own land to both cultivate coca and rent out to other coca farmers. Coca's profits also facilitated access to credit, often a problem for farmers—particularly the many without legal titles to their land—who need to invest in planting and fertilizing crops months or even years before harvests. Local stores sold on credit to coca farmers with the expectation that they would be paid once the farmers sold their harvest. This custom was so widespread that one former storeowner told me he had to offer credit, because otherwise coca farmers would simply take their business elsewhere. It was a custom, notably, that did not extend to farmers of legal crops, and which has largely disappeared along with coca.

Even those who did not directly work in the coca economy benefited. As coca farmers abandoned subsistence agriculture, those who continued cultivating food found a new market for their crops. Pig and chicken farms popped up as coca pickers who had once lived on beans, rice, plantains, and eggs began to expect meat for every meal. Perhaps no one benefited more than local merchants. Coca farmers must buy herbicides and fertilizers for cultivation, chemicals for processing, and food to sustain agricultural workers. Briceño's village center filled with stores offering these goods as well as "luxury items" like cell phones, new clothes, and kitchen appliances. Bars filled with young men who came to the village center after weeks on isolated coca farms with money to spend.

Coca was the rising tide that lifted the economic fortunes of all—men and women, poor farmers and affluent merchants, landowners and landless campesinos.

The Moral Meaning of Coca:
Bread, Roses, and Preserving Valued Rural Lifestyles

Cultivating coca allowed campesinos to buck global trends of smallholder exclusion, turning Briceño into a boomtown. At the same time, as a stigmatized illegal drug whose profits were associated with both violence and vice, coca offered a significant challenge to traditional campesino morals. Dominant policy narratives tend to explain the cultivation of illicit crops through stark economic calculations, whether rooted in the greed or the destitution of coca farmers. However, how campesinos resolve coca's moral ambiguity—as source of violence and social decay, but also as the only crop that allowed them to preserve valued rural lifestyles—is a critical element in both coca's spread through the village and campesinos' later willingness to give up their coca through the substitution program.

"This village changed with coca," Felipe, a forty-year-old coffee farmer and local merchant, tells me as we stand in Briceño's nearly empty main square on a Saturday night in early 2018, half a year into the coca substitution program.

Two men ride horses in circles around the square. One blasts traditional *porro* music from a small portable speaker that hangs from his shoulder. The speaker is not quite up to the volume he demands of it, and the *porro*'s bass line crackles in complaint. The men seem to be showing off for someone, but the square is nearly empty.

"But when *patos* started seeing the profits that came from coca," Felipe continues, they started planting their own on rented land."

"What are *patos*?" I ask him. The world literally translates as "duck," but I have yet to see the first mallard in Briceño.

He points toward a bar across the plaza. "You can see them over there, *pateando*, drinking, playing billiards." Four or five young men hold beers and cue sticks around a pool table.

Felipe explains that with the coca, these previously impoverished young men suddenly had money in their pockets. "All of this used to be full," Felipe says, gesturing at the relatively empty street. "The billiard halls, the bars." He explains that *patos* would pick coca until they had saved up some money, then come to the village to gamble, drink, or engage in other immoral pursuits.

"This was when drugs came to the village," he says. "And prostitution." Felipe explains that a brothel was established on the outskirts of town, below the swimming pool. Its proprietors would bring in different sex workers every week, from Medellín.

"Did all the prostitutes come from outside?" I ask.

"Yes," he says, "but many girls from here also got into trouble. The paramilitaries would ask them 'How much?' or even force them. There are many kids in this village right now with paramilitary fathers."

Another thing coca brought was violence. Felipe outlines a few scenarios. Drunk or stoned *patos*, apparently, have a propensity for fighting. The paramilitaries themselves would get into disputes while drinking in the village center—disputes they often resolved with guns. They, along with the guerrillas, also used violence against either civilian supporters of the other side or enterprising community members who sought higher prices for their coca paste with other buyers. "Many children were left without fathers," he said. "And many women were left widows."

Felipe repeats often that things are much better without the coca. Violence is gone. The town has little to no crime, and drug addiction has also nearly disappeared. Without the large amounts of disposable income available from the coca, the brothel has also closed.[2]

Nevertheless, narratives of the social decay brought by coca are counterbalanced by the ways coca rescued embattled campesino livelihoods, as described above. Even beyond economic calculation, coca became associated in the local collective imagination with two elements that Briceño's campesinos value highly in moral terms: the ability to build a better future for their families, and the preservation of living on and from the land.

A classic hymn and demand of the US labor movement reminds us, "Hearts starve as well as bodies; give us bread, but give us roses." In similar terms, while scholars of both the rural and the urban poor have long been understandably focused on the question of survival (Auyero 2001; Phillips 2018; Scott 1977), the politics and livelihood strategies of Colombian campesinos rest not only on economic security but on a better and more meaningful life—roses with their bread. Feeling we are making progress toward meaningful aspirations is a human need nearly as motivating as subsistence. For decades, coffee provided roses for many: farmers used its profits to build up their homes, acquire livestock, and give their children land or education. When coffee prices cratered, coca took its place, with its economic advantages opening even more opportunity for advancement. While campesinos associate coca with vice, they also talk about how it allowed them to buy farms, educate their children, and enjoy themselves—including, in one commonly mentioned example, being able to make a first visit to the beach.

But in the face of the very real existential threats occasioned by the plummeting prices of legal crops, coca also came to represent the preservation of morally valued rural lifestyles and campesino identities. Importantly, the potential of abandoning farming to take up residence in urban slums represents cultural as much as economic dislocation. Like the experience of Dideison, fortunate to find work through his aunt's business but condemned to a long and uncomfortable commute, city living brings distressing changes in both lifestyle and physical environment. Campesinos who have relocated to urban slums from Briceño often describe their loss in sensuous terms, expressing nostalgia for the beautiful landscapes, clean air, and birdsong of the countryside. And while the urban poor, often through tremendous ingenuity, may have increased access to cash income, they give up the subsistence crops that guarantee their families' basic nutritional needs.

Indeed, a central element of campesino identity is self-sufficiency—the ability, through physical labor in concert with the land, to provide for their families' needs. Like Dideison and his stepfather, campesinos who move to cities often describe themselves as feeling lost, lacking the sense of purpose offered by a daily routine of leaving the house, machete in hand, to tend to their crops and animals and return home with sacks of yuca, plantains, and corn for lunch (fig. 1.3). This purposelessness exists in tension with a sense, particularly among parents, that cities hold the promise of a better future for their children, fed by both increased educational opportunities and the

FIGURE 1.3. Working in concert with the land to provide for their families' sustenance provides campesinos with both nutrition and purpose.

significant difficulties of agricultural economies. Still, campesinos describe cities as places of crime and moral depravity, where their children may be corrupted and where meeting basic needs requires access to cash.

The dislocations of urban living are more than simply theoretical. Even as coca brought prosperity to Briceño, increasing levels of violence forced some campesinos to leave, many ending up in Medellín. Even those who did not leave heard about the experiences of neighbors and family who had fled to cities. Often these served as cautionary tales, highlighting the struggles of city life.

Victor is a young man whose family left Briceño in 2007 in the wake of a military eradication campaign—more on this shortly—that decimated the municipality's coca crops. While most farmers replanted their coca, the local economy stalled for the seven months it took for the plants to grow back. Victor's family were not coca farmers; they operated a small butcher shop in the village center. But with coca's disappearance, business ground to a halt. There was no work for *raspachines*, and thus no need (or money) for coca farmers to buy meat to feed them. When Victor's father slaughtered a cow, more than half the meat would go bad before the family could find buyers for it. Even worse, many of their coca farming clients had long bought meat on credit, and those debts were never repaid.

Facing destitution and with no economic opportunities in Briceño, Victor's family moved in with his aunt in Medellín. The home was in a *barrio de invasión* (squatters' community), where masses of farmers displaced by economic difficulties and rural violence erected houses that were often little more than tarps draped over wooden poles. Victor's aunt's house was a small shelter for the five people who already lived there. With the addition of Victor, his five sisters, and his mom and dad, there was hardly room for everyone to lie down at night.

"When it rained," Victor remembers, "yellow mud would stream down the hillsides and cover the dirt floor." They often woke up to find ooze trails left by slugs that would pass directly over sleeping children.

To feed the family, Victor's parents would go to large outdoor markets, rifling through dumpsters filled with spoiled fruits and vegetables to find something salvageable. After a few months, Victor's mom took over the operation of a small food stall in the local elementary school, selling candy and homemade meat pastries to students. This gave the family some economic stability, but she lost the business when city inspectors found that without running water, it did not meet sanitary standards. Victor's father worked construction jobs off and on when he could find them. Victor dropped out of school after sixth grade, going to work helping a local shoemaker. His sisters continued studying to finish high school. "But when you hear stories about people who have to choose between paying for transportation or food, that's true," Victor says. "My sisters experienced that. They would come home from school fainting after all day without eating."

Given the alternative of urban struggle and suffering, it's not hard to understand why coca became a morally acceptable option. However, this understanding of coca's morality directly contradicts dominant national narratives that present coca growers as criminals (Ramírez 2011)—attitudes of which coca farmers are well aware. In response to this stigmatization, Estefanía Ciro (2019) has shown how coca growers in southern Colombia invoke a particular set of narratives to turn coca cultivation into a legitimate rather than a criminal activity: they grow coca because they have no other alternative, they make only a pittance compared to the narcotraffickers who are the true criminals, and they use coca profits for virtuous ends like educating their children. As I have shown, these narratives have a significant basis in reality. But the crucial point is not these narratives' accuracy. What matters is that, in the face of broader transformations that threaten morally valued rural ways of life, communities like Briceño collectively understand coca cultivation as a legitimate if morally fraught behavior. And this has important consequences for their relationship to competing local authority figures—both the state forces who destroy coca livelihoods and the armed groups who organize them.

Coca, Violence, and Armed Group Legitimacy

The strategies that locals choose to meet their everyday needs and fulfill their aspirations—and specifically their decisions as to whether they turn to armed groups or state actors—are central to the development of peace and authority. Armed group authority predated coca in Briceño—campesinos had turned to the FARC to fulfill governance functions since the early 1980s (see chapter 5). However, coca changed local authority dynamics in three related ways: it motivated the entrance of the paramilitaries, an additional armed group that violently contested the FARC's control of the territory; it directly tied local livelihoods to both the FARC and the paramilitaries, who regulated the coca economy; and it provided the basis for an increase in interactions through which campesinos turned to armed groups as local authority figures.

Paramilitary groups arrived in Briceño around the year 2000, helping a burgeoning coca economy to spread by encouraging farmers to grow coca and even loaning them money to offset start-up costs. They set up purchase points in the village center and obliged farmers in areas under their control to sell only to them. Local police and the military only contributed to their impunity, receiving monthly payments from paramilitary commanders, standing guard at coca purchase points, and openly referring to them as their "cousins" in the face of their common enemy, the FARC.

The paramilitary incursion turned Briceño into a war zone. Previously, the FARC had seen the village as a place of rest from nearby areas of pitched combat, and traveled in small groups of a half dozen combatants, often with only a couple of pistols between them. This all changed in the face of violent competition with paramilitaries for control of the territory and its drug economy. Many more guns and guerrillas entered the territory, and the FARC began using violence to dissuade collaboration with the paramilitaries, who themselves used violence against supposed guerrilla collaborators.

The stories locals tell of this period are terrifying: massacres that left the streets covered with dead bodies; a black truck controlled by the paramilitaries that picked up supposed FARC collaborators, never to be seen again; a period of time when the guerrillas fired from the hillsides above into the village's main square and police station every other day. Many civilians were caught in the middle, targeted for supporting one side or another or simply unlucky to be hit by wayward bullets. Through 2022, the municipality, with a population of 8,000, had 9,499 registered victims, including 8,639 victims of forced displacement and 918 victims of homicide (Unidad para la atención y reparación integral a las víctimas 2022).[3]

The guerrillas' role in the coca economy was more ambiguous than that of the paramilitaries. Many farmers from the area under guerrilla control described the FARC as the direct buyers of their coca. However, an ex-guerrilla commander I interviewed in Briceño admitted to charging a 10 percent tax on all coca sales, but insisted that the guerrillas only organized outsider buyers to protect campesinos from drug gangs who might take advantage of them.[4] Like the paramilitaries, however, they also imposed a death sentence on farmers who "pirated" by selling their coca elsewhere.

Whether they directly purchased or only taxed the crop, the coca economy transformed the dynamics of FARC authority. Indeed, guerrillas had long performed statelike functions such as resolving disputes, keeping law and order, and organizing communal work groups to repair mule paths (see chapter 5). Coca, however, provided the basis for an intensification in the patterned interactions through which campesinos treated the FARC as the local authority and turned to the guerrillas for their everyday needs. Coca farmers anxiously awaited the FARC commanders' announcements of when and where the group would set up coca purchase points. At these points, they stood in lines organized by the guerrillas before paying—if begrudgingly— the 10 percent tax. With the entry of the coca economy, the FARC also defended the rights of agricultural laborers, imposing—and subsequently raising—a minimum daily wage and ensuring that workers had breaks of thirty minutes for breakfast and an hour for lunch.

Thus, if the coffee economy had previously helped establish the "stateness" of Fedecafé, coca provided the basis for the FARC to extend its governance practices and local authority.[5] And even more important than what the guerrillas did was the patterned behavior of community members. To borrow from Beetham's (1991) classic description of the legitimation of power, repeated interactions through which coca farmers treated the FARC as local authority both provided public evidence of consent to its power and exerted a "subjectively binding force" on the farmers themselves. And particularly as state actors made inroads on Briceño, the coca economy established material incentives for farmers to publicly side with the guerrillas against the state.

Just before dawn a few years earlier, Eduardo tells me, a tactical team of fifty soldiers had descended from the jungle to surround a home where the local FARC-supported coca buyer slept with his lover and three guerrilla bodyguards. They were taken by surprise and quickly captured, with thirty kilos of coca paste, several thousand dollars, and a stash of guns. Word quickly spread. "All of us campesinos met together," Eduardo says, "and we said, 'How can we let them take him?'" Their interest in saving the buyer, however, was more than loyalty. The man had received their coca but had not yet paid them. "He owed us millions," Eduardo continues, "and he was the only one who knew about it. So in less than half an hour, four hundred people showed up, with more on the way." The campesinos, fearing they would lose their money, surrounded the soldiers. They finally reached a compromise: the soldiers took half the coca, half the money, and all the weapons, but let the buyer go. Within a month, he paid off his debts to the community.

In an ethnography of the Mohawk nation of Quebec, Audra Simpson (2014) uses the term "refusal" to describe a political stance that rejects the authority of the Canadian state (by rejecting, for example, Canadian law, passports, and voting), insisting on the group's right to maintain political sovereignty. The FARC are not governors of a long-standing Indigenous sovereign nation any more than Briceño's campesinos identify as members of one. Nevertheless, the campesinos' defense of the coca buyer represented nothing less than a refusal of state law—and the soldiers' authority to enforce it. And while the campesinos were primarily motivated by the money the buyer still owed them, coca's moral meaning constituted a critical element of their refusal. The coca economy had created the basis for a situation in which communally validated livelihoods were set directly against the rule of law. Soldiers—outnumbered and unwilling or unable to resort to violent force— found themselves reduced to bargaining with lawbreakers to partially enforce national law and avoid the embarrassment of returning empty-handed. Meanwhile, the FARC guerrillas, even when caught sleeping, were able to draw on community support to negotiate their release.

Neither the refusal of state authority nor the acceptance of guerrilla authority were absolute; the compromise campesinos reached with soldiers at least recognized the soldiers' right to take something. But this compromise indicates the major limitations in the establishment of the symbolic power of the state as taken-for-granted authority (Bourdieu 2014), particularly when set against the FARC. Indeed, the "stateness" of the soldiers' intervention was decidedly limited in comparison to how we usually think of states. The ideal form of the modern state, in Weber's (1947) influential characterization, operates according to a clearly defined set of laws and procedures carried out by a massive and impersonal bureaucracy—a system which traps its subjects within an inflexible iron cage but also grants the state its legitimacy by creating the appearance of both impartiality and justice. Of course, states that actually exist the world over are filled with agencies and actors that fail to achieve the ideal of impartial rule following. Nevertheless, experiences like Eduardo and his neighbors' defense of the coca buyer are particularly striking in the extent to which they unmask the myth of the "the state" and "the law" as standing above the society they govern (Hansen and Stepputat 2001, 15).

It was not only that locals turned to armed groups as authority figures through the coca economy. Like the campesinos who refused to recognize the soldiers' right to detain the FARC-sponsored buyer, they also turned away from the state, and particularly from military coca eradication campaigns that threatened local livelihoods.

Eradication, the War on Drugs, and Turning Away from the State

"We saw that the government was going to enter, so we hid [coca] seeds. And four hundred soldiers and eradicators came in, and they pulled out everything. The government left, and immediately we planted our seeds, because if the government does a forced eradication and doesn't bring projects, what are campesinos going to live from? So the eradication did not last, because that's one thing coca has going for it: after only seven months, you can harvest it. That's what happens everywhere the government does forced eradication."

EDUARDO

Beginning around 2003, two forms of military eradication campaigns have periodically targeted Briceño's coca crops: manual eradication, where men accompanied by soldiers pull coca plants out by hand; and aerial fumigation, where small crop-dusting planes bathe coca with the toxic herbicide glyphosate. These expensive and sustained campaigns failed to eliminate Briceño's coca economy, as farmers mostly replanted their crops. Eradication was, however, one of the most consequential ways local farmers experienced state power, establishing the state as a force that attacked rather than supported their livelihoods.

It's not hard to understand why farmers whose plants were eradicated rushed to replant their coca. They faced losing the crop they were counting on to provide for their families. Often they were also in debt from what they'd invested in the anticipated harvest. They needed a crop that would pay off, and quick. They knew that traditional crops like corn and beans were now sold below the price of production. Even when the price of coffee was in a boom cycle, farmers couldn't afford to wait the nearly two years it would take for the crop to mature—a time by which, they had learned, its price would probably go bust. The seven-month turnaround of coca, along with the fact that local merchants and at times armed groups would offer them supplies on credit to plant it, made it the clear choice.

Statistics back up Eduardo's assertion of forced coca eradication's general ineffectiveness. Studies from the United Nations Office on Drugs and Crime

(UNODC), state agencies, and independent institutes have calculated coca replanting rates between 38 and 67 percent after manual eradication, and between 69 and 80 percent after aerial fumigation (Jaramillo 2019; Redacción Judicial 2019a; UNODC 2021). Aerial fumigation is particularly ineffective because it does not even require farmers to replant; in Briceño, farmers whose coca was fumigated either bathed their plants in a mixture of milk and molasses or simply cut off the tops of their plants before the poison spread to the roots. In five months, the plants grew back as good as new.

Aerial fumigation with glyphosate, however, did more damage to any food crops, water sources, or people unfortunate enough to be in the vicinity. Some readers may recognize glyphosate as the active ingredient in the world's most popular herbicide, Roundup. Since 1996, it has been sold alongside seeds like corn, soy, and canola genetically engineered by the agribusiness company Monsanto to resist glyphosate; farmers can indiscriminately spray their so-called Roundup-ready fields, and only the weeds will die. But if glyphosate has become a central element in corporate food production, its use for coca fumigation was devastating for campesino food crops. Briceño's farmers told me that planes usually flew high to avoid being shot at, and the wind would blow the streams they dropped far afield. Within a few days, corn, beans, and fruit trees as far as a kilometer away would shrivel and die as the glyphosate reached their roots.

Fumigation with glyphosate has also been associated with cancer, miscarriages, and dermatological and respiratory illnesses in coca farmers (Camacho and Mejía 2017). In 2015, Colombia's Constitutional Court finally banned aerial fumigation over health concerns, though right-wing Colombian politicians and the Obama, Trump, and Biden administrations all pushed for its resumption even as glyphosate was subject to some of the largest legal settlements in history, with more than $12 billion paid out since 2020 to US farmers based on claims that their use of Roundup gave them cancer (Farrell 2023).

Even if, as many policymakers argue, the major benefit of counternarcotics is to drive up prices to make drugs less accessible, there is little reason to believe that eradication affects drug prices. Cocaine's large profits have very little to do with the physical drug itself; instead, its value is generated as it passes international borders and is exchanged in consumer markets (Ghiabi 2022). As Tom Wainwright (2016) points out, the leaf itself may constitute only 38.5 cents of the roughly $122 a gram of pure cocaine will eventually fetch in the United States—even a wildly successful eradication campaign that managed to triple the price of coca leaf would only raise the eventual price to the consumer to $122.77.

When forced eradication campaigns have reduced or eliminated coca in a

FIGURE 1.4. In plant form, coca's unassuming green leaves give little clue of its symbolic and political weight.

given area, we have four decades of evidence that cultivation has most likely only shifted to new areas—often bringing violent organizations along with it (Dest 2021; Gootenberg 2008). This so-called balloon effect, in which squeezing one area of the cocaine trade only leads production centers or trafficking routes to shift elsewhere like the air in a balloon, describes the outcome of many anti-cocaine campaigns of the War on Drugs.

But although eradication campaigns have done little to advance their stated goals, they have been central to both coca-cultivating communities' experiences of the state and the Colombian state's engagement with the international community—its effort to show it is doing its part to target drug production. And just as coca cultivation is rooted in a global history of agricultural transformation, coca eradication emerges from a US-led international drug control regime that has long held rural Colombia in its sway.

FROM PLANT TO DRUG TO ENEMY

The term "war," normally used to describe an enduring violent conflict between two groups of people, is an awkward fit when applied to drugs (fig. 1.4). What does it mean, after all, to cast a substance like a coca bush or a baggie of heroin as, in Richard Nixon's famous declaration of the War on Drugs, "public enemy number one?" Do the very real human costs of drugs—the innumerable families destroyed by overdose and addiction—count as an act of belligerence? Does it even make sense to keep talking about a "War on Drugs" when it seems mostly to attack marginalized communities while drug economies continue prospering as much as ever?

The definitional confusion is only deepened if we turn our interrogation to "drugs" themselves. In fact, while cultures across the world have ingested a wide array of consciousness-altering substances throughout recorded history, the concept of "drugs" was only brought into existence in the twentieth century by the very laws that prohibited them (Porter 1996). It is the law, as the legal scholar Kojo Koram (2022, 2733) argues, that "ties together as one group cannabis, cocaine and opium and then places that group in contradistinction to alcohol, tobacco or caffeine." The law casts plants like coca and those who grow them as an existential threat to social order and our very humanity. As I have argued above, the law also insulates coca from the competition of the corporate food regime. However, even as legal prohibition helps coca farmers protect valued rural lifestyles, it sets their livelihoods directly against the state, putting them in the crosshairs of a War on Drugs in which they are a reluctant enemy.

And while empirical evidence suggests that the War on Drugs has been a failure, its criminalized and militarized approach is difficult for countries like Colombia to avoid. Since the UN 1961 Single Convention on Narcotics Drugs, antidrug laws have been imposed in standardized form across the world in the international drug control regime led by the United States (Idler and Garzón Vergara 2021). As Lina Britto (2020, 158) writes in an insightful history of Colombia's 1970s marijuana boom, when the Cold War created an imperative to consolidate US power in Latin America but the US failures of the Vietnam War made the American public averse to overseas military intervention, drug control allowed the United States to extend its influence while "claim[ing] it was fixing a whole host of social, political, and economic problems by marrying counterinsurgency efforts and modernization-informed policies with antidrug missions." Both during and after the Cold War, militarized drug control has also served US economic interests by enabling the extraction of resources like oil, gold, and coal (see chapter 4) (Mercille 2011; Paley 2014).

The United States promotes this agenda with billions of dollars in foreign aid earmarked for drug control, but also uses coercion to push countries like Colombia to fall into line. Countries that host either drug production or transit zones are subject to annual reviews based on codified drug control objectives; in Colombia, these are mostly based on measurements of coca cultivation and eradication. Countries judged as failing to do their part receive major sanctions: the suspension of loans or development assistance from international organizations like the International Monetary Fund and the World Bank; tightening trade controls; and a decertification process through the US Congress that limits the foreign aid they can receive (Mansfield 2016, 17).

Ironically, it was counternarcotics policies implemented through just this kind of political pressure that brought cocaine economies to Colombia in the first place. Human use of coca, native to the Bolivian, Peruvian, and Colombian Andes, dates to before the Spanish conquest, when the leaf was chewed by the Incas and other Indigenous groups for both energy and nutrients (Gootenberg 2008). After cocaine was first produced in a German laboratory in 1860, its commercial production for a global market was long centered in Peru and Bolivia,[6] first during a nineteenth-century period when cocaine was legal and seen as a wonder drug, and then in a subsequent black market led by Chilean and Cuban smugglers (Gootenberg 2008, 2021).

Only two years after Nixon officially declared the War on Drugs, Augusto Pinochet's 1973 US-supported military coup against Salvador Allende's democratically elected government in Chile ultimately pushed drug economies to Colombia. Under heavy US pressure, Pinochet went after Chilean smugglers, creating a vacuum that a fledgling group of Colombian smugglers was only too happy to fill (Gootenberg 2008, 2021; Tate 2015). Colombian traffickers, most famously Pablo Escobar, began by importing coca paste from Peru and Bolivia, refining it in Colombia, and then transshipping it to a burgeoning US market (Gootenberg 2021).

In the 1980s and 1990s, as US domestic consumption spiked and racially charged panic over the crack epidemic gripped national politics, US foreign policy continued pushing Latin American governments to squeeze the balloon, this time targeting coca cultivation in the Bolivian and Peruvian Andes (Gootenberg 2017; Grisaffi 2018). Colombian drug traffickers facing a reduced supply brought seeds to remote colonization zones in their own country, and coca cultivation steadily shifted north. While Bolivia and Peru accounted for 87 percent of global cocaine production in 1980, Colombia was responsible for three-quarters of the global crop by the time coca took over Briceño's economy around 2000 (Durán-Martínez 2021; Gootenberg 2017).

Enter Plan Colombia, a US foreign aid initiative that sent $10 billion to Colombia from 2000 to 2015, turning the country into the primary ally of the US in the War on Drugs, and promising to simultaneously eradicate coca, strengthen the state, and defeat insurgent forces to bring peace (Gootenberg 2021; Tate 2015). Eighty percent of its funds went to the Colombian Armed Forces, driving coca eradication campaigns and helping the military to double in size (Ballvé 2020). The strengthened military reclaimed national territory from the FARC, killed a series of guerrilla commanders, and arguably pushed the FARC to the negotiating table for the eventual 2016 peace agreement. By nearly any measure, however, violence peaked in the early years of Plan Colombia as millions of innocent campesinos fled the countryside; they were collateral damage and in many cases direct targets of the escalated conflict (CEVCR 2022; Restrepo-Ruiz and Martinez 2009).

Plan Colombia's effect on coca cultivation was also mixed. Colombia's coca export capacity did halve by 2013, but it rebounded to all-time highs by 2017 (Gootenberg 2021). Intensified aerial fumigation and manual eradication campaigns mostly just temporarily cut into coca's bottom line or displaced cultivation elsewhere. While Plan Colombia did ostensibly provide for development programs to help replace coca, most farmers targeted by forced eradication, like those in Briceño, received nothing.

But this is not to say that Plan Colombia failed to impact rural economies. It included its own amendment requiring trade liberalization, and was seen by Colombian officials as a precursor to the Free Trade Agreement with the United States (Paarlberg-Kvam 2021; Paley 2014). The irony is clear: the policy package intended to attack coca also helped drive economic policy that worsened the exclusion of smallholding farmers, pushing them even further from the state—and toward coca.

And even more than jeopardizing rural livelihoods, eradication campaigns contribute to a broader sense, in the words of a social leader interviewed by Camilo Acero and Frances Thomson (2022), that "everything campesinos do is illegal." The criminalization of local livelihoods also extends to other economic activities they often simply cannot carry out legally. For example, Briceño's slaughterhouse was closed in 2016 because it failed to live up to prohibitively expensive requirements for solid waste disposal. With the closest legal slaughterhouse an expensive fifty-kilometer trip away in the neighboring village, campesinos responded by establishing makeshift illegal slaughterhouses that both stocked local butcher shops and were used by families for personal consumption. In coca-producing areas, the repressive and regulatory arms of the state are set directly against local livelihoods, jeopardizing the development of state legitimacy (Acero and Thomson 2022; Stepputat 1999).

"THEY ALWAYS COME HERE TO FUCK WITH US": AN ETHNOGRAPHY OF ERADICATION

In folding counternarcotics into peacebuilding, counterinsurgency, and economic development, Plan Colombia followed a widespread policy narrative that calls for international intervention to help so-called fragile states extend territorial control, develop effective institutions, build prosperous economies, and stamp out illegal economies and armed groups (Mansfield 2016). But while accounts of the synergy between counternarcotics, peacebuilding, state building, and development make for a compelling narrative, an ethnographic perspective tells a different story (see also Goodhand et al. 2021). In criminalizing coca cultivation, which was both collectively authorized and morally valued in Briceño, eradication campaigns set state law directly against an economic activity that was locally seen as legitimate (Acero and Thomson 2022; Ciro Rodríguez 2019). Thus, if organizing the coca economy made armed groups essential to local livelihoods, eradicating coca did the opposite for the state, establishing state power as something to be avoided.

I experienced this firsthand in 2020, when military eradicators made a puzzling return to Briceño, which was nearly three years into the coca substitution program. Locals often talked about replanting coca in the wake of the program's delays (see chapter 2), but the territory still had very little coca, particularly in comparison to neighboring villages. Nevertheless, on a Friday afternoon, Tomás, a longtime community leader, hailed me: "There's a *paro* [literally, a stoppage; this term is used for various forms of collective action including shutdowns, strikes, and road blockages] against military eradication in Las Auras," he said. "Do you want to go?"

Ten minutes later we're heading there on motorcycles, following a road that climbs from Briceño's village center to reach nearby farming communities. To our right, steep slopes drop down to the Espíritu Santo River. Not long ago, locals tell me, large portions of these hills had been covered with coca, partially hidden among stretches of untouched jungle. Now they are mostly pasture for cattle, broken up by guava trees and the occasional plot of coffee or corn. We reach a Y-shaped intersection named La Virgen for its white statue of the Virgin Mary. Historically, this point was an invisible border. Take a left and you were in an area controlled by the FARC guerrillas; go right and you would reach paramilitary territory. We turn right. With the disappearance of coca and the increased presence of state forces in the context of the peace process, paramilitaries have mostly disappeared. A FARC guerrilla group, however, has rearmed in Briceño. Their presence is visible in graffiti that adorns the walls of sheds and abandoned homes along the road: "FARC 36th Front Present;" and "We Are Indestructible 36th Front."

The guerrillas are also reflected in today's social action. Tomás explains to me that yesterday the FARC called the presidents of the three closest community action boards, telling them to organize a *paro* with all the men of their community to pressure military eradicators to leave.[7] The troop of eradicators has been camping in an open field by one of Briceño's most populous hamlets for nearly a week. It only eradicated for one day, destroying two small coca plots left behind by farmers who left the territory before the substitution program began. More recently, a few young men from the community have reclaimed the overgrown plots from the jungle, turning back to coca in the face of economic struggles. Now the coca is uprooted. Still, for reasons that are unclear, the eradicators, themselves young men without other economic opportunities (Redacción Semana 2023), have stayed put. Yesterday, local men heeding the guerrillas' call gathered to demand that the eradicators leave the territory. The eradicators agreed to do so, but still haven't left. The guerrillas have called for another *paro* today, this time telling the presidents of four additional hamlets to bring their communities' men as well. Tomás adds that guerrillas will be there, keeping track of those who participate. Those who do not show up will later be called upon to explain their absence.

By the time we arrive, the troop is already on its way out, walking from its camp to the road. There are maybe thirty in all, half eradicators and half soldiers entrusted with protecting them. The soldiers carry assault rifles and are wearing black leather boots and camouflage. The eradicators are unarmed, dressed in dark blue with the black rubber galoshes favored by campesinos. Two hundred community members walk alongside them, triumphantly whistling and cheering. Nearly everyone—soldiers, eradicators, community members, and plainclothes guerrillas—are men. The troop, split into groups of two to five with campesinos interspersed between, begins walking toward the village center on the dirt road, trudging under the weight of heavy backpacks (fig. 1.5).

We join a group of community members who walk behind two soldiers. Some of the campesinos bang sticks on the metal barriers, whistling and yelling, "¡Que se vayan! [Get out of here!]." The mood is in equal parts tense and festive. Suddenly, three shots ring out fifty meters up the road. A group of campesinos run toward us, away from the shooting. Our group is paralyzed, unsure of what to do. News of violent confrontations between military eradicators and coca farmers trying to protect their crops have lately filled the news. In several incidents, campesinos were killed. I point my camera up the road, filming in case something else happens. Nothing does. (When I later review the footage, it will appear blurry and jumpy, my hand unsteady.) Tomás breaks the silence, enjoining us to keep walking. "When there's shooting, that's when we most need to support our *compañeros*," he says.

By the time we reach the point where the shooting has occurred, the soldiers have continued down the road. A group of six campesinos has stayed behind. They point out the bullet holes in the dusty road and explain what happened. A soldier, angered by their taunts, turned and fired into the ground

FIGURE 1.5. Soldiers and manual eradicators are escorted out of the community.

in front of them, yelling at them to shut up. As the men tell their story, a group of soldiers catches up to us from behind. I gather that one of the soldiers is the commander; while the others are barely in their twenties, his close-cropped hair is graying at the temples, and he carries himself with an air of authority. He blames the campesinos for the shooting. "You need to recognize that they are cooperating with you," he says loudly. "There's no need to attack them."

"No one attacked them, no one threatened their lives, no one touched them," says a young man I recognize as the president of a nearby community.

"No, no, no!" the commander shouts, interrupting the man. "You're yelling at them, you're whistling at them, you're treating them like livestock!" He punctuates his point with a chopping motion of his right hand. "You know that you're inciting them! There's no need, because you're not herding cattle!"

The argument continues for another five minutes, but when the soldiers move on, the community members stay behind, excitedly recounting the story of the shooting to new arrivals. Their story is punctuated by references to the soldiers as "sons of bitches" who "always come here to fuck with us [jodernos]," a reaction that is both understandable from people who have just been shot at and related to long-standing negative experiences with the military, stemming in large degree from coca eradication campaigns.

Volatile though it was, the stakes of this confrontation were limited by the fact that the men facing off with the soldiers no longer had coca of their own. But when similar encounters took place as recently as 2015, not only were community members defending their livelihoods, but their encounter with soldiers marked one of the few and arguably most consequential ways in which they directly felt the state's impact on their lives—and it felt like the War on Drugs was the state's war on them. In that context, farmers not only depended on armed groups to organize the coca economy, but also turned to those groups to defend them from the state.

In the incident I witnessed, some campesinos later privately expressed resentment that the guerrillas had forced them to participate in the *paro*. Because they no longer had coca, the eradicators' presence did not bother them. However, the *paro* fits into a longer history (see chapter 5) of the guerrillas enforcing participation in collective action, including both political demonstrations and communal work parties to maintain local paths. Communities often granted significant legitimacy to the guerrillas' enforcement, recognizing that it helped ensure that everyone contributed to meeting collective needs. And for decades, one of those collective needs was that of defending the communities' coca against the military.

Locals who generally resisted taking sides in the region's bloody conflict silently celebrated when the FARC shot down a military plane that was fumigating their coca crops. The guerrillas also installed land mines around coca crops during manual eradication campaigns, warning farmers of their location. This practice claimed multiple soldiers' limbs and lives, and still endangers local inhabitants today, but many people identify it as a factor in stopping eradication. When soldiers set up checkpoints to prevent farmers from transporting coca processing supplies to their farms, those farmers called on the guerrillas to stage military operations to draw the soldiers away. And campesinos reciprocated the support, as in Eduardo's story of gathering to defend the captured guerrillas and the FARC-supported coca buyer. The farmers' primary concern, of course, was to avoid losing the money that was owed them. The point, however, is that through coca, their economic interests and behaviors aligned *with* the FARC and *against* state authority. Even in the action I witnessed, many locals' enthusiastic participation suggested that they relished the opportunity to kick the eradicators out—perhaps in revenge for their years of helpless frustration as eradicators destroyed their crops.

The finding that drug eradication jeopardizes rather than promotes the development of state authority will be of no surprise to anyone who has witnessed an eradication campaign. For all the missteps of the US invasion of Afghanistan, by 2010 army strategists began ordering soldiers to stop eradicating opium poppies, which were seen as funding al-Qaeda. "We don't trample the livelihood of those we're trying to win over," explained US commander Jeffery Eggers to *The New York Times* (Nordland 2010). But as Winifred Tate (2015) found in an ethnography of US military and diplomats in the context of Plan Colombia, policy is not produced through a rational process to determine the most effective course of action (see also Mosse 2010). Instead, the policies that get implemented are those able to maintain political support—from a US military turning to drug repression to justify its continued bloated budget after the Cold War, and from presidential administrations facing the political imperative of appearing tough on drugs (Tate 2015). Even as the US military in Afghanistan stopped eradicating, other agencies continued (Keane 2016). And to this day, US foreign aid to Colombia explicitly pushes eradication (Meyer 2023).

Conclusion

Coca cultivation, despite its material advantages, is not a means to incredible wealth. In 2018, shortly after the coca substitution program was launched in Briceño, UNODC estimated that coca farming families made an average monthly income of only $130, roughly 56 percent of the minimum monthly wage. While popular representations call to mind images of the wealth produced by the cocaine trade, the simple fact is that cocaine money goes overwhelmingly to traffickers (24 percent of cocaine sales prices) and to wholesalers and retailers in consumer countries (75 percent) rather than to Andean coca farmers (1 percent) (Mejía and Rico 2010; Organization of American States 2013; UNODC 2010). When you consider the limited returns combined with the violence, risk, and negative stigma associated with growing coca, it seems a bit of a puzzle that coca cultivation persists at all.

It's less puzzling, however, when compared with the alternatives for campesinos. In the context of trade liberalization and a corporate food regime, smallholding farmers the world over have been integrated into global markets where they must compete with prices that often fall below their costs of production. These pressures have left huge populations excluded from the global economy, driving farmers to abandon untenable rural livelihoods and concentrate in urban slums.

The anthropologist Phillipe Bourgois (2018, 390), who has spent decades researching both drug dealers and addicts, uses the term "predatory accumulation" to describe the highly profitable licit and illicit drug economies that have developed at the expense of "populations expelled from the licit economies of the Global North and South." Excluded bodies are sacrificed for profit across all links of drug commodity chains: from farmers who see clouds of industrial poison dropped on their crops and families to members of armed groups who battle over territories of drug cultivation; from Central

American gangs fighting over smuggling routes to drug mules risking decades of imprisonment; from small-time dealers facing state repression to American drug consumers who seek to numb the pain of their uncertain place within a society transformed by deindustrialization and the rollback of social services. And even if the predatory accumulation of the global drug trade routinely kills off its best customers, workers, and soldiers, it can draw on a nearly limitless supply of excluded poor who turn to drugs to make a needed income, gain coveted status, preserve valued customs of living on and from the land, or find some measure of pleasure in an unkind world.

The simple reality confronting many people who make a living through drug economies is that illicit livelihoods are often the only available options that can provide them with both bread and roses—the chance to meet their basic needs and to build a better and more meaningful future for their families. Drugs may threaten their lives, ravage their communities, and turn them into the targets of state repression, but they also provide them with an otherwise elusive productive niche within global capitalism. Rather than being criminals deviating from social norms, coca farmers are struggling to preserve rural lifestyles and build better lives for their families. Coca's place within the moral world of the village, linked to valued practices of living on and from the land, is critical to explaining its spread through Briceño.

But if coca's illegality insulates it from the competition of the corporate food regime, it also ties campesinos' livelihoods to the extralegal groups that regulate it. In Briceño, this helped establish the authority of both the guerrillas and the paramilitaries by providing the basis for a series of patterned interactions through which campesinos treated those groups as the local authorities. Terrifying violence became a feature of everyday life as the guerrillas and paramilitaries fought over control of the territory and its coca. Coca's illegality also placed coca farmers in the crosshairs of state eradication programs as part of the US-led War on Drugs. Even more than establishing state power as something to be avoided, these ineffective programs pushed campesinos to further turn to armed groups to protect them from the state.

The evident failures of the War on Drugs on a global level have led to an increasing clamor to simply legalize all drugs. It is a compelling argument. The illegality of drug economies pushes them outside the purview of the state, leaving their regulation to a variety of gangs, cartels, guerrillas, paramilitaries, warlords, and other violent actors. In the United States, antidrug laws and initiatives have been a central element in the criminalization of Black and Brown communities, the development of a racist and bloated prison system, and the waste of a trillion dollars of US taxpayer money (Alexander 2012). Treated as criminals, addicts are subject to jail sentences rather than needed treatment. Meanwhile, efforts to stop drug production and trafficking in the Global South have not only led to violence but have caused both drug economies and violence to spread through the balloon effect. Legalizing drugs, it seems clear, would reduce violence, inequality, and human suffering.

We cannot forget, however, that coca's illegality brings significant and meaningful advantages in a world where legal agricultural production is beholden to global markets that increasingly exclude smallholding farmers. We need look no further than newly legal marijuana markets in the United States, where marginalized populations that previously participated in the illicit trade have been squeezed out by wealthier and whiter cannabis entrepreneurs. It is highly unlikely that as a legal commodity, coca would continue to offer campesinos a unique productive niche in the global economy.

The next two chapters describe an alternative to both militarization and legalization: a substitution program that seeks to help farmers transition to legal crops. Through this program, however, Briceño's farmers have found that the legality of the post-coca world poses a major challenge to their efforts to stay on and live from the land. Until agricultural production is freed from the logic of comparative advantage, and is organized around a model of inclusion rather than one of competition, they will be faced with the Sophie's choice of abandoning rural lifestyles or embracing illegality along with the armed groups and violence it brings.

The State Is Coming

Eugenia and Suso, Act One

Eugenia's memories of her youth center on poverty. "My mom would send me to school with a bag of plantains fried with onions for lunch," she says, laughing. Eugenia was the youngest of fourteen, and resources were tight. "The first shoes I ever had were when I was nine. We walked around barefoot every day, until finally we went to a shop in El Valle [a neighboring village] and my big brother told me to choose a pair of sandals. So I bought one, and I was like this, so everyone could see that I had sandals." Eugenia lifts up and wiggles her feet, miming the joy of a young girl showing off her fancy new footwear.

Eugenia, now in her mid-thirties, spent much of her childhood along the Cauca River, a three-hour walk from her family's farm. While agricultural labor was customarily masculine, gold panning along the river was a common economic activity of local women, including Eugenia's mother. Eugenia often accompanied her. They would stay from Monday to Friday, setting up camp on the beach and eating plantains and yuca from their farm, stewed with fresh fish from the river. Eugenia helped her mother dig out sand from the riverbanks, washing it in a large wooden bowl called the *batea* to leave behind tiny nuggets of gold (fig. 2.1).

The local school only went up to fifth grade. Eugenia finished at the age of fourteen. "You graduated from fifth grade and that was it," she says. "That was a big achievement in those days." Continuing her studies was unthinkable, with the closest secondary school in El Valle, a four-hour walk away.

Eugenia began working for a daily wage at the age of thirteen, during the yearly coffee harvest. She would wake up at 4 a.m., walking two hours uphill to a large coffee farm. She washed the coffee pickers' clothes by hand, and even performed traditionally male labor by picking coffee and cutting away weeds with a machete.

FIGURE 2.1. Eugenia pans for gold.

In 2000, just as coca, paramilitaries, and violence spread through the region, Eugenia met Suso at a party at the community school. She was seventeen. They shared a few dances, and he asked if he could see her again. Soon he was visiting her home on Sundays, under her mother's watchful eye. After three years of off-and-on chaperoned dating, they married.

Like Eugenia, Suso remembers his mother as always traveling down to the Cauca River to pan for gold. "But I rarely went down; I never liked gold panning," he tells me as we drink sweetened lime juice and sit on plastic chairs on the outdoor corridor of the small house. Eugenia bustles around the kitchen cleaning up after lunch. Their oldest children, Adrián and Sebastián, aged sixteen and fourteen, have retreated to their room for the afternoon nap. Their daughter Susana, eleven, plays with their two-year-old son Dubian, pushing him back and forth on a toy jeep with a missing wheel.

Suso explains that at the age of seven he began helping his father on the family farm. By fifteen he was administering his own food crops: beans, corn, and yuca. When he was nineteen, he and an older brother picked a large bean harvest, taking it to a nearby village to sell. It was 1987, three years before Colombia's economic opening would begin driving agricultural prices downward. They used their profits to visit a cousin in the neighboring village of Valdivia. They found their cousin living and working on an isolated farm, picking a crop they had never seen in Briceño: coca. Suso stayed, and over seven years he worked in every stage of coca production: planting the seeds, fumigating it to kill weeds, picking the leaves, and finally treating it with chemicals to make coca paste. By the end of his time, he specialized as a "chemist," making four dollars a day, four times the standard wage. "I made good money, but spent it all on clothes, trips, and liquor," he says.

In 1994, Suso returned to Briceño, planting coffee on a plot of land he had inherited from his father—the farm he now shares with Eugenia. Coffee had already lost the protection of the International Coffee Agreement, but drought and frost in Brazil had driven down global supply and prices were high. Suso used his coffee profits to build a house out of *tapia*: dirt compacted between wooden boards fashioned into meter-thick walls.

Within a few years, coffee prices plummeted. Suso bought coca seeds from a farm a couple hours' journey away, planting them in a relatively hidden section of the farm. It was the first coca plot in the hamlet. As they saw coca's profitability, his neighbors quickly followed his lead.

The paramilitaries, Eugenia and Suso recall, arrived on the heels of coca. They began by targeting people they identified as guerrilla informants, shooting them and then throwing them off a bridge into the Cauca River. Suso and Eugenia weren't informants, but like everyone else in the community, they were terrified. "Just being from here, we have the reputation of being guerrillas," Suso says. Two of their neighbors were kidnapped by the paramilitaries and held for several days. Fearing the paramilitaries might come for him, Suso spent several nights sleeping in the jungle. Heated battles between the groups became common, with the sound of explosions filling the community.

For years, coca brought a measure of prosperity to the hamlet. Suso no longer drank his profits away, instead reinvesting them in the farm and adding additions to the house for his growing family. Like many rural farmers, he and Eugenia invested coca windfalls in cattle, fattening them on pasture before selling them at a profit to area dealers who would take them to local butchers. Later, they used coca money to buy a small property in the hills of Bello, a peripheral urban community to the north of Medellín. As violence spread through the community, they began to think of pursuing a future outside of Briceño.

Eugenia went back to school, taking a two-hour trip each way on a mule once or twice a week to reach the closest secondary school. This was not an opportunity available to most area women, who were shackled by domestic responsibilities. Eugenia credits Suso for shouldering child care responsibilities and supporting her. At the age of thirty she graduated from high school, the first in her family to do so. But as she studied, coca's profits began tailing off. The cost of the supplies needed to process it skyrocketed. A fungus infected area coca plants, cutting their productivity in half. Like most farmers in the area, Suso would often buy supplies on credit from local stores, squaring up when he sold his harvest. "One time I took out a harvest and couldn't even pay back my debts," Suso says.

In 2011 a small propeller airplane began making its way through Briceño, dropping streams of the controversial herbicide glyphosate on the area's coca crops. Suso was traveling on a mule to a clinic with his newborn daughter for her vaccinations. His mother called his cell phone to warn him, and he rushed home, shutting his family in the house and watching as the plane made three rounds over his coca fields, bathing them in white streams of industrial-grade poison. In less than two hours, the plane had covered the community's coca.

Area farmers rushed out to their fields, either chopping off the plants' upper parts before the chemical reached their roots or bathing their coca in a mixture of milk and molasses. "It came back really beautiful," Suso says. Within five months, they were harvesting coca again. Food crops fared worse. Even when a direct stream didn't fall on them, vapor clouds destroyed vegetable gardens and fruit trees.

Unlike his neighbors, Suso let his coca die. "People were telling me to chop the tops off my plants. But I used it as an excuse to get out [of growing coca]." Suso, facing the plant's risk and diminished profitability, had long wanted to give up coca. However, the guerrillas had expressly prohibited destroying coca crops. With the aerial fumigation, he had an excuse. He converted the fields into pasture for cattle.

Also in 2011, construction began on the Hidroituango hydroelectric dam over the Cauca River just below their farm. The dam company promised to bring progress to the region, but eliminated traditional fishing and gold panning economies. Legally obligated to financially compensate people whose livelihoods were compromised, the company behind the dam conducted a local census in 2008. Suso and Eugenia were fortunate to be included. However, many people, including longtime gold panners, were left out.

The Hidroituango dam also intensified conflict in the region, as the military entered the river valley to clear the region for it. The soldiers pushed the guerrillas up the valley walls and into the populated area of El Orejón. The guerrillas began laying land mines in the area to stall the military's advance. Eugenia describes her fear at sending her children to school, knowing that a single misstep could prove fatal. In addition to permanent land mines, the guerrillas would mine the paths at night to prevent the military from catching them unawares, and then remove those temporary mines by dawn.

In 2013, tragedy struck in an event that would forever mark the community. At 9 p.m. a loud boom echoed through El Orejón. A temporary mine had exploded not far from Eugenia and Suso's farm, killing the guerrilla who was placing it in the middle of a community path. At dawn, community members gathered to see what had happened. They stood in a circle around the guerrilla's mangled corpse.

They had no idea that the guerrilla had successfully laid an additional land mine before the accident. When it exploded, it injured ten people and killed a young woman. Miraculously, her newborn child, in her arms at the time of the explosion, was unharmed.

Dozens of people abandoned the region in fear, including the schoolteacher. With no one to teach their children, Eugenia and Suso also left, taking their family to live on their property in Bello. They slept all together on an air mattress in the middle of their unfinished living room and borrowed a gas stove from relatives. They stayed for two months with no work, living off a small subsidy a government agency gave them as registered victims of displacement.

In 2015, with national news reports calling it "the most heavily mined village" in Colombia, the government announced that El Orejón would host a land mine removal program. It was the first collaboration between the FARC and the Colombian government in the context of their ongoing peace negotiations. While news reports focused on the quantity of land mines, locals suspected El Orejón was chosen because of its proximity to Hidroituango. Pacifying the region had become a matter of great strategic importance.

While fighting continued not far away, a ceasefire was declared in the area surrounding El Orejón. In short order, El Orejón went from forgotten mountain community to the subject of great national interest for its symbolic importance to a peace agreement still under negotiation. Eugenia was elected community president, meeting with the FARC and military commanders, high-ranking state officials, journalists, and international peacekeepers who visited the community. But land mine removal was only the beginning of El Orejón's symbolic importance to the peace process. One day, state and FARC officials stood together, announcing to the community that Briceño had been chosen to host the pilot for a coca substitution program that was being negotiated in the peace agreement.

Eugenia tells me about the beginning of the coca substitution program on laundry day. "They told us that if we did it the easy way [*a las buenas*] they would give us money," she says, scrubbing one of Suso's button-down work shirts, permanently stained with the dirt of agricultural labor. "But if we wanted the hard way [*a las malas*], they would pull out the coca anyway."

"And what did the community think about substitution?" I ask her.

"There were many people who participated because they had no option. But we thought that with the FARC accompanying the program, it was more likely the government would live up to the program."

"Did people mistrust the government?"

"Of course. Because the government has never followed through [*nunca nos ha cumplido*]. And the communities here have suffered from a terrible abandonment by the state." After decades in which the FARC had taken over many of the governance functions the formal state had shirked, it was critical that the guerrillas stood behind the substitution program.

Briceño's role as peace laboratory went beyond hosting the substitution and de-mining programs. Even before the substitution program began, its details were to be worked out with the participation of the FARC, the state, and the community. Representatives from UNODC served as facilitators and guarantors. While the land mine removal program was headquartered in El Orejón, the substitution program set up shop in the neighboring hamlet of Pueblo Nuevo, a little more than an hour's walk away. The area filled with FARC, UNODC, and state representatives who moved into community members' houses and into with several wooden cabins specially constructed to house them.

Eugenia dries her hands to go through a stack of folders filled with papers she has faithfully saved from half a decade of state programs and meetings. She finally hands me a thick packet that explains the structure of what was called the Joint Effort (Esfuerzo Conjunto). It established six thematic tables: community outreach; earth, water, and environment; infrastructure (including roads, cell service, and internet); economic development; social development (including education, health, culture, and recreation); and security. Each table included representatives from each of the eleven hamlets included in the program, who were expected to identify the communities' needs and propose projects to meet them. Eugenia was elected as one of four community representatives to overlook the whole process. For a year, she traveled to Pueblo Nuevo for meetings three days a week. Again, she credits Suso's support with letting her develop her leadership. "Imagine, I was in Pueblo Nuevo every other day, and Suso stayed here, taking care of the family. Even if he put Ana's diaper on backward," she says, laughing.

However, Eugenia feels that the time she and the community invested in the process was a waste. "In the end, they didn't take what we said into consideration," she says. "That was for them to be able to say to the world that the community was present. And look what happened with substitution; they've given us only the smallest part of what they promised."

The substitution program was finally launched in June 2017, promising beneficiaries a yearlong cash subsidy plus three levels of productive projects: goods they could choose from a permitted list to help them establish legal economies. Eugenia and Suso requested cows, and other goods to help them grow their herd of cattle. For the first year they traveled to the village center every two months, collecting the subsidy. They waited, as did everyone else, for the promised projects. As their wait continued, they increasingly felt that trusting the promises of state representatives had been a mistake. Fourteen months in, with the subsidy having already run out, they finally received the first and smallest level of projects, designed to promote food crops for family subsistence. Four years in, they received part of the second level. They're still waiting for the rest.

Introduction

In May 2017, Colombian President Juan Manuel Santos arrived by helicopter to El Orejón, one of Briceño's most isolated hamlets, to symbolically launch Colombia's coca substitution program and inaugurate a new school and library. "Before, [soldiers] came, they eradicated [coca], and they left families to their own devices," he said into a microphone, with a white flag of peace and the yellow, blue, and red flag of Colombia billowing behind him. "Now the state is coming to give you a hand, to offer you an alternative so that you can permanently substitute coca for licit crops. The state is coming, not just with productive project, but with infrastructure, roads, and schools. . . . Most people want to leave coca behind because they know it brings violence, brings a future that is not what most campesinos want. They want a better future for their children, they want the state to come." Santos ended his speech with a promise to "bring progress to these areas that have never had it, because the state has never been present."

Santos's words conjured the imagination of a postconflict state and reflected an understanding of Colombian history that links violence to the illicit coca economy, and each of those things to state absence. Conceived within this paradigm, the coca substitution program was meant not only to transform rural economies but also, in combination with other rural development programs, to provide the support campesinos needed to provide their families with comfortable and meaningful lives. It was a message, in short, of inclusion—that after decades of limited useful presence, the state would finally bring Briceño within its prosperous and protective reach.

After his speech, Santos walked to a steep hillside covered with light green coca plants, accompanied by a FARC commander turned peace negotiator.

News cameras rolled as they watched the community leader Ocaris Areiza (whose death is chronicled in chapter 7) drive a shovel into the ground to expose the roots of a plant. Ocaris tucked the plant, fully as tall as he was, under his right armpit and pulled it out with both hands. Then it was the president's turn. His face shaded by a traditional off-white sombrero, the sleeves of his button-down shirt rolled up to the elbow and his slacks tucked into calf-high rubber galoshes, Santos took a plant that was handed to him. He placed it into the hole left behind by the coca and proudly announced that he was replacing coca with cacao—and, by extension, cocaine with chocolate, armed groups with state control, and violence with peace. Briceño, the peace laboratory, was to be an example for the rest of the country as it sought to end a half century of civil war.

Prominent in local retellings of the event was the president's agricultural confusion: rather than cacao, Santos had planted a plantain seedling, a distinction that humorously symbolized the disconnect between campesino communities and the urban elites who run the country. On this joyous occasion, someone gently corrected Santos, and the faux pas didn't make the nightly news. What no one had the temerity to tell him was that the country's economic model excluded smallholders from selling plantains at a profit. What no one had the foresight to tell him was that in little more than a year he would be replaced by an opposition president who would imperil the peace process. And what no one imagined was that seven years later, the government still wouldn't have distributed most of the productive projects meant as an alternative to coca.

Indeed, since the optimistic high of the president's visit, local experiences of substitution have been marred by delays, broken commitments, and uncertainty. The plan called for beneficiaries to receive a year's worth of bimonthly subsidy payments ($4,000 total) to support their families while transitioning away from coca. In that first year, assisted by agricultural technicians, farmers were to execute two levels of projects: food security projects to promote subsistence agriculture (with a value of $600) and short-term productive projects ($3,000) that would let them begin drawing income by the time their subsidy payments ran out. Then in the program's second year, and with the continued help of agricultural technicians, they would execute long-term productive projects ($3,300).

The reality, however, was that they began receiving subsidy payments, pulled out their coca, and waited. The first year and the subsidy ended without any projects. The farmers did receive food security projects in the second year, but there was widespread dissatisfaction with the quality and price of the goods. From there, local experiences diverged on the basis of the different

FIGURE 2.2. A sign from a protest march protests the "*incumplimiento* of the agreement between the government and communities." It adds that the community is "tired of waiting for the short- and long-term projects. Because of these delays, families are suffering from [an inability to meet] our basic needs. We demand *cumplimiento*."

agricultural economies they chose to pursue, with projects for coffee, cacao, and cattle all managed by different nonstate contractors. Roughly half of the beneficiaries hadn't received any part of the short- or long-term projects after five years, while in the best case, the small number of farmers in the coffee line received nearly all the promised resources within three years.

When community members evaluate the state and substitution program, they repeatedly come back to one word: *incumplimiento* (verb form *incumplir*). *Incumplir* is the negation of *cumplir*, which is usually translated as "to fulfill, comply, or live up to." Local invocations of *incumplimiento* accuse the state of a failure to fulfill in two senses: the violation of its agreement to provide former coca farmers with resources to develop legal crops; and in a deeper sense, the state's long-standing failure to live up to its responsibilities to its citizens (fig. 2.2).

Briceño's experience of *incumplimiento* is captured by anthropologist Valentina Pellegrino's (2021) memorable description of how state actors "*incumplir cumpliendo*" (comply incompliantly) by generating evidence that they are fulfilling their legal responsibilities even as they utterly fail to produce intended results. The coca substitution program has failed to deliver promised resources and establish strong legal economies. At the same time, state actors have repeatedly drawn on the village for evidence of their effectiveness. But discussions of *incumplimiento* do more than contradict these optimistic accounts. In establishing a baseline of the state's responsibilities, they contribute to the development of shared ideas about the state's rightful role as provider of the public good—understandings critical to the state's symbolic power that cannot be taken for granted in communities where the FARC has long performed governance functions.

While the next chapter of this book describes the livelihood strategies that locals have pursued in the wake of coca's disappearance, here I focus on how the state/society relations established through the peace process contribute to state formation. First, I explain locals' highly consequential decision—turning, in a way they never had before, to the state as local authority—to give up their coca. I show how their decision emerged from a combination of ecological factors and state actions that diminished coca's profitability, community desire for the state as bearer of peace and progress, and guerrilla authorization. Second, I describe the forms of collective claims-making that have emerged in response to state *incumplimiento* and the opportunities opened by the peace process. Even when these claims express frustration with state inaction, they contribute to the development of the state's symbolic authority by implying commonsense understandings of the state's rightful role and responsibility. Finally, I show how the coca substitution program's outsourced structure has been central to local experiences of the state. Contracting out the program's implementation has caused delays, confusion, and a crippling uncertainty for beneficiaries—but has also allowed state officials to outsource blame for its *incumplimiento*. This provides a ready-made excuse, but denial of state responsibility also threatens the development of the state's symbolic power. The ironic result is that even as community members affirm the state's rightful role in their lives, state officials themselves deny it.

Setting the Stage for Substitution

> The truth is that we have always mistrusted the government. We didn't believe in the government, that they were going to *cumplir* everything they were saying. We thought about it a lot before we agreed to substitution.
>
> EDUARDO

It should be clear by now that Briceño's campesinos had little reason to trust the state, and perhaps even less reason to trust legal agricultural economies. Nevertheless, nearly all the campesinos voluntarily agreed to pull out the crop that had long provided for their families' livelihoods. This decision was not merely puzzling; it was also of great consequence. With the disappearance of the coca economy, so too disappeared the repeated interactions in which campesinos turned to armed groups as the local authorities. Instead, these same campesinos turned increasingly to the state. They attended hundreds of public meetings on the program's execution, traveled to the village center to wait patiently in line to receive their bimonthly subsidies, and hosted agricultural technicians who toured their farms and told them what they could and could not cultivate. Where earlier the actions of state entities had been of little consequence to their lives—or had compromised their livelihoods, as in coca eradication campaigns or the hydroelectric dam—substitution made Briceño's farmers depend on the state for their everyday needs and future projects. And through repeated interactions in which they treated state officials as authority figures, as well as through the foundational act of voluntarily uprooting their coca, they provided public evidence of their consent to state power (Beetham 1991).

Thus, the farmers' decision to voluntarily destroy their coca is worthy of explanation. Why did they willingly uproot the crop that had long provided for their families' needs? And what does this tell us about the potential for building peace, state authority, and legal economies?

Three factors help unravel this puzzle. The first is material: coca's profits and importance to the economy had nosedived long before the substitution program, due to a combination of human-driven and ecological factors. The second is symbolic: local desire for the state, related to a widespread discourse that attributes violence and poverty to the state's absence, casting its presence as the source of peace and progress. And finally, the third factor depends on authorization from an alternative authority: the FARC guerrillas.

COCA'S DOWNTURN

Briceño's farmers had begun to sour on coca even before substitution sounded coca's death knell. While Suso's response to fumigation—letting his coca plants die and pursuing legal agriculture—was atypical, it was telling of a broader phenomenon: as time went on, the crop's profitability dipped significantly and its hold on the municipality's economy weakened. The simplest explanation was that the prices paid for coca paste never increased to match the growing cost of living. From 1999 to 2017, just to keep up with the cost of inflation, the price of a kilo of coca paste should have risen from 2.2 million pesos (roughly $1,100) to 5.4 million pesos ($2,700). It stayed the same. Local accounts, however, centered on two elements that highlight the human and ecological factors behind local acceptance of the substitution program.

The first factor behind coca's downturn was a major rise in the cost of the supplies needed to process and grow it. "When I started," Suso says, "the supplies were much cheaper." He begins listing the price change of the dizzying array of chemicals used to turn coca leaves into coca paste. Sodium permanganate went from $7 to $43 per kilo, gasoline from $50 to $133 for a thirty-six-gallon drum, caustic soda from $3 to $13 for two kilos, and sulfuric acid from $1.70 to $17 per liter. The cost of the chemical inputs to produce one kilo of coca paste went from roughly $60 to $200.

"And that's not even counting the herbicides and insecticides, which also went way up in price," Suso says. "Or what you paid the coca pickers, or their food." The worst indignity, he says, were the bribes. In fact, military attempts to stop or extort the entry of chemical inputs into Briceño helped drive up the price of supplies in the first place. But farmers often had to pay an additional bribe to soldiers or police officers they encountered while transporting these goods to their farms. Eradication campaigns also cut into coca's profits, putting coca economies on hold for five to seven months as farmers' crops recovered.

Just as consequential as rising costs, however, were the ecological factors that sunk coca's productivity. A species of ravenous worms ate its way through Briceño's coca, sometimes devouring entire harvests. Even more insidious, a fungus spread throughout the territory, drying out local plants and greatly reducing their production of the cocaine alkaloid. Suso and other coca farmers paid pickers by the *arroba*, or twenty-five-pound sack of coca leaves. The amount of coca paste Suso could extract from each *arroba*, he says, began at twenty-five to twenty-seven grams. But as the fungus took over his plants, it dropped to fourteen grams. This reduction could mark the difference between a profitable harvest and producing at a loss. The worms and fungus also drove production costs even higher as farmers bought expensive chemicals to protect their crops.

In 2008, Briceño's hillsides were covered with 2,400 hectares of coca. By 2016, with many disillusioned farmers having moved on, the municipality was down to 504 hectares.[1]

As Timothy Mitchell (2002, 10) has provocatively argued about the importance of nonhuman forces to the formation of the Egyptian economy, unraveling the myriad forces that drive social processes often reveals that "human agency appears less as a calculating intelligence directing social outcomes and more as the product of a series of alliances in which the human element is never wholly in control." We may not usually think of worms or fungus as the advance troops of state formation. Nevertheless, allied with state initiatives, they drove the changing material calculus that helped persuade campesinos to give up their coca—a precondition of their turn to state power.

DESIRING THE ABSENT STATE

In addition to material considerations, coca farmers who had lived in a war zone for decades were motivated to accept substitution by a deeply held desire for peace and prosperity. Social theorists have long understood that the state is as much an ideational as an institutional achievement (Abrams 1988). The belief in the idea of "the state" as a unified entity over and above society that guarantees order and provides for the public good generates what Bourdieu (2014) would call the state's symbolic power, essential to explaining why people consent to state authority—for example, by agreeing to join the substitution program. But how, after years in which the state's presence was marked largely by coca eradication initiatives and a hydroelectric dam that imperiled their livelihoods, did Briceño's campesinos come to hold ideas of the state as the guarantor of peace, order, and the public good?

In Briceño, and to some extent in all of Colombia, the state-idea has been rooted not only in how people encounter the state, but in how they do not—specifically, in the state's absence and the violence and poverty that are understood as its consequences. While I focus throughout this book on exclusion from global economic markets, the lives and livelihoods of campesinos have also been marked by their exclusion from what are widely considered to be the benefits of state power: roads, security, and access to good health care and education, among other things. The understanding of state absence as the cause of suffering implies state presence as the solution. Thus, the idea of the absent state helps establish the state's symbolic power by framing access to peace and prosperity in terms of proximity to the state. Based on this logic, campesinos who dreamed of a better and safer future for their children desperately desired inclusion within the state's protective reach, including through coca substitution.

It's hard to exaggerate how often local and national political actors invoke state absence and link it to violence and poverty. Indeed, it has already come up multiple times in this text: Eduardo's point that farmers had to cultivate coca because Briceño has been "very forgotten by the state," Eugenia's argument that they "have suffered from a terrible abandonment by the state," and finally President Santos's claim that Briceño has never had progress "because the state has never been present."

Even as state presence increased through coca substitution, locals drew on the language of state absence to articulate an idealized vision of what the state should be, particularly in the face of economic collapse. In a meeting with a substitution program official, a social leader said: "Our hope is that we won't be abandoned by the state. In fact, we are abandoned. We need more help. We need goods, we need social investment, and we need the projects we were promised."

The official disputed her claim: "I don't think you can say that you're abandoned. Here you've had more investment than anywhere else in the country."

Another woman spoke up, defending the point: "For me, and for this community, we are abandoned. The state was never here. And then you come, and you promise alternative economies and development, but we are in the same situation."

What the anthropologist Margarita Serje (2005, 2012) has called the myth of state absence has permeated Colombian political discourse, coming to represent what Roseberry (1994:363) calls a "common discursive framework: a shared, state-authorized language of cognition, control, and contestation" (see also Ballvé 2020; Ramirez 2015). This discourse is central to understandings of purportedly stateless places like Briceño, defining them in terms of their savagery and violence, and the state itself in opposition as the impartial provider of a modern and secure social order (Serje 2005, 2012). Why is this a myth? First, because far from being absent, the state is often complicit in violent processes of social control and capital accumulation in purportedly stateless areas (examples in Briceño include the Hidroituango dam and coca eradication campaigns); and second, because this idealized state does not actually exist anywhere in Colombia (Ramírez 2015; Serje 2012).

But local understandings of state absence as the cause of poverty and violence do not only represent the adoption of a broader public narrative. Whenever people left Briceño to visit areas like Medellín that are closer to the centers of state power and resources, they encountered firsthand evidence of what the presence of the state could mean: paved roads, people with cars to drive on them, sewers, parks, relatively modern public hospitals,[2] public universities, commuter trains, and superior schools. Even if people from Briceño usually stayed with family members on the marginalized urban periphery, the proof of the advantages of state investment was always nearby.

Now that at least some of this investment has come to Briceño, the fact that campesinos continue speaking of state absence is telling. The state they desire, the state they conjured through joining the coca substitution program, is not the real existing state. Instead, as Winifred Tate (2015, 110) wrote of the political imaginaries of coca farmers in southern Colombia's Putumayo department, they desire an aspirational state: "caring, responsive, generous, and abundant, rather than distant, repressive, and extortive." It is a state that promises security, well-being, and a better future for their children. This hopeful idea largely rooted in state absence has been somewhat tarnished by negative local experiences with the state through the substitution program—though, as I describe in the following section, even local denunciations of state *incumplimiento* have served to articulate and spread collective expectations for the state. Nevertheless, the idea retains its allure, particularly because violence has indeed diminished. And as the substitution program was launching, campesinos' desire for this state was critical to their decision to participate.

GUERRILLA AUTHORIZATION

Even while campesinos desired an imagined state that would bring peace and prosperity, they were disinclined to trust the existing state, which had given them little reason to do so. Nevertheless, the FARC guerrillas—long the state's most powerful competitor—stood behind substitution, giving people more reason to believe, and fewer alternatives to doing so.

Communities generally learned of coca substitution through the guerrillas, in meetings the FARC led either on their own or in a united front with state officials and UNODC representatives. While coca farmers had spent years flouting state law, they were accustomed to following the rules of the guerrillas. The FARC had performed governance functions and solved community problems for decades and were seen as a legitimate authority by many community members (see chapter 5). The FARC's credibility also depended greatly on individual guerrilla leaders who were personally known to the community.

Ronaldo, the FARC delegate to the substitution program in Briceño until 2020, was the man who most often spoke on the guerrillas' behalf. He was from a campesino family in a nearby municipality and had served as a commander in Briceño for more than ten years. Though locals generally sought to avoid too-close relations with the members of any armed group for fear of being painted as collaborators (a potential death sentence), community members knew and respected him. Fabio and Angélica, Suso and Eugenia's neighbors in El Orejón, describe how he slept at their farm one night, staying up late to tell them stories of how he had joined the FARC to fight for a better Colombia after seeing the dirt-cheap prices his father had received for his *panela* (unrefined cane sugar). Eduardo recounts how Ronaldo caught a man smoking a joint laced with coca paste, against the FARC's express orders. Ronaldo let him go, telling him that he could kill himself if he wanted to, but that if he got any of the local youth into drugs, the FARC would execute him.

Ronaldo had gained a reputation of being tough but fair, and interested in the community's well-being.

So when Ronaldo publicly stood behind the substitution program, people listened. In front of community meetings, he told farmers they had a unique opportunity to leave violence and coca behind, and that the FARC would be there to accompany the substitution program and make sure it lived up to its promises. Moreover, he said, the FARC would no longer organize buyers for their coca, nor protect the coca from the military. If the farmers refused to join the substitution program, the state would send manual eradicators to destroy their crops, and then they would receive nothing.

Of course, the state had long been sending manual eradicators and providing farmers with nothing. But after decades in which the FARC had fought state power and expressly prohibited farmers from giving up their coca, the sight of Ronaldo joining state officials to tell them to join substitution was impactful. Local farmers, often resentful of the state's failure to live up to the agreement, stress that the FARC's support pushed them to believe in the program. But the fact that the FARC would no longer protect their coca was also important.

"The truth is that this became an area where it would be very difficult for campesinos to live from coca," Eduardo told me, "because those who supported coca were no longer there. . . . If there was a forced eradication coming, we lost those who were going to shoot it out with the soldiers and mine the plots of coca. We were exposed."

* * *

Why did Briceño's farmers place their faith in a state that had done little to deserve it, voluntarily tying themselves into dependence on state resources and providing public authorization of state power? On the one hand are the factors, both human and ecological, that changed farmers' material calculus around coca: the worms and fungus that plagued coca crops; the rising cost of supplies to process it; and state eradication campaigns, promising to become particularly damaging without the FARC's protection, that further hurt coca's bottom line. On the other are symbolic elements: the FARC's authorization of the program and a deep-seated local desire for state presence that is paradoxically rooted in narratives of state absence that cast more of the state as the key to ending violence and poverty. These myriad elements suggest a distinct way of thinking about the formation of state power: not simply as emanating from the actions of state officials, but as being also rooted in the agency of local populations that pursue distinct livelihood strategies motivated by calculations both material and symbolic.

Use versus Opportunity:
Collective Claims-Making and Believing in "the State"

Briceño is not just any village. As host first of the land mine removal and then of the pilot coca substitution program, Briceño's experiences as peace laboratory have become symbolically consequential, invoked by both supporters and detractors of Colombia's controversial peace process. In the context of *incumplimiento*, these accounts have often strayed from reality, making campesinos feel used. At the same time, Briceño's symbolic importance to the peace process has opened political opportunities for the community, allowing for distinct forms of claims-making that have at times achieved real material gains. In this section, I describe the power effects of this tension between use and opportunity, showing how the authority of the state has been configured through the collective action that farmers have undertaken in response.

Christian Lund (2017) has shown that rights-based claims-making and political authority are mutually co-constitutive, involving a reciprocal recognition in which the state grants citizenship rights and citizens grant state authority. We may think of a student asking a teacher's permission to use the bathroom: the very request authorizes the teacher's power, while the teacher's granting of the student's right to a toilet is simultaneously a claim to her own authority to do so. Of course, not all collective action directed to the state recognizes state authority. In the previous chapter I described how the coca economy created the basis for the refusal of state authority (Simpson 2014)—a mobilization that prevented the military from arresting a coca buyer. The "coming" of the state to Briceño has more recently created the basis for collective action based instead on what Lisa Mitchell (2023, 10) calls "hailing the state": "collective mobilizations that appeal to authorities and seek their recognition and response," and which, in so doing, "acknowledge and, in the process, reify state authority."

This reification—a word sociologists use to describe the process of treating an abstract idea as if it were concrete—is critical to the state's symbolic power. If previous desire for the state was rooted in its perceived absence, the peace process era has made state actors and institutions increasingly present in community life. As Phillip Abrams (1988) famously argued, their legitimacy depends on their being cast as "the state," a coherent and unified entity that serves the common good. When we believe in "the state," we consent to state power, seeing its exercise as natural, legitimate, and inevitable (Bourdieu 2014; Loveman 2005). When we do not believe, a police officer, soldier, or tax collector may seem like just another armed thug. And like Eduardo's community defending the coca buyer, we may even band together to stop them.

The story of this book is to no small degree the story of how a community begins to believe in the state—albeit in an incomplete fashion, at times reluctantly, and with significant disappointments. But the state is not only an artifact of belief; it is also a dynamic field of power which different actors compete to control (Bourdieu 1999). For at least the last three decades, questions of how to resolve Colombia's internal conflict have been the central issue animating these struggles for political power, coming to a head with the highly controversial 2016 peace agreement. As peace laboratory, Briceño became central to these struggles, utilized by both the Santos presidential administration in its efforts to legitimize a nascent peace process, and the Duque administration that followed, which was hostile to the peace agreement. This change affected the substitution program's execution, the political opportunities available to Briceño's campesinos, and the way their experiences as a peace laboratory were exploited to either discredit or support the peace process.

In this section I detail this national context before describing three instances of claims-making on the state across these two presidential administrations to show how a new moment of state/society relations—one in which communities are hailing rather than refusing the state—has emerged through the peace process. Even when these claims come out of frustration with the state's *incumplimiento*, they express a recognition of state authority, allowing for commonsense assumptions of the state's rightful role and responsibility—a belief in "the state"—to spread. At the same time, the elusive promise of state resources has had power effects by pushing the communities to make claims through formal institutional channels rather than through contentious politics.

POLITICAL CONTEXT:
A NATIONAL STRUGGLE OVER PEACE

Santos's 2017 visit was an inflection point for Briceño, when the state came to a forgotten mountain village to occasion a wholesale transformation. But much as it *made* history for Briceño, it was also a moment deeply made *by* history—not only by the village's legacy of coca and conflict, but by a national struggle over peace that has dominated Colombian politics for more than a decade. In the introduction of this book, I situated Briceño's experiences within a broader account of state transformation: how the pressures of democratization push Global South states to take an increasingly active role in distributing goods to their poorest citizens even as they implement policies that exclude these same people from legal markets. Yet while the power of the vote has been a useful bargaining chip for Briceño's poor in their desperate struggle to access state resources (see chapter 6), just as powerful has been their status as coca farmers, victims of the armed conflict, and residents of the peace laboratory. Here I explain how this happened: a peace agreement that has opened new symbolic bases and institutional pathways for people in conflict-affected territories to make claims on state resources, and the associated political struggles in which both the supporters and the detractors of peace have invoked the example of Briceño.

Perhaps the best starting point to understand the struggle over peace is the political rivalry between its two primary antagonists: Álvaro Uribe (president from 2002 to 2010, and power behind the presidential throne from 2018 to 2022) and Juan Manuel Santos (president from 2010 to 2018). Uribe—from the Antioquian capital of Medellín, a few hours south of Briceño—presented an image different from that of the elites who had long ruled the country. He often appeared on a horse with a traditional poncho and hat, conjuring an image of frontier white masculinity: a strongman promising security to a population fed up with decades of living in fear (Burnyeat 2022; Cuéllar Sarmiento 2009; Lobo 2017). He has been investigated for his role in hundreds of crimes, including assassinations, paramilitary massacres, and the "false positives" scandal, in which soldiers murdered thousands of innocent campesinos and dressed them up as guerrillas to inflate body counts. Yet he was wildly popular during his presidency for his military successes against the guerrillas; and while his support is flagging, many Colombians still identify as *Uribistas*.

Whereas Uribe presented himself as a (strong)man of the people, Santos came from one of the country's most powerful Bogotá families. Like many in the traditional elite, Santos had extensive international experience, with master's degrees from the London School of Economics and Harvard's Kennedy School (Burnyeat 2022). When Santos won the 2010 presidential election, endorsed by Uribe after serving as his defense minister, he was expected to continue his predecessor's militarized approach. Instead, he opened peace negotiations with the FARC, a move Uribe denounced as a betrayal.

As peace talks progressed, Santos was highly successful at mobilizing support and funding within the international community. While Uribe had succeeded in attracting foreign capital, his heavy-handed tactics had made international investors nervous. Santos, "the type of Colombian that the foreign investor can feel comfortable dealing with" (Bunce 2019, 188), promised to use peace negotiations to turn Colombia into a liberal market democracy whose untapped resources would be up for grabs, freed from the specter of violence. However, even as Santos's plans for peace were popular with the international community, Uribe, by now a senator, led a major opposition movement. After the FARC and government negotiators came to an initial agreement, the pro- and anti-peace forces squared off around a referendum meant to give the Colombian people the final say on the agreement, with a national vote set for October 2016.

The No campaign's most powerful and oft-repeated script invented the term *Castrochavismo* to associate the peace agreement with authoritarian left-wing governments in Cuba and Venezuela. In this logic, the agreement would attack private property and democracy, turning Colombia into socialist Venezuela—a prospect that became increasingly threatening as Colombia filled with millions of Venezuelan migrants fleeing economic collapse. The *Castrochavismo* script proved so effective that it was repurposed in 2020 Spanish-language "Latinos for Trump" attack ads that ran in Florida and alternated clips of Joe Biden with Hugo Chávez, Nicolás Maduro, and Fidel Castro. *Uribistas* also manipulated popular discomfort around the 2016 legalization of gay marriage and pedagogical programs designed to promote LGBTQI tolerance to accuse the peace agreement of promoting a feminist and pro-gay "gender ideology" (Gomez-Suarez 2017). Catholic priests and evangelical pastors preached against the accords, while one popular social media pastor called the peace agreement the "antichrist" (Nadal 2016).

Finally, the opposition accused the peace agreement of surrendering Colombia to the FARC and offering impunity and excessive material rewards to the guerrillas. Like the *Castrochavismo* and gender ideology scripts, these arguments were widely transmitted through social media in messages that included major exaggerations and outright lies (Arroyave and Romero-Moreno 2023). Millions of Colombians read and forwarded untrue WhatsApp messages claiming that if the peace agreement was ratified, their pensions would be seized to pay FARC ex-combatants, that the peace agreement would install FARC commander Rodrigo Londoño as president, or that ex-combatants would receive three times the national minimum wage (Burnyeat 2022).

While members of the Santos administration were barred as government officials from actively campaigning, they promoted the agreement through educational initiatives and news stories that trumpeted the inspirational potential for peace. The image of Briceño, where FARC guerrillas, army soldiers, and state officials were still collaborating on the land mine removal program, was often central to these efforts—a status that, as I'll describe, established a leverage point for locals to demand state resources. Leading up to the October 2016 referendum vote, surveys indicated widespread support for peace, expected to garner as much as 72 percent of the vote. However, the referendum was defeated by a razor-thin margin of 50.2 percent to 49.8 percent.

Only five days later, Santos was announced as the winner of the Nobel Peace Prize, a bittersweet recognition following the shocking electoral loss.

The agreement was renegotiated with the *Uribista* opposition and ratified by Congress in late November 2016 without going to another referendum vote. The new version banned the expropriation of unused land to address rural land inequality, stipulated the right of the government to continue forced coca eradication, and removed language that recognized the rights of the LGBTQI community (Romero 2016). But even if the agreement was eventually pushed through, the failed referendum dealt a major blow to the already fragile legitimacy of the peace process.

National controversy notwithstanding, the peace agreement provided the basis for transforming state/society relations in conflict-affected rural areas. Woven throughout was the notion of "territorial peace," described by High Commissioner of Peace Sergio Jaramillo (2014) as a "logic of territorial inclusion and integration, based on a new alliance between the State and communities to jointly construct institutionality in the territory." It proposed to build peace from within the rural regions that had suffered most from conflict by establishing spaces of local participation through which state agencies could identify particular territorial needs and address the underlying social, economic, political, and cultural conditions behind conflict (Cairo et al. 2018; Lederach 2023; Olarte-Olarte 2019). In concrete terms, this meant that a slew of agencies and programs, many created through the agreement, entered territories like Briceño to distribute resources, carry out trainings, and hold thousands of meetings. These programs changed the way people like Eugenia and Suso were seen and engaged by the state: they became victims deserving of state aid through newly created programs like coca substitution, rather than narcos and objects of suspicion as potential guerrilla sympathizers.

However, the political struggles did not end with the agreement's signing. Santos's visit to Briceño occurred in the context of two struggles to set peace on the right track. One was legislative, as effectively carrying out the agreement required the National Congress to pass multiple laws. Those efforts largely failed, as many legislators who had been Santos's allies saw the referendum's defeat as an example of Uribe's continued strength, and began jumping ship (Gutiérrez Sanín 2019b).

The second battleground was the 2018 presidential election, which came down to a runoff between candidates from opposing poles: the right-wing *Uribista* Iván Duque and the left-wing pro-peace candidate Gustavo Petro, a former member of the M-19 guerrillas. Petro was the first Colombian leftist to even get as far as a presidential runoff. In the so-called Pink Tide of the early 2000s, nearly all South American democracies pushed back against neoliberal reforms to elect left-wing heads of state, while Colombian voters turned further right in electing Uribe. But in 2018 the unprecedented electoral success of the left pushed Colombia's elites, previously divided over the issue of peace, into some semblance of unity. After their own candidates were defeated, parties that had originally supported peace as part of Santos's governing coalition (the Partido de la U, Cambio Radical, the Conservatives, and Santos's own Liberal Party) all backed Duque despite his party's promises to "rip up the peace accords" (Gutiérrez Sanín 2019b). Duque won an election marred by significant accusations of voter fraud.

Under Duque's watch, funding for key elements of the agreement dried up, and its implementation ground to a halt (Isacson 2021). Yet even if the election had seemingly provided him with a mandate to dismantle the peace process, Duque faced significant civil society and international pressure to respect the legally binding peace accords. Despite becoming one of the least popular presidents in Colombian history, he achieved what Gutiérrez Sanín (2020) calls a "small political miracle": secretly sabotaging the agreement while nevertheless maintaining relative international goodwill and funding streams by seeming to comply—a perception that, like Santos's earlier efforts to popularize peace, the Duque administration repeatedly used the image of Briceño to promote.

LAND MINE REMOVAL AND LEVERAGING THE SYMBOLIC IMPORTANCE OF THE PEACE LABORATORY

In June 2016, the Facebook page of the Colombian presidency published a video titled "Briceño, Antioquia, prepares itself to be the Peace Laboratory." The video begins with the image of Humberto de la Calle, the chief government peace negotiator, seated in front of a blue banner announcing, "Dialogues of Peace, Havana Cuba."

"The first joint pilot project for humanitarian de-mining in Colombia is now a reality," de la Calle announces, as soft piano music begins to play. The screen fills with images of FARC and government delegates getting off a helicopter to greet El Orejón community members. De la Calle continues: "For the first time, after more than fifty years of conflict, a battalion of the Colombian army and the FARC are jointly carrying out actions that favor a population that has been severely affected." The camera zooms out to show a helicopter taking off from El Orejón's soccer field, green hillsides in the background.

Cut to de la Calle: "El Orejón is a small hamlet in northern [Antioquia] which has more explosive artifacts than inhabitants. It is the terrible reality of war." The scene shifts to the inside of a campesino home, where white men in brown vests project laptop images onto a dirt wall as attentive community members look on. "Alejandro is a campesino who trusts that his son can grow up in a territory free of mines. It's not enough to de-mine. We have to give new opportunities to these communities. But the seed of hope for peace has been planted in this population. We must safeguard it." The piano music intensifies, reaching inspirational notes. A campesino leads a mule, weighed down with luggage, on a dirt path. "What is happening in El Orejón is a potent message of peace. . . . De-mining a hamlet like El Orejón is a fact that shows it is possible to end war."

The video shifts back to de la Calle at the Havana negotiating table, repeatedly bringing down his right hand to punctuate his words. "We are here because we think it is possible to inaugurate a future of peace. It is the moment to end the war. No more deaths. No more suffering."

✷ ✷ ✷

Fully two years before President Santos's visit, the land mine removal program first planted the seed of hope for peace and inclusion in the community of El Orejón. As the subject of state pro-peace messaging and nightly news segments, community members felt that their well-being had become a national priority. After decades of violence, they were playing informal soccer games with guerrilla and army soldiers—as well as with Norwegian humanitarian aid workers and state officials from Bogotá. After a lifetime of feeling abandoned by the state, they lived alongside national state officials for months, developing relationships that persist to this day. They observed and participated in meetings that felt historic, with high-ranking FARC and military commanders discussing how to achieve shared goals after having been sworn enemies for decades.

As the program unfolded, however, community members began to feel they were being used. As community president, Eugenia helped organize meetings where campesinos drew maps showing the locations of mines. Her neighbors Fabio and Angélica participated, excited at the idea of being able to walk through their community free from fear. But as Fabio says, "After we gave information about all the sites where there were possible mines, they decided to de-mine . . ."

Angélica finishes his sentence: ". . . in another area."

Fabio continues: "Where they de-mined were the lands that Hidroituango had bought, land we barely used."

The community had requested that the program target a strategic and heavily mined point on the top of the ridge that allows access to many neighboring communities. Officials in the land mine removal program explained that because the guerrillas who had laid the mines in this area were dead, it would be too difficult to find and remove all the mines. But community members, taking stock of where land mine removal had taken place, suspected other motives. The program had cleared the lower areas of the hamlet, on property that had been taken over by the hydroelectric dam. It had also cleared an additional area that was rumored to be the planned location of a military base. "The land mine removal program was for Hidroituango, not the community," Fabio says. "Because if it had been for the community, they would have de-mined all the area that we told them, an area that is now abandoned. But it's still mined and is going to stay that way for life."

The military base was never built, and I have no direct evidence to suggest that Hidroituango officials influenced the decision of which areas would be de-mined. However, local suspicions of the land mine removal program were also stoked by the national government's disingenuous messaging around its achievements.

By 2016, just as the Santos government was trying to drum up support for the national referendum on the peace agreement, national headlines were trumpeting the accomplishments of land mine removal as testament to what the peace process could achieve: "El Orejón, free of mines." One nightly news segment was typical. The newscaster began: "The hamlet of El Orejón, in Briceño, Antioquia, which at one time was known as the most heavily mined place in the world, is the first in Colombia to be declared free of mines." The report goes on to refer to El Orejón as "a reference of what can be achieved with the peace agreement."

Nevertheless, if you walk on the path that goes uphill from the community center, you will quickly find evidence that El Orejón is far from land mine-free. The path seems literally cut into the jungle, roughly three feet wide with dirt walls as much as ten feet high. I'm walking with Eladio, who at seventy-seven years old still traverses the route several times a week to work on a plot of land where he plans to graze a herd of cattle. "They used to warn us that if we need to go to the bathroom, to take care of our necessities directly on the trail," he tells me, referring to the guerrillas. We are reminded that this is still the modus operandi by red skull-and-crossbones signs mounted on wooden posts that appear periodically on the trail, often less than two feet apart (fig. 2.3). They read:

DANGER
EXPLOSIVE ARTIFACTS
STAY CLEAR

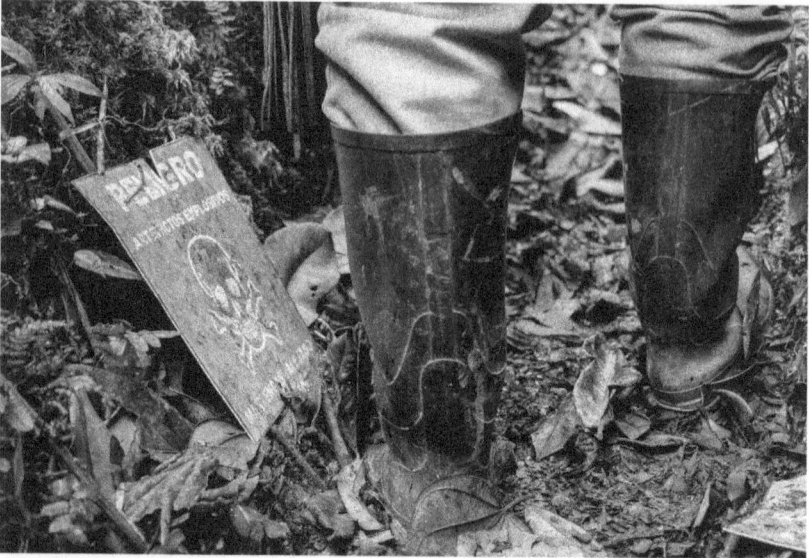

FIGURE 2.3. In the areas where the program has installed warning signs instead of removing land mines, a single misstep can still prove fatal.

Eladio's two dogs are with us, and they periodically run into the underbrush after jungle creatures real and imagined. Each time they push through the green wall of the jungle to reappear, I feel my pulse quicken, listening for what I imagine as the click of a mine's syringe being activated. Eladio himself still suffers from hearing loss from the 2013 explosion of a mine that—as I've detailed earlier, in the story of Eugenia and Suso—killed one community member and injured ten more. He seems relaxed, accustomed to a coexistence with land mines. He does, however, warn me against leaning on the trail walls: "You never know."

The anthropologist Diana Pardo Pedraza (2022), who researched land mine removal in El Orejón firsthand, has written that communities like El Orejón are left with "landscapes of suspicion" in two senses: one, community members find their relations with the land forever reconfigured by the fear of hidden mines; and two, they mistrust the intentions and effectiveness of land mine removal, and are skeptical of state actors' real motives.

In this context, a community that felt state officials were exploiting its experiences began to discuss ways to gain some collective benefit from the land mine removal program. The farmers realized that even if the program was not motivated by community needs, it had opened opportunities for them to demand social investment in the community. After years of anti-dam activism (see chapter 4), they also had a well-developed repertoire of collective action to draw on. They planned a *paro*, in which they would stall the program by blocking the road and preventing the arrival of needed supplies. Program officials, however, got wind of the plan. Public images of a protest against land mine removal would have contradicted the government's characterization of El Orejón as a "potent message of peace."

One of the program officials called Eugenia to get the community to desist, asking her what the community wanted. The community sent a list of eighteen demands to Havana, where representatives of the FARC and the Colombian government were carrying out peace negotiations. In response, the national government funded a bridge that connected El Orejón to the village center, the Turkish government paid for a new school as part of a broader financial commitment to support the peace process, and Norwegian People's Aid—an NGO that was already collaborating with the land mine removal program—funded a new community meeting house and fixed up the local soccer field (fig. 2.4).

The land mine removal program represented a critical learning experience for the campesinos of El Orejón. Their initial hopes for a significant community transformation were largely frustrated, even as media accounts distorted the program's achievements for political ends. But the exploitation

FIGURE 2.4. The community took advantage of political opportunities brought by Orejón's symbolic importance to the peace process to demand (from left) a new school, a community meeting house, and an improved soccer field.

of their experiences also brought political opportunity; they were able to leverage their symbolic importance to the peace agreement to draw unprecedented state investment.

The relationships through which this investment arrived are also of critical importance. The state officials who lived in El Orejón during the land mine removal program enacted the state's newfound presence, putting a face to the state (Burnyeat 2022) while also giving locals a means to access it. Through these ties, alongside the new community buildings, "the state" became real and familiar. Indeed, the simple fact of a community president like Eugenia having the phone numbers of national state officials—and of them having hers—is critical to state/society relations (a point I will return to in chapter 7, where I describe how Eugenia drew on these officials to get resources to build the community road). While the exceptional and newfound state presence in El Orejón brings this point into clear relief, personal relationships between community members and state officials make overlooked contributions to state formation across the world. In frontier areas where state authority is still an open question, turning to the state as authority and provider of the common good is a function not only of believing in "the state" as abstract idea, but of having the concrete ties—a phone number one can call, an advocate one can depend on—through which to do so.

PARTICIPATION, EXPECTATIONS, AND DISILLUSIONMENT

In 2016, as the land mine removal program continued in El Orejón, the neighboring hamlet of Pueblo Nuevo hosted the Joint Effort (Esfuerzo Conjunto). The Joint Effort lasted more than a year, bringing together community members alongside government, FARC, and UNODC representatives to hammer out the details of the substitution program to be launched in Briceño and subsequently across Colombia.

These spaces for community participation in Colombia's peace process make up part of a broader global trend referred to by peacebuilding scholars as the local turn (Mac Ginty and Richmond 2013; Paffenholz 2015). For decades, Western peacebuilders pushed a one-size-fits-all approach to peacebuilding based on a sense that war-torn nations had only to institute the model of Western liberal market democracy to overcome violence (Paris 2002). In the face of evidence that nearly half of these externally designed and led peace agreements were ending in returns to violence, the local turn pushes for interventions that empower and include local people (Högbladh 2012; Paffenholz 2015).

Spaces of participation in Briceño gave locals an unprecedented opportunity to represent their communities, engage the state, and articulate their expectations of it. They provided for the emergence of a group of community leaders like Eduardo and Eugenia, who developed relationships with state actors and learned how to engage the state on its own terms—the world of bureaucratic procedures, meeting minutes, and requests for information sent in triplicate to Bogotá. They contributed to the development of a belief in "the state" by pushing communities to think through what the state could contribute to their lives. But after the inevitable *incumplimiento* of state officials' lofty promises, these spaces of participation also contributed to local feelings of being used, and a related disappointment with the peace process.

Ana, who was elected alongside Eugenia to represent community interests in the accompaniment group, estimates that she participated in more than two hundred meetings in the year leading up to the beginning of coca substitution. But after all the time spent and supposed participation, Ana struggles to identify one concrete impact the community's input had on the peace process: "The [officials] who were there from the government said they had to gather information, send it up [*elevarla*], and all that, because they couldn't make decisions. Supposedly all the information arrived, but we still haven't had responses. . . . They use us but they've never considered us, not when we give our opinions or want things to be done differently."

Ana and other local leaders can name dozens of ideas they pushed forward that fell by the wayside: classes in rural hamlets for adults who want to finish their high school education; a plan that would allow beneficiaries to replace their coca gradually rather than all at once; antennae to improve cell phone service in rural communities; and the ability to execute their projects communally, like a plan for multiple families to develop commercial fish ponds and pool their resources to buy a refrigerated truck.

Even more than ideas for how to implement substitution, spaces of participation elicited ideas for what inclusion within the state's prosperous and protective reach could contribute to the village. While this began with the Joint Effort to prepare for coca substitution, it continued with another element of the peace process, the Development Projects with a Territorial Focus (PDETs). The PDETs, destined for the 170 rural municipalities most affected by the armed conflict, are a central element in the peace agreement's first chapter, Comprehensive Rural Reform. The projects were meant to be designed and created by community members.

In 2018 I attended one such meeting, restricted to women (Colombia's peace agreement has been celebrated for several mechanisms to ensure women's participation). Carolina, a state official who lived in Briceño for a year as she led the PDETs' participatory processes, breaks the women into eight groups of three. She assigns each group one of the PDETs' eight pillars, which include infrastructure, health, education, and agricultural economies. She distributes markers and posterboard, telling each group to make posters explaining proposed solutions for the region's problems.

When the women present their proposals, they are ambitious. They request subsidies for single mothers to buy their own land, an office dedicated to women's issues in the village, guaranteed buyers for the agricultural goods they produce, health brigades of qualified doctors who will visit their communities every month, homes for women who don't have them, computers and projectors for rural schools, scholarships for children, and credit-free loans. Carolina takes photos of the groups' posters and sends their requests to Bogotá.

When these processes began, government officials led community members to think their requests would be fulfilled, and that the peace process would make up for what they understood as decades of state absence. In Eugenia's words, "They told us they needed to gather information on all the community's needs. We asked for many things because now they were going to give us everything. That now they were going to *cumplir*. We believed that."

The result, as Isabel Peñaranda (2020) found in PDET meetings in southern Colombia, was an "asking free-for-all" that produced a "grocery list" of requests divorced from discussions of budget or viability. While the PDETs brought nearly twenty small-scale projects to Briceño, mostly repairs of rundown schools and community meeting houses, not a single one of the women's proposals was realized more than five years later. This is in line with the experience of the other 170 PDET municipalities, which have received small public works projects rather than transformative investment, rooted in communities' self-identified needs, that might lift them out of poverty (Isacson 2021).

But even while failing to live up to the community's expectations, the spaces of participation established through the Joint Effort and the PDETs had important consequences for state power in creating and spreading these expectations in the first place. They helped fill in details of just what the state as a source of peace and prosperity might bring to the community. And like the land mine removal program, they helped establish ties between participants and state officials like Carolina.

PEACE IN THE HANDS OF AN ANTI-PEACE
GOVERNMENT: DISCIPLINING POLITICAL ACTION

Carolina, however, was unable to stay in her position. When Iván Duque took over as president in August 2018, her contract was not renewed—nor was she replaced. Instead, as it did on a national level with multiple elements of the peace process, the Duque administration used a combination of inaction and political appointments of hostile or incompetent officials to let implementation of the peace process grind to a halt (Gutiérrez Sanín 2020).

In a July 2019 public meeting in Briceño to evaluate two years of the substitution program, I get my first in-person look at the new Duque-installed national director of the substitution program, Hernando Londoño. Eduardo is one local leader chosen to speak on behalf of the community. "Our whole economy was illicit," he says. "And when you were telling us to pull out our coca, you promised productive projects in the first year. But now you're telling us to wait. We don't have resources to buy fertilizer, there's no economy, there's no work for the youth. So when will the projects arrive?"

After listening to more than an hour of complaints about state *incumplimiento*, Londoño responds. He first explains the delays: "The previous [Santos] government started a program that costs $1.5 billion. Why did they form it if they didn't have the money? We will respect what the previous government signed. But we've changed the times because we don't have the budget."

Then Londoño turns to the subject of Briceño: "Briceño received $14 million in little over a year. But you're saying the economy stopped because coca ended. Of course." His voice drips with sarcasm. "But you should know there are no other municipalities in Colombia that have received this level of investment. And their economies haven't been destroyed. With this reflection, you realize that you are privileged. . . . You need a change in attitude. A change in mentality. We need a substitution of people who are dedicated to licit crops."

Londoño's call for a substitution of people—pushing the blame back onto the coca growers—is exemplary of how the Duque administration turned back to the criminalizing approach of the War on Drugs. Accusing the Santos government of launching the substitution program without sufficient funds, the Duque administration capped the program at the 99,097 families that had already signed individual accords, excluding more than 87,000 families that had originally been part of collective accords (International Crisis Group 2021b). And the administration's promises that it would respect the agreement rang increasingly hollow as planned spending for an already underfunded substitution program dropped by 98 percent from 2020 to 2021 (Isacson 2021).

But even as it sabotaged the peace process, the Duque administration was under both national and international pressure to follow the legally binding peace agreement, or at least give the appearance of doing so. For this it turned, as Santos had done to drum up support for peace, to the example of

Briceño. As before, this opened political opportunities. But the promise of needed resources also disciplined the community's collective action by pushing its claims-making down permitted institutional channels.

In January 2019, while I was in the United States between fieldwork stints, Alberto—a program beneficiary and one of the locals most engaged in local spaces of participation around the peace process—wrote me excitedly that something important had happened. In an hour-long phone conversation, he explained that in December, local leaders upset about the substitution program's broken promises had met to organize a *paro* protesting state *incumplimiento*, in which they would block the highway where it meets the road leading to Briceño. The protest was planned to coincide with a December 23 visit to Briceño by the highest national peace process official and substitution program director. Alberto, involved in organizing the visit, said that the purpose of the visit was for the high-ranking officials to "spend Christmas with us and declare the municipality free of coca, showing it as a model of substitution and alternative development." State officials, however, got wind of the *paro* and canceled the visit. Local state representatives working with the substitution program also threatened that if community leaders carried out the protest, they would leave the region, and the substitution program's promised resources would disappear entirely. Alberto said this would have been a disaster, adding: "We need to convince, not force [officials]." He was disappointed that the visit was canceled, but told me proudly that he and another local leader intervened and managed to persuade local leaders to cancel the *paro*. Instead, they crafted a document with twenty demands, and in two subsequent meetings with substitution program officials, negotiated an agreement. "We demonstrated our commitment," Alberto aid. "We don't want to give motives to anyone to say that substitution doesn't work." Alberto worried that public demonstrations critiquing the substitution program could provide ammunition for supporters of the War on Drugs.

In February 2021, Alberto is finally able to organize the national officials' visit. "Other people want to have a protest," he explains as we sit in in a café looking out at Briceño's main square. "But I don't think this is the space for that." He refers to an Indigenous mobilization (*minga indígena*) a few months earlier that joined a broader movement against rising violence, government sabotage of the peace accords, and the country's economic model. "They went all the way to Bogotá, and Duque didn't even meet with them." The national context has been marked by major social mobilization against the Duque government, beginning with a November 2019 *paro nacional* in which hundreds of thousands took to the streets. The mobilization was put on hold by the pandemic, but has more recently been rekindled, with widespread outrage bolstered by police violence against protesters.

Alberto continues: "No, rather than an angry protest, to take advantage of the visit we need to show success, so that Archila [the head official of the peace process] says to give Briceño whatever it asks for.'" Alberto says he has been seeking "content" beneficiaries willing to give grateful rather than critical testimony at the event.

A few days before the event, a communications team working for the national government comes to Briceño to record testimonies from content beneficiaries. I travel with them to Eduardo's farm. Eduardo tells a simple and inspiring story for the cameras: Briceño's farmers lived from coffee until its prices collapsed and they were forced to cultivate coca. Coca, however, ushered in an era of terrible violence and fear. But now, thanks to coca substitution, people no longer have to participate in illicit economies. Coca has disappeared from Briceño and the village is enjoying a new era of peace. His community's coffee association now seeks to toast and sell its coffee under its own brand to guarantee high prices. Eduardo is grateful to the substitution program for all the resources to improve the quality and production of his coffee.

After the interview, the communications team follows Eduardo around the farm, filming him picking coffee beans and showing off the bags of fertilizer and the coffee pulping machine he received from the substitution program. When they finish and head to the next farm, I hang back. Not only has Eduardo's testimony contradicted his previous outspoken criticism of substitution, but I recall that only a few weeks earlier he took me to a ridge not far from his house to point out replanted coca plots. "Coca has disappeared?" I ask him.

He laughs out loud. "*Hombre* Alex, sometimes you have to tell them what they want to hear."

The day of the national officials' visit, a delegation of about twenty campesinos gathers to welcome the important guests, wearing matching shirts to commemorate the occasion. The shirts bear the name of the event: "Briceño, Model of Peace with Legality." The phrase "Peace with Legality" is the Duque administration's rebranding of the peace process, an allusion to the *Uribista* attack on the peace agreement as illegally offering impunity to FARC guerrillas and rewards to coca cultivators. The visitors include the highest state peace process official, Emilio Archila, along with Londoño and a dozen other highly placed officials. After they arrive by helicopter and visit a nearby farm, we go down to the village coliseum, whose worn-down soccer/basketball court is decorated for the occasion. Hanging from the crossbar of the soccer goal, a placard reads "Briceño, Model of Peace with Legality." On the other side of the court, tables are set up with samples of regional products—chocolate, honey, panela, and coffee, including Eduardo's brand—in front of a massive sign reading "Farmers cultivate hope and harvest the future."

The event begins with a string of speeches by the important guests. When Archila speaks, he highlights the pride that campesinos are taking in their legal products, and in being able to show that they are good people by abandoning such a terrible thing as coca. The videos produced by the communications team are projected onto a screen hung from the wall, with multiple beneficiaries posing with the crop they've been able to develop thanks to substitution, and saying how happy and grateful they feel to live in peace. Alberto and other campesino leaders then give certificates to each of the guests, along with gift baskets filled with products from Briceño. They read each certificate into the microphone: "Special recognition granted to Doctor Emilio Archila, for his labor in closing the gaps of inequality and the construction of peace in territories affected by the armed conflict." Archila has neither medical training nor a PhD, but the title "Doctor" is traditionally used in Colombian society to express deference to powerful authorities—particularly when you are hoping they will send you resources under their control. The ceremony ends with a group of five children who come up to read a poem, handwritten on a green posterboard, titled "Peace Begins with a Smile."

Following the event, the Duque administration milks the example of Briceño for all it is worth. On the social media platform Twitter, Archila posts a photo of Eduardo along with a message: "In a recent visit to Briceño, Antioquia, model of #PeaceWithLegality we toured the crops of various #EntrepreneursOfTheCountryside who previously cultivated #coca, and today have prosperous businesses, like Eduardo who harvests one of the best #coffees of the region." Eduardo also appears in a video released by the peace process TikTok page, as well as on *PodPaz*, the government-produced podcast on the "advances of peace," which dedicates an entire episode to Briceño. The episode highlights how the Duque administration's handling of the substitution program has allowed farmers like Eduardo to overcome violence and illegality to establish successful brands. President Duque himself turns to the example of Briceño a couple of weeks later, playing one of the videos produced by the communications team as part of a presentation for international diplomats and social media, titled "Ten Realities of Peace with Legality."

Alberto sends me a WhatsApp voice message, his tone triumphant: "I think that the problems the [substitution] program has had, if we don't fix them with this message of solidarity and commitment from the beneficiaries, we'll never resolve them. We achieved the objective, having [Archila] and the institutions speak about Briceño. They made us an example. From here, it's more about the *gestión* of things that are missing." The word *gestión* is normally translated as "management," but within Colombian politics it's used to describe the process of procuring resources from powerful institutions or state officials. Alberto is betting that the characterization of Briceño as a "Model of Peace with Legality" will become a self-fulfilling prophecy, with ties to national officials resulting in more resources for the village.

Consent to power, some scholars have argued, is rarely a matter of subject populations being duped. Rather than truly accepting the ideology of a dominant group, subordinate groups act as if these representations of the world are real because they have material incentives to do so (Sayer 1994). It's not that they enthusiastically embrace a social order that disadvantages them; rather, they don't seek to remake it because they are too busy trying to meet basic needs and incrementally improve their lives within that structure (Przeworski 1985). To the dismay of revolutionaries and scholars alike, poor people's politics are usually rooted less in overthrowing an unjust world than in ensuring their own survival—and perhaps their material advancement— within it (Auyero 2001).

But if Eduardo and Alberto told officials "what they want to hear," allowing themselves to be used to prop up claims they knew were false in the hopes of gaining resources for their families and village, many others favored contentious action, including a march I will describe in the next section. Even as they critique a particular regime's performance, these actions, rooted in an understanding of the state's rightful role and responsibility, contribute to the construction of the state's symbolic power. The belief in "the state" as guarantor of public good, however, has been compromised by the fact that the substitution program has been implemented by nonstate actors.

The Outsourced State

"If you're criticizing the state for not living up to the [substitution] agreement, you don't understand how the state works." It is February 2020 and Hernando Londoño, the substitution program's national director, is back in Briceño. While during his previous visit, described above, he blamed the Santos administration for leaving the program without sufficient funding, now he turns to a different excuse in the face of thirty angry campesinos who have spent the last three hours complaining about the program's delays, substandard goods, and general *incumplimiento*. Londoño explains that the state has contracted out the substitution program's implementation to third parties, and thus cannot be held responsible for its shortcomings. Indeed, he says, the money to complete the program in Briceño is available, but they're still seek-ing a contractor to execute it. Though their frustration grows, the campesinos are mostly silenced. Is it possible that the state they so fervently desire, one that would bring peace and progress to overcome decades of violence and exclusion from social investment, is simply a misunderstanding?

Political ethnographers have long known that people's understandings of the state greatly depend on their everyday interactions with state officials (Gupta 1995). The so-called coming of the state to Briceño has intensified both the number and the stakes of these encounters, as campesinos now count on state resources for their families' livelihoods. These interactions, however, have often been with third parties the state has contracted to ex-ecute the substitution program, a complex assemblage of thirteen different entities including international agencies, local and national producers' asso-ciations, NGOs, local political associations, and consortia of businesspeople.

Londoño's point that contracting out program implementation is funda-mental to how the state works underscores the fact that outsourcing public goods provision has become a central element of state practice across the world. This outsourcing is commonly associated with neoliberal reforms—whether to market actors based on the claim that the competition of the pri-vate realm adds efficiency, or to NGOs that step in to fill gaps created by cuts in state services (Birch and Siemiatycki 2016; Cammett and MacLean 2011). This not only affects the quality of public services offered but also changes the very meaning and identity of the state.

In Briceño, this outsourced structure has led to delays, frustration, and a paralyzing uncertainty for beneficiaries waiting for needed resources. It has also given state officials like Londoño a convenient scapegoat, allowing them to outsource blame for the program's *incumplimiento*. In doing so, however, they disclaim state responsibility for the common good, compromising the development of local belief in "the state."

"WE'RE ABOUT TO START":
THE UNCERTAINTY OF AN INDEFINITE WAIT

Dideison was eighteen years old when the coca substitution program started. With seven years of experience picking coca as a *raspachín* but no crops of his own, he entered the program as a coca picker, entitled not to productive projects but to a year's salary while he did work for the community and par-ticipated in vocational training. Due to a bureaucratic error, Dideison did not start with the first group in early 2018. Not knowing when he would begin and with no work in Briceño, he asked for permission to travel south, where he'd been offered a job. "They told me that if I left to another municipality, they would remove me from the program," he explains as we sit on the terrace of my apartment in February 2020, overlooking Briceño. Desperate for a salary, he left anyway.

After Dideison had been working for four months, the president of his hamlet's community action board called him. The program was about to begin, and if he didn't return to Briceño he would miss out. Dideison quit his job and came back. The program, however, did not start. The Women's Association of Briceño, which had been contracted to execute the program for coca pickers, dropped out, describing the program as an administrative headache. An NGO focused on sustainable agriculture took over the program, but also dropped it before Dideison's group could begin. Dideison waited for more than a year, becoming increasingly frustrated. As he describes it, the official message was always the same: "'We're about to start, we just need this entity to do this paperwork, don't despair, don't leave the municipality.'"

Finally, in October 2019, another local association took over the project and Dideison began working. By this time, vocational training had been abandoned after state officials couldn't find a contractor to provide rural classes. After Dideison was paid for October and November, the money dried up. The rumor was that the UNODC employees who were overseeing the program were on vacation. In early February 2020, work was halted until the coca pickers were paid.

Dideison is again contemplating leaving the municipality to work elsewhere. "But you feel like if you leave, they won't pay you [the two months owed], or maybe they pay you and they kick you out of the program." He tells me that two and a half years have passed since he last picked coca. The substitution program has given him four months of work, paid him for two, and offered him none of the originally promised educational programs. For Dideison and many others, however, the true harm lies not in what they haven't received, but in the frustration, uncertainty, and even hope generated by the program. Having grown up in an environment where it was essentially taken for granted that young men would work in the coca economy, Dideison welcomed a program that would compensate for the coca economy's disappearance with work and vocational training. However, he says that if he had known from the start how long he would have to wait, he would have abandoned it to pursue other opportunities. Instead, because of the confusion generated by contracting out its implementation, state officials, contractors, and even well-meaning community leaders kept stringing him along, in the belief that it was "about to start."

The Colombian state, as Julieta Lemaitre (2018) has insightfully argued in her work with female conflict victims, always arrives late: after decades of war, after years of requests for social investment, and in situations where alternative competing authorities and local mistrust of the state may already be well established. Even when state resources are promised, locals quickly realize that "the times" of the state are not their own—they are instead marked by the hurry to demonstrate legitimizing spectacles (as in President Santos's helicopter entrance and bold proclamation that the state was coming), followed by indefinite delays in the delivery of needed services (Lederach 2023). The experience of waiting—combined with attendant emotions of uncertainty, boredom, and frustration—is a central element of how the poor experience state power and social marginalization, in the process learning, as Javier Auyero (2012, 9) wrote of Argentinian welfare recipients, a "subtle . . . daily lesson in political subordination."

OUTSOURCING RESPONSIBILITY

On February 21, 2020, hundreds of beneficiaries of the crop substitution program gather at the beginning of a cobbled road leading to Briceño's most isolated hamlets. Chanting, "*Alerta, alerta, el pueblo se despierta* [Alert, alert, the people are awakening]," they march to the village's main square. A group of campesinos leads the march, carrying a banner nearly as wide as the street that reads, "Government: Cheating campesinos means destroying communities." In the square, a community leader takes to the bullhorn: "They haven't lived up to the agreement we made when they had us uproot our coca, the only livelihood we had in our communities. We're demanding that the national government *cumplir* just as we did."

Pedro, the local state representative of the substitution program, meets with the protest organizers. The major source of the delays, he says, is the protocols required by state contracts. He addresses complaints about products that beneficiaries received through the program. "If the products were of poor quality, they shouldn't have signed for them. People are saying the state is robbing them. But the state doesn't buy anything; it only transfers [the money]," he says, deflecting blame to the program's contractors. He goes on to say that they have an emergency plan that will be executed by the Pan American Development Foundation (FUPAD), a Washington-based NGO, to implement productive projects with the remaining families. They are resolving a problem with the contract, he says, but they should begin soon.

For Pedro, facing a room full of local leaders who have publicly criticized the state of *incumplimiento* and cheating campesinos, the program's outsourced structure is productive in at least one sense: it allows him to deflect blame. The delays, he says, are inherent to state contracting processes. And if people are unhappy with the products they received, it is the fault of the contractors who provided them. While leaders grumble and challenge him on some points, his logic is hard to refute—at least given the assumption that the state's responsibility is to fund the program rather than execute it. At the same time, however, this logic contradicts a different set of assumptions: local expectations that in coming to Briceño, the state itself would guarantee peace, progress, and goods to develop legal agriculture.

The kind of state that emerges in this narrative is one that is responsible not for living up to its explicit commitments or guaranteeing a particular level of service, but simply for carrying out and funding contracting processes. In contracting FUPAD to execute an emergency plan, Pedro implies that the state is doing everything it can. By extension, there is nothing local leaders can do, either. They can only wait and hope that the next contractor delivers.

Less than a month later, in the meeting described at the beginning of this section, Londoño, the substitution program's national director, expands on his point that locals misunderstand the state: "I want you to understand that here I have an operator who is United Nations, who does the monitoring, who contracts the operators of technical assistance. They're the ones who cause a six- or seven-month delay for technical assistance to arrive. The substitution program, we're not executors of anything; I don't have the authorization to buy a single cow. . . . [The problems come from] the execution of the United Nations and the local operators."

It only gets worse. In the month since the meeting with Pedro, Londoño announces, the agreement with FUPAD has collapsed. "And is the program to blame?" he asks theatrically, jabbing his index finger at his chest. "It's not the program's fault. . . . We lost five months of the contracting process. And we had to publish another call for applications on Friday." Within one month, he says, the application process will close, and within three months, "we will surely start implementing the productive projects." In fact, this start, which includes less than half of the beneficiaries and involves only a portion of the missing projects, is delayed more than a year—a year in which the promises, uncertainty, and disappointments continue.[3]

In the introduction to this book, I argued that resource distribution has become the central way Global South states extend their power through generating recognition, loyalty, and the community relationships that officials depend upon to govern. However, outsourcing the distribution of goods and services to nonstate actors has the potential to compromise state formation through altering the state/citizen relationship and even the meaning of the state itself (Birch and Siemiatycki 2016; Cammett and MacLean 2011). In Briceño, contracting out the implementation of the coca substitution program has complicated the development of popular recognition of "the state" and the symbolic power that comes with it. Locals have encountered the state as a complex and confusing assemblage of actors that has repeatedly failed to live up to its commitments, generating mistrust, frustration, and a paralyzing uncertainty. Collective mobilization around these failures has created an ironic duality: while the community seeks to establish the state's responsibility for providing needed public goods, state officials themselves disclaim responsibility for the direct delivery of services. For locals, the result is a feeling of impotence and a growing disinclination to turn to the state as solution to their problems (Diamond 2022).

Conclusion

The state, as President Santos promised, has come to Briceño. This is not, after years of coca eradication campaigns, its first appearance in the village. Communities did not blindly trust it; instead, their acceptance of the coca substitution program had as much to do with coca's decreasing profitability and the FARC's authorization as with a desire for state presence. With implementation outsourced to nonstate entities and wrapped up in national struggles over the peace agreement, the state has not lived up to the commitments of the substitution program. Nor has it ushered in a new era of prosperity. The fact, however, is that coca substitution and the peace process have driven a broader transformation through which Briceño's campesinos newly turn to the state for help in meeting their daily needs and future aspirations. Even when they organize protests or complain about its *incumplimiento*, they affirm a belief in "the state" as the guarantor of order and provider of the public good.

This analysis, rooted in community members' everyday experiences and livelihood strategies, offers four lessons in how to build state power in areas where it has long been lacking. The first is related to why campesinos initially put their trust in the coca substitution program, and through it the state. I have shown that a critical element of this decision was a material calculation based on a conjuncture of human and ecological factors that slashed coca's profitability: skyrocketing costs, eradication campaigns, and the spread of worms and fungus. At the same time, it is impossible to deny the seductive power of the promise of inclusion within the horizon of state protection and investment, particularly for areas that have suffered from long-standing violence and poverty. While much scholarly work has described state formation as an imposition on reluctant populations (Matsuzaki 2019; Scott 2009; Tilly 1990), communities like Briceño can also be enthusiastic co-participants in helping to spread state authority. In these communities, which are increasingly connected to the outside world, the promise of "the state" may arrive even before state institutions themselves do. This promise becomes all the more seductive to the extent that local economic transformation—whether driven by ecological factors, by global market forces, or by communities' own decisions of how to make a living—make state resources essential to their livelihood strategies.

Second, while both symbolic desire and material need for the state operate as preconditions of state formation, the establishment of direct relations tying communities to individual state actors is a critical mechanism for building state authority. In so-called modern societies, the state operates in a largely impersonal manner: traffic lights function as if by magic to ensure a smooth commute, our phones invite us to connect to free internet in a public park, and taxes disappear from our paychecks. In contrast, for isolated communities with limited institutional penetration, community leaders depend on direct connections with state actors to conjure needed state resources (a point to which I will return in chapters 6 and 7, on local elections and the village's roads).

Third, collective claims-making plays a critical role in the building of the state's symbolic power by spreading commonsense expectations of the state's rightful role and responsibility. This process, like local desire for the state, is related to economic transformation. When coca dominated Briceño's economy, campesino collective action was more likely to refuse to recognize the authority of state actors who attacked their livelihoods. As legal farmers, dependent on state resources for their livelihoods, communities have begun hailing the state (Mitchell 2023)—recognizing state authority by pushing state actors to guarantee their rights as citizens.

Finally, even while collective claims-making affirms the state's role as provider of the public good, its symbolic power is complicated by campesinos' direct encounters with a real existing state that outsources delivery of goods. Across the Global South, NGOs and international humanitarian aid serve as a stopgap to provide needed services that so-called weak states are unable to provide (Ferguson and Gupta 2002; Hanlon 1991). While some scholars suggest that these services may help enhance both state capacity and legitimacy (e,g., Brass 2016), an ethnographic description of the state/society relations that play out through outsourcing suggests that they compromise developing beliefs in "the state." Campesino leaders find themselves in the paradoxical position of insisting on the state's responsibility to them even as state officials disclaim it. Thus, even as the disappearance of coca has pushed campesinos to depend on the state for their livelihoods, their communities have become increasingly resentful of the need to do so—and increasingly willing to seek alternatives.

3

Substitution and Its Discontents:
Post-Coca Livelihood Strategies

Eugenia and Suso, Act Two

Eugenia and Suso first began to imagine a future outside of Briceño in the 2000s, when violence was spreading through the community. In 2009 they used coca profits to buy a small property in the urban slums of Bello, just north of Medellín. Then in 2012, shortly after construction on the hydroelectric dam began, they were one of the lucky families who received a legally mandated payment from the dam company—a compensation for the dam's destruction of traditional gold panning and fishing economies. They combined this money with a substantial loan to begin building a small home on the property. "We thought that it would be very nice to have a house in the city," Suso says, "[for our children] to study, or, if we were displaced, to have somewhere to go. Because at any time there can be a displacement here."

In 2018, it was Eugenia's pregnancy with their youngest child Dubian that pushed them to move semipermanently to the city. Her pregnancy had been a surprise; Eugenia, unaware, visited Briceño's small hospital complaining of stomach pain. The doctor, a brand-new graduate, told her she had gas.

"And seven months later, the gas was born," Eugenia says, laughing. Dubian, an incorrigibly naughty toddler saved only by his cherubic grin, giggles in the background as he smacks their impressively tolerant orange cat on her back. The pregnancy was high-risk. Understandably mistrustful of the medical care available in Briceño, the family went to stay in their Bello home so that Eugenia could attend regular doctor's appointments.

"We always told people we were only in Bello for the pregnancy," Eugenia says. "But we ended up staying for our children's education." Their eleven-year-old daughter, Susana, had attended El Orejón's new two-story school, inaugurated during the president's visit to launch the substitution program in 2017. But it only had classes for the first through fifth grades, with one teacher teaching everyone the same material. A school in the nearby community of Pueblo Nuevo enabled their older sons, Adrián and Sebastián, sixteen and fourteen, to study through the ninth grade; but to graduate from high school they would have had to commute to the neighboring village of El Valle, in a program where they would finish the final two years in one year, studying only one day a week.

Eugenia thinks back to her own experience of finishing high school: "There were up to sixty students, from sixth to eleventh grade, with one poor teacher. And only forty chairs, with students sitting on the floor. And what could the teacher do? Grab a textbook and teach the same thing to everyone. Students leave those programs very poorly prepared for the university." She and Suso resolved to give their children a shot at a university education and a salaried job that would enable them to avoid a life of rural poverty.

"Adrián started ninth grade in Bello," Suso says, "and at the same time, he's studying with the SENA [the National Learning Service], and after he graduates, can enter immediately to finish a *técnica* [a vocational degree program of between one and two years, offered free by the SENA]. Where can you find something like that around here?" Sitting in the outdoor corridor of their Briceño home, Suso gestures to the beautiful yet isolated valley walls around us, green with cow pasture, coffee plants, food crops, and the occasional patch of jungle. It is May 2020, and the spread of Covid-19 has pushed classes online. Suso and Eugenia have temporarily moved back full-time to the countryside, where we are social distancing together.

"Look at everyone who graduates from high school around here," Suso continues. "They continue doing the same thing, swinging a machete on their farms."

"Right now, everything we do is for our children," Eugenia adds. "So they don't have the same future."

With their children enrolled in urban schools, they live, like many rural smallholders transitioning to urban futures, between the city and the countryside (fig. 3.1). They still come back to their farm during school vacations and global pandemics, and Suso often makes the four-hour motorcycle trip to spend a few days taking care of their crops and animals. The kids are always excited to arrive at the farm; Adrián and Sebastián make plans to go hunting or fishing with their friends, while Susana finds and hugs the cattle herd's cutest calf. They usually stay as long as they can, enjoying the freedom of the countryside.

Along with a life split between rural and urban areas comes a patchwork of livelihood strategies. Over time, Eugenia and Suso have built three apartments on top of their Bello home that they rent out for a monthly income.

FIGURE 3.1. After years teaching his sons to do agricultural work, Suso sees a better future for them in the city.

These construction projects, however, have left them in debt. They periodi-cally sell off a cow from their herd to meet payments. If they have a little extra money, they often invest it in an additional cow to fatten up on their pastureland and later sell at a profit. The yearly coffee harvest offers a signifi-cant windfall—though whether it covers the costs of fertilizer, insecticides, and labor to pick the beans depends on coffee's highly variable price. In good years, they use money from the coffee harvest to take a family trip up north to the Caribbean coast.

Many of their monthly bills are covered by Families in Action, a state wel-fare subsidy for poor families with children. When they are in El Orejón, their farm meets most of their nutritional needs. Whenever Suso travels back to Bello, he straps bags of plantains, yuca, and avocados to his motorcycle to offset grocery bills. Over the years, Eugenia has found temporary paid work with the land mine removal program, which hired her as a community liai-son, and with another NGO interested in promoting women's leadership in the area. Suso briefly worked for a road repair project (described in chapter 4) which was funded by the hydroelectric dam company.

Like nearly all their neighbors, they also turn to local electoral politics as part of their livelihood strategies (a phenomenon I will describe in detail in chapter 6). Eugenia, a respected community leader, has been able to leverage her political support to get resources for both her family and the community, primarily to build and then fix up the community road and a long driveway that leads to their home (see chapter 7). These improvements cut heavily into agricultural transport charges, and let them travel more easily between Bello and Briceño. Nevertheless, other commitments from the mayor have gone unfulfilled. Most recently, the mayor has broken promises to provide them with materials to fix a leaky roof and a sewing machine Eugenia hoped to use to get a piece-rate job making clothing from home.

"I don't want to support any [candidate] anymore," Eugenia tells me as we sit in her Bello home in 2023, as another mayoral election is heating up. The home is well kept and orderly, but the contrast is clear with her house in El Orejón, where social life revolves around the open-air corridor with a 270-degree view over the Cauca River valley. Dubian zooms by on a small push bicycle, occasionally running into my feet in the cramped living room.

"I want my children to get an education so they can work for a company and not depend on some mayor," Eugenia adds.

The children themselves largely share her vision, though their rural upbringing also informs their goals. "Life is too hard in the countryside," says Susana, referring to her mother's struggles to split branches to light their wood stove and feed a hungry family. Drawing on her experiences raising animals on the farm, she wants to be a veterinarian.

Sebastián hopes to become a professional soccer player—a dream that has itself been aided by their move to the city. When Eugenia and Suso first moved to the city, they enrolled him in a soccer school run by a famous local player. Even after graduating, Sebastián continues practicing, but he has also entered a local university to study environmental engineering.

Adrián, the oldest son, graduates from high school and finishes his *técnica* with the SENA. As part of the *técnica*, he completes an internship with a dairy company. He gets good reviews from his bosses, and they offer him a permanent job. At only nineteen, five years after his family's semipermanent move to the city, he achieves the elusive goal of a salaried position. Nevertheless, he still dreams of studying biology and eventually returning to Briceño to do conservation work with the village's flora and fauna.

Eugenia and Suso are proud of their children's achievements and happy to see their sacrifices begin to pay off (fig. 3.2). Still, they speak of El Orejón, where they spend less and less of their time, with regret—particularly after all the time and hope they invested in the peace process. And they're not alone in leaving the community. Where before coca provided a guaranteed and relatively high daily wage, now there is little work available. The beaches where gold panning always offered a guaranteed backup plan for the community have been flooded by the dam reservoir. Those who try growing food

FIGURE 3.2. Suso and Eugenia's love for their children has brought the family to the city, but all miss the freedom and beauty of the countryside.

crops operate at razor-thin profit margins. Like Eugenia and Suso, still hoping for the cattle they expected to receive four years earlier, they await the substitution program's promised resources. In 2016, eighty-eight people lived in the community. Now there are less than fifty. Peace and the economic collapse associated with coca's disappearance have displaced more people than violence ever did.

"Look, Alex, the countryside is beautiful and free, but it never rewards you," Eugenia tells me. We're back on their farm, drinking coffee as we contemplate the setting sun.

"You plant and plant, harvest your products, and you can't sell them, or they're worth less than your cost," says Suso. He has just returned from picking coffee all day in the fields. A sack of yuca he uprooted for our dinner sits at his feet. "And we don't want our children to have the same future."

"Look at this beautiful school that's here—what for?" Eugenia gestures in the direction of the ostentatious two-story school building they successfully demanded during the land mine removal program. The school is down to seven students spread from first through fifth grade, with one teacher teaching them all the same material. After devoting years to community leadership, Eugenia has stepped down as community action board president.

"All my life, I've wanted to do work for the community," she says. "But

I have other things to fight for. Right now, what we're thinking about is the future of our children. We live well here, growing our food. But what opportunities are there here? For a better future, nothing."

"No one has a future here," says Suso. Ana, forever the doting daughter, has climbed up to sit on his right knee, her left arm draped around his suntanned neck. "There's only one future here: to kill yourself working day and night."

Introduction

Roughly two years into the coca substitution program, Hernando, a jovial man in his early sixties, decided to plant a bean crop on a section of his farm. Though he was a program beneficiary, Hernando had not been a coca farmer. Instead, throughout coca's apogee in Briceño, he made and sold beautiful leather saddles in a small shop that faced Briceño's main square. The end of coca, however, spelled the end of the local disposable income needed to sustain a business of ornate and expensive saddles. Hernando decided to return to the agricultural activities of his youth and entered the substitution program with the support of the community action board president. Hernando set about recovering his overgrown farm, planting coffee, pasture for cows, and now beans.

As an older man now unaccustomed to agricultural labor, Hernando contracted local labor to help him plant and pick the beans—forty days total, from neighbors who were grateful for the work. After harvesting the beans, Hernando reserved a portion for his personal consumption, then awakened before dawn to load the rest—336 kilograms total—onto his mules. He traveled an hour to the point where he could catch the daily local transport, then paid to take the beans on a truck to the village center, two hours away. He made the rounds of local shops, but was unable to find a buyer: the shopkeepers were already stocked with dried imported beans. Hernando caught a bus to neighboring Yarumal, paying for a second ticket and a second transport charge for the beans. There he sold the beans for $330, returning quickly to Briceño to avoid having to pay for a hotel that would cut into his earnings. Between his tickets and freight charges for the beans, he paid $45 to get the beans to market.

"And how much did you invest in cultivating them?" I ask Hernando, jotting down numbers in my notebook as I sit on the patio of his farm. Aside from his own time, he says, he paid $350 for labor and goods.

"With the beans," I tell him, "you lost $60, not counting the use of your land and your days of work."

Hernando gives a little laugh. "That's the hard thing about the countryside," he says. "That you take out your products, but they're not worth anything."

In his struggles to sell his beans, Hernando was coming face-to-face with the corporate food regime, which (as described in chapter 1) has exposed Colombian smallholding farmers to competition with cheaply produced imported goods. As he told me his story, I couldn't help but think of the bean crop that Suso had sold—more than thirty years earlier, before Colombia's economic opening—to finance his trip to a nearby village. While simply producing a large and high-quality food crop had once been enough to turn a modest profit, Hernando was realizing the hard way that he was now effectively excluded from local, national, and global agricultural markets.

For nearly two decades, coca insulated Briceño's campesinos from the corporate food regime, offering them a crop that, because of its illegality, maintained relatively high prices. Their struggles to make a living in the face of the disappearance of both coca and gold panning economies speak to three related trends that characterize the lives of the excluded poor across the Global South.

The first is that, like Eugenia and Suso's patchwork livelihoods, these strategies tend to be varied. Auyero and Servián (2025, 41) evocatively refer to the Global South poor as "hard-working bricoleurs" who piece together a precarious living through combinations of formal and informal labor, small-scale ventures, and help from anyone within their social orbit. The replacement of stable waged labor with temporary jobs and the rise of the gig economy in the Western world suggest that the patchwork livelihoods of people like Suso and Eugenia are not limited to the Global South, nor even to the poor (Denning 2010). Yet these strategies take on added immediacy for those who are pushed to them by the specter of hunger and destitution.

The second trend is that while specific livelihood strategies vary widely, ethnographic literature on how the Global South poor make ends meet suggests that assistance from the state or from alternative governors is a ubiquitous element. Small-scale enterprises use state cash transfers to get off the ground and state contracts to stay afloat (Ferguson 2015; Krohn-Hansen 2022); armed groups organize economies around drugs, diamonds, and illegal mining (Felbab-Brown 2017; Keen 2000); jobs working for the state or armed groups may constitute the only available wage labor (Shah 2019; Zarazaga 2014); and in the face of calamity, the poor rely on emergency aid from state officials or competitors to its authority (Arjona et al. 2015; Auyero 2001; Phillips 2018). While some parts of their livelihoods may be more autonomous, only in rare cases do the excluded poor of the Global South patch together a living without recourse to those who would govern them.

Third, within rural communities, modernization has made the classic figure of the peasant as isolated subsistence farmer increasingly rare.[1] Scholars of rural economies have long warned that as part of the advancement of corporate agriculture and widespread rural-to-urban migration, peasants are disappearing, "outdistanced by contemporary history" (Kearney 1996, 1). Many consider this a good thing; economists call countries in which a large proportion of the GDP and workforce are devoted to agriculture "underdeveloped" (Gupta 1998), while classical Marxist theory sees the incorporation of peasants into the working class as a political advance (Edelman 1999). However, given that rural populations continue to grow in absolute terms and still make up 43 percent of the world, a different interpretation is that peasant ways of life have reconfigured rather than disappeared. As exemplified in the example of Suso and Eugenia, and fitting within the two trends mentioned above, peasant livelihoods have become increasingly patchwork and cash-dependent, crossing rural/urban divides and combining wage labor, subsistence farming, production for markets, and state aid (Breman 2013; Edelman 1999; Phillips 2018; Smith 1989).

Increased integration into markets brings with it both vulnerability and opportunity. As one example, in a twenty-year ethnographic engagement with highland Indonesia, Tania Li (2014, 4) describes how farmers who began planting cacao for global markets entered a world of "capitalist relations in which their capacity to survive was governed by rules of competition and profit." As time went on, some peasants accumulated wealth while others lost their land to cycles of debt, and had to seek out wage labor. Critically, the whole process was set in motion not by their land being ripped away, but rather by peasants' desires to improve their lives by leaving "behind their condition of backwardness and acquir[ing] goods they associated with a modern life" (Li 2014, 165).

In similar terms, Briceño's campesinos were mostly subsistence farmers who turned increasingly to market production as first coffee and food crops and later coca provided profits that let them buy consumer goods, acquire land, and educate their children. And once they are drawn into market economies, the alternative of turning back to subsistence farming becomes unthinkable—what Suso describes above as a non-future of "kill[ing] yourself working day and night" with no cash rewards or opportunity for advancement. Thus, while subsistence farming is a critical element of how families meet their nutritional needs, patchwork campesino livelihood strategies necessarily include a means of accessing cash.

Daniel Tubb (2020) has described how rural Afro-Colombian communities establish dual household economies by complementing subsistence farming and hunting with money from small-scale gold mining. In his analysis, the true value of the small amounts of gold they pull from artisanal mines is not as a generator of wealth. Instead, the gold's worth comes from its emancipatory potential, providing access to enough cash to guarantee these marginalized populations a "self-directed freedom" they understand as a "good life" (Tubb 2020, 23)—similar to how coca profits previously enabled Briceño's campesinos to preserve morally valued rural lifestyles. In the wake of the disappearance of coca and gold panning economies in Briceño, which sources of income with this emancipatory potential remain?

This chapter describes four major livelihood strategies that have emerged in the peace process era in Briceño (chapters 5 and 6 detail two others: joining the rearmed guerrillas and participating in electoral campaigns to get a municipal job). First is farmers' (pipe) dream of becoming campesino-entrepreneurs and selling products under their own brands, which I describe through an analysis of coffee farmers and state development programs that seek to turn them into better capitalists. Second is the raising of cattle, which offers a relatively guaranteed income but binds locals into dependence on state resources and drives widespread deforestation. Third is the replanting of coca, which has shifted from potential to reality, and threatens to reestablish armed group authority at the expense of the state. And finally, many like Suso and Eugenia abandon a future in Briceño and use outmigration to leave, primarily to urban slums or coca-producing areas elsewhere in Colombia. An ethnographic perspective shows that these strategies are decisive to local relationships to the land, global markets, and distinct authority figures.

Making Better Coffee and Better Capitalists

Coffee's wild price swings (explained in chapter 1) have been critical to the experiences of coffee farmers in the post-coca era. When the substitution program began in June 2017, coffee's global price was low, around $1.25 a pound, with production costs slightly over $1 per pound. The price dipped below $1 by late 2019 before beginning a recovery to a high of $2.50 in early 2022 in response to a global coffee shortage driven by frost in Brazil, civil war in Ethiopia, and Covid-related disruptions of Vietnam's harvest. The price boom came at the perfect time for Briceño's coffee farmers; while other substitution program beneficiaries were still waiting for promised goods, the National Coffee Federation (Fedecafé) disbursed projects to the 476 families in the coffee line. Production skyrocketed as farmers fed their hungry bushes with thousands of pounds of fertilizer under the guidance of Fedecafé technicians.

Nevertheless, Briceño's coffee farmers knew that coffee's high price—like their access to free fertilizer—was only temporary (indeed, it dipped to $1.60 a pound by December 2022 and stayed between $1.50 and $2.00 for the next year). They seek to lessen their exposure to global price swings by roasting, packaging, and selling their beans under their own brands. When I first arrived in Briceño in early 2018, the municipality had one coffee brand. Three years later, there were six, with each struggling to find a place in national and global markets. This shift was in part a logical response to the difficulties of legal agriculture. But it was also driven by a series of trainings and agricultural development programs that sought to turn Briceño's campesinos into better capitalists, changing their attitudes and behaviors.

In Briceño's post-coca era, these programs have become a ubiquitous feature of campesino life. A tour of Eduardo's farm, for example, is a history lesson on local development programs: avocado trees from a program provided by Public Enterprises of Medellín (EPM), the public company behind the hydroelectric dam; cacao trees supported by a program from the municipal secretary of agriculture; houses for honeybees that came, along with beekeeper's suits, from a US Agency for International Development (USAID) program; and finally, coffee bushes that have benefited from both coca substitution and another USAID program called Territory of Opportunities. All are examples of how farmers turn to state officials and resources for help with legal agriculture; even USAID programs are implemented in consultation with the municipal government. But these initiatives and countless others like them also provide trainings and the "accompaniment" of agricultural technicians to change campesino attitudes and behaviors.

These programs have even introduced a new lexicon to Briceño. Campesinos speak readily of "making the countryside profitable" (*volver al campo rentable*), "seeing their farm as a business" (*ver a la finca como una empresa*), and producing "added value" (*valor agregado*) through the "transformation" of their products. This language and the proliferation of coffee brands can be understood through the Foucauldian concept of governmentality, which describes how experts direct people's conduct by shaping their desires and the actions to fulfill them (Foucault 2007; Miller and Rose 1990; Rose and Miller 2008). In this understanding, power operates from a distance through a diffuse web of actors (in Briceño, agricultural technicians, development experts, and political officials) who transmit particular ways of understanding and acting in the world—for example, by creating a village worth of campesino-entrepreneurs who see their farms as microenterprises, their life stories as fodder for marketing campaigns, and their neighbors as economic competitors.

As Tania Li (2007) wrote of rural Indonesia, these development programs and their technologies of the self emerge from a well-intentioned "will to improve" the lives of marginalized people rather than a sinister plan for domination. Still, through particular ways of defining and attributing problems, they imply particular solutions while excluding others (Rose and Miller 2008). They turn the rescuing of Briceño's ailing agricultural economies into a matter of promoting rather than restraining unchecked market competition. To borrow from Li's (2007, 267) description of a World Bank program, they see "capitalist enterprise and the search for profit . . . only as a solution to poverty, not as a cause."

✳ ✳ ✳

Eduardo has become the local symbol of the coffee farming campesino-entrepreneur, featured in tweets, videos, and podcasts released by substitution program and USAID officials. But when I attend the graduation ceremony for a course in coffee transformation and commercialization organized by the National Learning Service (SENA) in collaboration with USAID, I realize that more than being a nominal figurehead, he is the linchpin of the Territory of Opportunities program. The ceremony, appropriately, is at Coffeebri (short for Coffee Briceño, but pronounced *Coe-FEH-bree*), the café facing the main square that I visit on a near-daily basis—because locals gather there to discuss village politics, and because the baristas make a delicious caffè latte, always with local coffee. A specialty café of this sort in a village like Briceño is unusual. Though Colombia produces the best coffee in the world, most is slated for export, and most Colombians outside the urban elite are used to drinking cheap coffee made from beans that don't make the cut for export.

A silver plaque on the wall by Coffeebri's entrance explains how the café came about: Colombia Responds, a USAID program which began in Briceño in 2012. One part of the program strengthened a coffee growers' group called the Association for Social and Economic Development of Briceño (ASDESE-BRI), providing an industrial roaster, computers, aid in developing a brand, and all the equipment for the café. The idea was for the association to take over the commercialization of Briceño's coffee to provide farmers with higher prices. Nevertheless, ASDESEBRI struggled to open markets beyond the café itself, and now buys from just one local producer. His coffee is sold on the shelves of Coffeebri under Briceño's original brand, and is used to make the café's drinks.

Following the graduation ceremony, I sit in the café with Óscar, a Colombian specialist in economic development who has worked with USAID for twenty years. He freely admits that the previous program was a failure. "We've learned from programs like Colombia Responds," he says to me. "We can't try to democratize aid, to give too much to people who aren't ready. It's like giving a motorcycle to your child who can't even walk yet. They're going to crash." Óscar, I quickly learn, draws on equal parts patronizing metaphors and right-wing discourse as he explains the USAID's new vision for alternative development.

"We need to move away from *asistencialismo*," he says, "where people expect the government to give them things rather than taking control of their own lives." *Asistencialismo* is a concept used to criticize government welfare programs that may deincentivize hard work and create dependency on state subsidies—kind of a Spanish-language equivalent of the Reagan-era denunciation of "welfare queens." The moralizing discourse has also been adopted by campesinos, particularly to attack locals who wasted the yearlong cash subsidies of the substitution program. The most humorous example is the video for the song "Coca por copa" ("Coca for Cup" [of alcohol]) by the Briceño band Voces del Recuerdo, which shows a group of ex-coca farmers sitting in a park waiting for the substitution program's cash subsidies, drinking away the money in local bars, and eventually having to pawn their worldly possessions.[2]

"Instead," Óscar continues, "we pick a 'positive deviant' who is already succeeding, and we give them resources so they can succeed more." He gives the example of someone who starts selling empanadas and is so successful that all their neighbors begin selling empanadas as well. Program officials have tabbed Eduardo as the positive deviant, and plan to support him until he becomes Briceño's version of the successful empanada trailblazer. In the first phase of Territory of Opportunities, they helped Eduardo found a new association, taught its members about the business of coffee, and financed a coffee exporter who is supposed to connect the community to international markets.

However, Óscar continues, "coffee is not the goal, but rather a pretext to develop other capacities, to help people learn how to lead their own processes. The idea is to change the culture."

"What needs to change?" I ask. I'm familiar with the history of USAID, founded in 1961 with the mandate of using international development to counter communist insurgencies from Vietnam to Latin America. More recently it has been criticized for initiatives aimed at undermining Pink Tide leftist governments in Venezuela and Bolivia, with Bolivia even expelling

USAID in 2013 (Dangl 2010; Grisaffi 2018). Nevertheless, I'm surprised by a response that seems rooted in Cold War–era red-baiting—though he may also be tailoring his response to what he thinks a gringo researcher wants to hear.

"We have a culture that's strongly influenced by socialism," he responds. "Russia and China seek to weaken the allies of the United States, while Venezuela is funding leftist political campaigns in Colombia. We need people to understand that they can have their own enterprises, that the government won't just give them everything."

Territory of Opportunities is initiating a second phase in Briceño, one in which it will provide both machinery and technical assistance to help farmers improve the quality of their coffee. It will also continue to connect farmers to potential national and international buyers. It has already sent many farmers, including Eduardo and four others who have their own brands, to business roundtables (*ruedas de negocio*) where they have met potential buyers.

Turning the village's coffee farmers into businesspeople whose brands profitably circle the globe with the help of state and USAID-sponsored programs certainly seems to have the potential to turn them against both socialism and the rearmed guerrillas who ostensibly espouse it. However, despite embracing both the language and behaviors of campesino-entrepreneurs, Briceño's coffee farmers are still excluded from specialty markets for their brands. Coffeebri carries five different local brands of coffee, but only one of them is sold anywhere else, in a store in a neighboring village. In Coffeebri, they mostly sit on the shelf until outsiders working in the peace process or in development programs arrive in search of gifts or souvenirs. Eduardo has sent coffee samples all over the world for four years in the hopes of finding a consistent buyer, without success. Once I even accompanied him to a state-sponsored campesino market at a military base in Medellín. State funds paid for his hotel, transportation, and meals, but he sold fewer than ten bags of coffee—a triumph of pro-capitalist counterinsurgency only to the extent that the officer who grilled him about Briceño's guerrilla forces learned anything from his evasive answers. The actual sales of Eduardo's brand are primarily to personal contacts. In 2021, out of a 2,000-kilogram harvest of green coffee beans, he sold 300 kilos (which, after roasting, represented 390 one-pound bags). The rest he had to sell wholesale to Fedecafé, at a slight markup of less than twenty cents per kilo over the standard global price, in recognition of its quality. With coffee's price booming, he still made a modest profit. But he knows the boom is only temporary.

Only one of Briceño's coffee brands is succeeding. Its owners have not participated in a single USAID program. Instead, one of Briceño's relatively few well-to-do families draws on a network of middle- to upper-class urban business owners to sell its coffee in stores owned by friends. More recently, the family launched its own café in a middle-class suburb of the city. All the coffee produced in its Briceño farm is sold under the family brand, at far above the global market price. However, without its contacts and resources, campesinos like Eduardo struggle to access similar markets for their products.

"I only need one," Eduardo says, referring to the one café in Medellín, the one bakery in Italy, or the one roasting company in the United States that will fall in love with his coffee and buy his harvest directly. He may find it. But as coffee's price falls back to earth and their brands continue to lack commercialization routes, Briceño's farmers are likely to find that being a better capitalist depends more on their connections and financial resources than on their attitudes and behaviors.

Cattle, State Power, and Deforestation

With coffee's reputation sunk by its price volatility, the agricultural economy to which farmers have most often turned is cattle farming (fig. 3.3). The reason for this, according to a local woman from a milk-producing family: "Cattle have the right name. *El ganado está ganado.*" Her play on words makes sense only in terms of the grammar of rural economies and the vocabulary of Spanish, in which *ganado* can mean either cattle or some combination of won and earned. "Cattle [*ganado*] is a win [*ganado*]." Many cattle farmers raise cows for what's known as a double purpose: the daily income from milk, plus the larger and more sporadic windfalls from selling fattened steers for meat. As distinct from agricultural crops that may be difficult to sell or subject to prices that drop below the cost of production, locals see cattle as a sure thing, the only guaranteed win in rural economies. But the growth of cattle economies has had two critical effects. First, particularly for dairy farmers who must get their perishable milk to the market on roads, it has made local livelihoods directly dependent on state resources. And second, the need to create pastureland has driven massive deforestation.

Cattle herds, in fact, grew slowly even as coca took over Briceño—farmers would often invest their earnings in buying cows, using them as a sort of rural bank deposit. Those who had land for pasture could turn their animals loose, wait for them to fatten up, and then sell them at a profit. Thus, as the substitution program was ending, Briceño already had an established cattle economy, and most program beneficiaries chose productive projects that would give them resources to support cattle ranching.

FIGURE 3.3. The hopes of most of Briceño's farmers now rest on cattle.

The cattle economy, however, has several preconditions. The first is access to land. While some programs have sought to institute land-efficient models based on the cultivation and cutting of tall grass, the vast majority of Briceño cattle farmers turn their animals loose to graze. With each cow requiring more than half a hectare of cleared pasture, even a modest herd of ten cattle requires a relatively large farm. Second, cattle farming has significant start-up costs, both to buy the animals and to vaccinate them.

And critically, if coca tied campesinos' livelihoods to armed groups, farmers who want to receive the guaranteed daily income of dairy farming become dependent on state resources. They need to be able to get their milk onto the refrigerated trucks—essentially motorized aluminum cans—that visit Briceño every day. This requires roads that let the milk trucks get relatively close to their farm. While communities have mostly led roadbuilding initiatives themselves, they depend on state resources not only for road construction but to maintain roads so that their production doesn't spoil following periodic landslides (see chapter 7). Additionally, the milk economy has more recently been supported by the installation of milk tanks, funded by the municipal government, that allow campesinos to bring their production to a nearby shared collection point. Thus, campesinos' ability to establish dairy economies depends directly on access to state resources. Without nearby milk tanks, and with community roads too steep and precarious for a milk truck to enter, neither Eduardo nor Suso can even consider becoming dairy farmers.

But many of their neighbors and Suso himself have turned to cattle ranching for meat even when dairy is not an option. Briceño's landscapes have therefore been transformed, with campesinos turning large swathes of jungle into pasture. Farmers have long cleared jungle to plant coffee, coca, or subsistence crops. However, the land requirements for pasture are exponentially larger, leading to massive deforestation. In many areas, the only forest left is on the steepest sections of land, too dangerous for cattle grazing. According to figures from the municipal ministry of agriculture, Briceño is now 80 percent pastureland.

Farmers clear jungle in two ways. First are controlled burns, which usually take place in the dry season from February to March in anticipation for planting just before the April rainy season (fig. 3.4). During burn season, Briceño's normally clean air and spectacular landscapes are visibly contaminated by smog trapped between its steep river valley walls.

Second is the spraying of herbicides. On a gloomy morning, I help spray Suso and Eugenia's pastureland. They are not, properly speaking, clearing jungle; instead, their idea is to kill weeds on pastureland that Suso is already using to house a herd of eleven cattle. The grass is of a special variety that has been genetically engineered to resist the herbicide. All we must do is cover the fields with chemical poison and voilà—the weeds will disappear, and the grass will grow back stronger than ever.

FIGURE 3.4. Controlled burns destroy not only plant life, but village air quality as well.

Suso has hired Juan, a man from a nearby community, to do the actual spraying. "I could do it myself," he tells me, "but after all those years spraying poison [chemical herbicides and pesticides] on my coca, I don't want to risk any more damage [to my health]." In fact, he says, he would prefer not to use herbicides at all. But he has little choice. If he tried cutting away the weeds with a machete, it would take him forty-five days of labor—not to mention that the chopped-off weeds would just grow back stronger than ever.

We mix the powdered herbicide with water in two-hundred-liter plastic barrels. A gas-powered pump, donated by an agricultural program implemented by the United Nations Food and Agriculture Organization, pushes the mixture through a hose as Juan begins systematically moving his way through the fields, covering every inch with herbicide (fig. 3.5). Along with Suso's son Adrián, I follow behind, trying to prevent the hose from getting blocked up while keeping a safe distance from the poisonous mist. Juan, about thirty years old, tells me he has specialized in spraying agricultural chemicals for twelve years. When the coca economy still existed, he also worked as a *raspachín*. Now spraying is the only work he can find.

When we break for lunch, Suso tells me he's planning to turn his two hectares of coffee into pasture as well; it's early 2020, before coffee's price recovers and Suso changes his mind. "I'd rather just have fifteen cows, instead of wasting all my time and money with coffee," he says.

In the face of the climate crisis, deforestation in South America and particularly in the Amazon jungle—which, as the "lungs of the planet," is responsible for one-quarter of the carbon dioxide absorbed by the world's forests—has become an issue of tremendous international interest. In 2019, global media outlets began publishing alarming accounts that the "Amazon is burning," accompanied by photos of fires used to clear land for cattle ranching and large-scale soy farming, primarily for livestock feed, in Brazil (Associated Press 2020; Sullivan 2019). In Colombia, deforestation surged following the peace agreement in areas previously under FARC control, where the guerrillas had often—if inconsistently—protected the jungle (International Crisis Group 2021a). Accounts from newspapers and environmentalists alike readily attribute guilt for this destruction to greedy ranchers, global meat consumption, and politicians who are either unable or uninterested in protecting forests. The villains created in these narratives are often more than deserving; the most high-profile among them, Brazilian President Jair Bolsonaro (2019–22), not only looked the other way as the Brazilian Amazon burned, but in one reserve even pledged to "give a gun and a course on how to use it to everyone and let the whole of the Chico Mendes Reserve be deforested to build ranches" (quoted in Kröger 2020, 465). Just as Chico Mendes himself was murdered for

FIGURE 3.5. Briceño's campesinos have used herbicides to convert large portions of their territory into pasture for cattle farming.

defending the rainforest in 1988, Amazonian Indigenous groups charge that cattle ranchers murder them to take over their land (Bayat 2022).

Nevertheless, Briceño's recently denuded hillsides suggest that clear-cut villain narratives fail to capture many of the forces and actors behind deforestation. Just as Briceño's farmers began cultivating coca to preserve valued rural lifestyles in the face of forces that excluded them from other agricultural markets, the same forces have pushed them to clear land for cattle farming in the wake of coca's disappearance. Briceño's farmers often have deep affective ties to the jungle and lament its disappearance. However, their environmentalism—which I take up in the next chapter in the context of the hydroelectric dam—does not extend to jeopardizing their families' livelihoods. Thus, the economic exclusion of the corporate food regime has made destroying the jungle central to the livelihoods of embattled rural farmers who try desperately to hold on.

Replanting Coca: From Denunciation to Reality

From the very start of my time in Briceño, I heard repeatedly that the village was going to fill again with coca. "Let's plant coca then," a young man said in a June 2018 community action board meeting in response to the announcement that the substitution program's projects would be further delayed.

"There's no work here," a campesino struggling to feed a family of seven told me a few weeks later. "But if we go to Yarumal [a neighboring village], we lose the [substitution] projects. So just to get food, people are going to be obliged to plant coca again."

And then, from a WhatsApp message forwarded around various community groups in July 2018: "We lived up [to the substitution agreement] but the government left us screwed. . . . I know they relax because they have everything, they don't know what it's like to see a child with hunger, they don't know what it's like to go to bed without a bite of food and thousands of worries. You know I'm a single mother, and at this moment like many I'm desperate, I don't know what to do anymore, that's why others are thinking about planting coca because if the government doesn't live up to the agreement with us, we don't have any reason to live up to it with them."

And finally, a year later, Eduardo said to me at Coffeebri: "If the government doesn't implement the projects as soon as possible, people will replant [coca]. It won't take even a year."

From roughly 2018 to 2019, replanting was a threat that locals invoked to denounce the substitution program's broken promises. This public narrative—repeated in community meetings, private conversations, and social media posts—held that Briceño's farmers had agreed to give up their coca in exchange for projects, the state had failed to live up to its commitments, the local economy had collapsed as a result, and farmers would be left no choice but to return to coca (Diamond 2023). And as time went on, narratives that replanting would happen were replaced by rumors—and then evidence—that it had. When I visited some rural areas, campesinos pointed out coca plots to me from a distance—more hidden than they had used to be, but visible nevertheless. The rearmed FARC guerrillas began attending community meetings to tell farmers the coca economy had returned, saying that they would buy their harvest and protect the crops from military eradicators.

If locals' decision to pull out their coca in the first place provided public endorsement of state power, the reappearance of coca on Briceño's hillsides offers a potential challenge to state authority. Just like that of state actors, civilian behavior is subject to a process of interpretation. Many interpret replanting as an immoral decision, and fear that it is part of a return to the era of violence. However, narratives that replanting *would* happen were long used to denounce the state's failure to live up to the promises of substitution. In the same vein, much discussion of the fact that replanting *has* happened makes sense of the village's new coca crops, less as farmers' deviance from broadly accepted norms than as a consequence of the state's failure to fulfill its responsibilities to the community. "What do you expect people to do if the state hasn't lived up to the [substitution program] agreement?" one campesino asked me as he gestured toward coca plants visible on an opposite hillside.

The amount of coca in Briceño is still limited. However, if it continues growing, the coca economy would again tie local livelihoods to the rearmed FARC guerrillas. And even more than being a conspicuous indictment of the failures of substitution, the increasing visibility of replanted coca fields would send a public message about who is in control. Where the state's authority is well established, crime is not eliminated, but is generally consigned to its rightful place, hidden in the shadows—a demonstration of popular acceptance of what state law considers acceptable or deviant behavior. To the extent that Briceño's hillsides again visibly fill with coca, they will serve as public evidence of defiance to state authority and the power of the guerrillas—not the state—to set the terms of everyday life (Beetham 1991; Corrigan and Sayer 1985; Sayer 1994).

Outmigration

In 2022 I ride my motorcycle, with Dideison on the back, through the community where he grew up. We pass dozens of abandoned houses (fig. 3.6). Dideison tells me where each house's owners has gone: "Don Arturo, he's in Medellín; Daniel is in Cauca, picking coca; Duván, he's in Nariño." Cauca and Nariño, departments in southern Colombia, are notorious for armed group rule and coca production; many of the young men Dideison used to pick coca with live there now, again pursuing their livelihoods through coca.

Dideison himself nearly went to Nariño at the invitation of a friend who moved there after coca's disappearance from Briceño. For years, his friend told him that it was easy to get established with a profitable crop. Landowners, he said, will happily sell you coca seedlings and rent you the land on which to plant them, charging a tax of roughly one thousand dollars every harvest. Dideison's friend started out with one lot with ten thousand plants. In his first harvest, after eight months, he paid off his initial investment. By the second harvest, three months later, his production doubled and he was able to invest in a second lot. He now has several lots, paying different people to manage them, and he makes good money. These stories, when they reach Briceño, inspire others to follow suit. Dideison even began traveling to Nariño to set himself up in the coca economy, getting as far as Medellín before he changed his mind, not wanting to return to a violent context. But many other young men have followed through. Dideison can readily name a half dozen coca-producing villages in Cauca or Nariño that have thriving *colonias Briceñitas* (settlements of people from Briceño).

FIGURE 3.6. In many of Briceño's most isolated areas, more than half the houses have been abandoned.

While coca cultivation is essentially limited to the Andean countries of Colombia, Peru, and Bolivia, the condition of moving around in the desperate search for income has become typical of the rural poor across the Global South. Over decades of research in India, the sociologist Jan Breman found that as large estates implemented labor-saving agricultural technologies, rural laborers who would have previously spent their lives working for one wealthy landowner have become a "footloose proletariat kept in a transient state between countryside and city as well as between various economic sectors" (Breman 2004, 1). They travel all over, seeking employment in economies like textile production, brickmaking, and construction, but they rarely establish a foothold (Breman 2019). In similar terms, throughout the course of my research I saw many people leave the village—chasing an income in illegal gold mines, a family member's small store, or construction projects— only to return home, usually having failed to make it big. Still, by far the largest *colonia Briceñita* is in and around Medellín; and for many, the city represents a permanent move. Most everyone in Briceño has family in Medellín, and many have lived there, whether displaced by violence or pursuing jobs or educational opportunities.

As I described at the beginning of this chapter, Eugenia and Suso maintain their farm in Briceño but spend most of their time in Bello, on the urban peripheries of Medellín, seeking a better education for their four children. From their hamlet of El Orejón alone, which at the height of coca held roughly eighty-eight people, fourteen now live in Bello.

Living in the city, however, has not meant leaving violence behind. Just as the FARC guerrillas in Briceño long provided law and order, in Bello the local drug gang acts as neighborhood authority. When I visit Eugenia and Suso's urban home, their elder sons Adrián and Sebastián excitedly tell me about the man who was caught shoplifting in the neighborhood store. "Do you know the *muchachos* who are always out on the street?" Adrián asks me, referring to a group of young men who stand on a corner near their home. A part of larger criminal structures, they engage in low-level drug dealing and also charge local business owners what's known as a *vacuna* (literally, vaccine) in exchange for protection.

Sebastián shows me, grabbing his brother's hand, how the adolescent drug dealers made the shoplifter hold out his finger and burned it with a cigarette lighter as a punishment. "We were right there when they grabbed him," he says. "He was screaming, but he couldn't take his hand away."

Eugenia is worried about her kids leaving their city home after dark. Children and parents alike prefer the freedom of the countryside to the contamination of the city, but see no future in rural economies. "Cultivating isn't profitable," Eugenia says. "Imagine, Alex; I heard the minister of agriculture on the news, and he said the countryside gets older, dumber, and poorer." Eugenia periodically repeats this quote to express an indignant sadness over the fate of rural communities. "And it's true. I haven't met the first farmer who's been able to buy a car."

Still, Eugenia and Suso know that there's a qualitative difference between urban and rural poverty. When they travel to Bello from their farm, they bring a box full of produce: plantains, corn, mandarin oranges, and yuca. Often, they share with their neighbors in Bello, including a few who are struggling to feed their children. Even the poorest campesinos in Briceño, as long as they have access to land, can at least meet their families' basic nutritional needs. In the city, however, food prices have skyrocketed, work is hard to come by, and impoverished children go to bed hungry.

Eugenia and Suso plan to return to their farm after their children have finished studying. They do not, however, want their children to join them. Instead, they dream of their kids becoming college-educated professionals, working for a salary. It is a dream that they know will likely push their children away from Briceño. Only one employer in the village offers salaried professional jobs: the municipal government, where the mayor uses positions to reward political supporters (see chapter 6).

This dynamic—in which families associate their children's success with an education that takes them away from rural economies and away from Briceño—is widespread. And while it began before the first coca plant took root in Briceño, the loss of coca and the difficulties of legal agricultural economies have accelerated the village's "brain drain," adding it to the long list of rural communities around the world that are emptying out.

Conclusion

Local struggles to develop new livelihoods in the wake of coca's disappearance are neither new in Briceño nor unique to rural Colombia. Instead, peasants across the world have shifted and diversified their livelihood strategies—motivated by material need and their desire to access the benefits of modernity, but hindered by a corporate food regime that excludes them from participation in increasingly globalized markets. Coca's original spread through Briceño was one such shift, driven by negative price shocks that made coffee farming unsustainable. The subsequent shock of coca's disappearance has occasioned another era of instability as campesinos seek livelihoods that will grant them not only bread but roses—meeting their everyday needs alongside the equally basic human goal of building a better future for themselves and their families.

In this chapter I have identified four distinct strategies, each with different consequences for local authority structures, relationships to the land, and participation in global capitalist markets. Coffee farmers inspired by state development programs that have trained them to become better capitalists seek to develop their own brands in the hope of establishing a profitable niche within global markets. However, despite a major outlay of state and USAID resources to support them, without the resources and connections to access these markets it's hard to imagine enough success to substantially change the region's economic future. Cattle now dominate Briceño's agricultural economy, providing a foothold for state authority by making local farmers dependent on state resources. However, cattle economies face the limiting factor of land; Briceño simply does not have much jungle left to deforest, which in the era of climate change is itself preoccupying. Coca requires less land and more limited start-up costs, but threatens to again promote armed group authority and potentially return the village to an era of violence. The fourth alternative is testament to the drawbacks of available alternatives, as many campesinos have simply left, often to other zones of coca production—or, like millions of peasants across the world, to urban slums.

To understand how these livelihood strategies impact dynamics of conflict, one demographic group is of particular interest: young men. Indeed, economists find that few if any factors show a stronger correlation with internal conflict across the world than a robust supply of poor male youth with little to do (Becker 1974; Collier 2008). In Colombia, impoverished rural young men have provided the troops to sustain more than a half century of conflict even as combatants consistently demobilize or are killed at high rates.[3] In providing a means for young men to earn a decent wage, plant their own crops, and acquire land, Briceño's era of coca limited the supply of local recruits. However, the alternatives of the peace process era are particularly—and dangerously— limited for poor young men.

Coffee, along with its unstable prices, requires land, and offers a harvest only after two years. As a result, young men who seek to make their fortune by establishing a new coffee crop are exceedingly rare. The only instance I encountered was a young man who ran a small business in the village center and planted coffee in partnership with his father on their family farm in the hopes that it would eventually offer a supplementary income. Establishing a cattle herd requires access to even more land, as well as the start-up capital to acquire animals. Some young men, seeking cattle's quicker and more secure profits, manage to do so with loans and the help of their families. However, families with some access to resources, like Eugenia and Suso, are more likely to discount a rural future. Like Sebastián and Adrián, their sons often pursue education and eventually wage labor that takes them out of Briceño.

In contrast, young men from poorer families are excluded from higher education or the possibility of acquiring the land and cattle to establish profitable herds. They can, however, rent small, isolated plots of land to plant coca in exchange for a portion of their earnings, whether in Briceño or in other parts of Colombia. Even more disturbingly, they may join armed groups. I will return to this point in chapter 5, where I describe how local narratives blame recruitment to the rearmed guerrillas on the widespread unemployment caused by coca's disappearance.

Briceño's campesinos, like peasants across the world, turn to patchwork livelihoods in the face of structural changes that imperil valued rural lifestyles. To some extent, the development of legal economies in the peace process era has helped promote state authority, and with it the potential for peace. The state's new role in the community is, however, a fragile achievement, imperiled by a distinct set of livelihood strategies that promote a return to coca cultivation and armed group authority. The strategies to which campesinos turn, limited by the dynamics of exclusion that have increasingly become a central feature of global capitalist economies, will be decisive to the village's future.

4

Water and Gold: Megaprojects, Peace, and the Struggle for the Future of the Countryside

Fabio and Angélica

Dedication to my Patrón Mono, *the Cauca River*
Hello! Do you remember me?
I am Angélica, your faithful admirer.
When I was just an innocent girl,
my parents, siblings, neighbors, and I used to visit you often,
to fish, to rest, to pan for gold.
Or simply, in a remote meeting place,
to music that broke hearts and a few *guaros*[1]
to admire the life that still beat and blossomed inside you,
because you were the source of nourishment and economy for many
generations of canyon dwellers.

Feeling the wind blowing over the crest of the mountain,
softly speaking to the gold panners,
saying, "Leave your name on these beaches, gold panner,
soon will come the moment to die with pride."

At that time I didn't think your price was so high,
the memories,
the economy
the culture,
the air,
the landscapes,
the fauna,
the flora,
the price of life itself.

Such was the wealth you possess that one day they took notice
and decreed you a death foretold.

Today I see with nostalgia that this foretold death is coming,
carrying hunger, misery, uprooting [*desarraigo*], sadness, rage,
and displacement,
in the limitless hurry to dominate nature,
to take revenge against that which has given us everything in life.

excerpted from a poem by Angélica

Angélica cannot get even halfway through reading her poem aloud before her voice breaks, her eyes fill with tears, and her hands, clutching a ripped-out sheet of notebook paper, begin to tremble. We are filming her performance for our documentary, and she apologizes for ruining the recording.

"It was perfect," I tell her. "Such a powerful representation of the emotions behind everything that has happened with the hydroelectric dam."

Community members have long known the Cauca River as the *Patrón Mono*. *Patrón* because, as in campesinos' expectations of the patronage relations I will describe in chapter 6, the river guaranteed their economic well-being, offering both fish and gold. And *mono*, a word that in Colombia is used to refer to people with blond hair, because of its light color against the dark green hillsides that surround it (fig. 4.1).

Beginning with the construction of the Hidroituango hydroelectric dam in 2011, however, local communities lost access to the river and their associated cultural and economic traditions. In response, Angélica and her partner Fabio have spent more than a decade engaged in collective action—first to stop the dam, and more recently to push the company behind the dam to make meaningful social investment in the community. The coming of the dam was deeply related to the outbreak of terrifying violence in the community, a conjuncture of factors that have jeopardized locals' ability to stay in the territory.

Fabio and Angélica fight to stay put, however, combining activism with agroecological farming practices that offer an alternative to corporate agriculture. They live in El Orejón, on a 48-hectare (119-acre) property on the walls of the Cauca River valley, around one thousand meters above and slightly upstream from the dam. Most of their farm is jungle: impossibly green steep slopes covered with ferns and broad-leafed tropical trees that are home to monkeys, tarantulas, and a variety of colorful songbirds. The farm, which they call the Portal to the Sky, stands out as a verdant oasis amid the pastureland, including Eugenia and Suso's farm, that dominates the area. Even the coffee plants and cacao trees that Fabio and Angélica cultivate around their house seem to come out of the jungle, interspersed among their mango,

FIGURE 4.1. Fabio on the path that leads to his home, with the Cauca River below.

mandarin, and lime trees. As agroecological farmers, they are part of a global movement that has been described by the ecologist Steve Gliessman (2018) as encompassing scientific research to create sustainable agroecosystems, Indigenous and campesino practices to cultivate in harmony with nature, and social change to transform power relations and inequalities around food distribution.

Fabio, in his late fifties and lanky with a prominent mole on one cheek, does most of the agricultural work on the farm. As he plants and harvests the crops and clears underbrush, he wears rubber galoshes, a threadbare button-down shirt, and a full-brimmed hat from Machu Picchu that someone brought him as a souvenir. Angélica is the same age as her life partner, with graying curly hair that she restrains with a hair net as she transforms the crops into products for sale. She toasts and grinds the cacao and coffee beans, dries and pulverizes turmeric root, and mixes together spicy peppers and homemade vinegar to make delicious hot sauces (fig. 4.2). Once a month they load their motorcycle with all the products it will carry and take them to an organic market in Medellín. Angélica is the salesperson. She draws in prospective customers, offering samples and explaining the virtue of the products. With the money she and Fabio make, they buy rice, cooking oil, and an occasional birthday gift for their grandchildren. Nearly everything else they eat—eggs, beans, yuca, peanuts, avocados, plantains, corn, fruit, chicken, fish, and more—comes from their farm.

Both Fabio and Angélica's farm and their livelihood strategies are relatively unique in the region. Most of their neighbors use genetically modified seeds and chemical insecticides, herbicides, and fertilizers to bend nature to their will and efficiently produce as much food as possible. These farmers find beauty in orderly rows of a single weed-free crop. For Fabio and Angélica, beauty means something else—cacao and coffee bushes interspersed with jungle plants, all fertilized by natural organic material (fig. 4.3). Their harvests are notably smaller, but so are their costs. And while selling the products themselves requires significant travel and labor, it fetches much higher prices.

Ironically for a couple who share a passion for organic agriculture, they were brought together by technology. In 1985, Fabio, who was born in a rural community on Colombia's northern coast and had grown up farming before training as an electrical technician, had his own electronics workshop on the rural outskirts of Medellín. One day, Angélica showed up at his shop. "I brought him a tape recorder to fix, and he couldn't fix it for me," she says.

"I fixed *her* up though," he says mischievously as they share a flirtatious laugh.

They each had two children from previous relationships; they had a fifth child together in 1990. Although in the first years of their relationship they owned and ran a succession of small urban businesses together—a fruit-and-vegetable store, a bar, and finally a restaurant—they shared an affinity for

FIGURE 4.2. Angélica opens cacao fruits.

FIGURE 4.3. Fabio harvests yuca cultivated in the midst of the jungle.

farm life that dated back to their respective childhoods. Angélica was raised near Briceño in the village of San Andrés, on a large farm that produced subsistence for her seventeen brothers and sisters as well as milk, coffee, and panela for sale. Fabio grew up helping his father grow flowers for sale.

In 2006 they visited one of Angélica's brothers in Pueblo Nuevo, the hamlet that neighbors El Orejón. Halfway through a six-hour hike to her brother's home, they passed a farm where an old man offered them water. Eventually he offered the farm itself for cheap. With their kids all having graduated from high school, they saw the opportunity to return to the rural lifestyle that they both remembered so fondly. In moving back to the countryside, they were reversing dominant trends of rural-to-urban migration. Even more unusually, however, they were going to an active conflict zone—and not to plant coca, the economy that dominated the region.

Fabio and Angélica's first move when they settled in was not to register the sale with government officials, but rather to visit the FARC. The guerrillas informed them of the rules: no one could leave their homes at night, they could not aid or give information to the paramilitary groups that were challenging the FARC's territorial control, and those who fought or stole would be made to leave.

In 2007 the Colombian military entered the region in force, occupying the area designated for the Hidroituango dam project. The FARC were pushed farther up the valley walls. "There were battles at all times of day," Fabio says, mimicking the sounds of shooting and explosions. "Pam, pam, pam. There were shots, bombs. It was a delicate situation between the army who was taking care of the [Hidroituango] project and the guerrillas who wanted to take care of the territory."

"Look," says Angélica, pointing to the ridge far above their farm. "That's the Alto del Oso. There were some battles up there, *por Dios*! It was like the apocalypse, they dropped some [bombs] that even split the trees. And I was so scared I couldn't sleep. And sometimes you would be sleeping, and when you least expected it, you heard 'bubububu,' and that sound came like it was echoing from inside a pipe."

As violence raged on in the valley walls above, the dam project below advanced. A crucial moment came when EPM, the public corporation that controls Hidroituango, arrived to conduct a census of the people who would be affected. The census fulfilled EPM's legal obligation to identify and compensate anyone whose economic activity would be harmed by the project. This should have been a long list of people. If coca was the primary driver of the economy, the Cauca River, their *Patrón Mono*, was second. It offered fish, sand for construction projects, and, most importantly, gold. Even before coca arrived around 2000, gold panning offered locals a lucrative and easily transportable source of income to supplement their subsistence farming.

Angélica has fond memories of gold panning on the banks of the Cauca with her father. They would stay for weeks on end, sleeping under a plastic tarp stretched across four tree branches they had driven into the sand. While the gold itself was important, she reminisces more about how gold panning brought together people who spent much of their time on isolated farms. On the beaches of the Cauca, they sifted through the silt in search for gold nuggets, shared stew made from freshly caught fish, and traded with each other.

One day in 2008, a group of people rushed by Fabio and Angélica's home. "'Hurry up,' they told us. 'They're doing a census in Chirí [a neighboring community] from one to two,'" Angélica says. It was already eleven in the morning. They briefly considered going, but didn't want to waste their day chasing a rumor. But it wasn't just a rumor. EPM was performing the census to determine who would be compensated for lost economic activity based on dam construction. They had just announced the census that same day, by radio, which made it impossible for workers on the beaches to be included. Angélica continues: "It was the worst that could happen, because they didn't do the census in the site on the beaches where people were working." Of nearly a hundred people in El Orejón, all of whom depended on the river in some way for their livelihood, only nine were able to participate in the census. Those who missed their chance never got another.

In 2011, EPM officially banned local access to the river. Rather than preventing the community from continuing to pan for gold, however, this prohibition turned a traditional livelihood into contentious politics. People from Briceño and surrounding communities started to meet on the riverbanks, figuring that coordinated occupations would give them safety in numbers and pressure EPM to include them in the census. "It looked like a city," Angélica says, describing agglomerations of plastic tarp huts that more than one hundred people in all quickly erected. During the day they would fish and pan for gold. At night they held *tertulias*, informational discussions where they spoke about their struggle.

EPM sent in a special battalion composed of private security and the army, who repeatedly used violence to remove them from the beaches. Soldiers pulled their tents down, often throwing them in the river, and forcibly pulled people from the beaches. The campesinos dispersed, only to reorganize themselves and move to another beach. This pattern of occupation and forced eviction repeated itself several times. "It started as our normal economic activity," Angélica says. "From there, they started to remove us, and we decided to stay as an act of resistance."

As dam construction started, Fabio heard a woman on the radio talking about the dam project: its responsibility for the violence in the community and its potential for destroying the environment and local livelihoods. The woman on the radio was from Ituango, across the river from Briceño. She was part of Ríos Vivos (Living Rivers), a new organization seeking to organize local resistance into a more concerted movement against the dam. Along with many in the community, Fabio and Angélica joined the movement.

In March 2013, supported by Ríos Vivos, five hundred campesinos gathered to block the highway, demanding that EPM extend the census to those who had been left out. Riot police attacked the protesters with nightsticks, arresting twelve people they identified as leaders and taking them south to Santa Rosa. The others took off walking toward Santa Rosa, a hundred kilometers down the road, to demand the release of their comrades. They carried signs to bring visibility to their cause: "No to Hidroituango," "We're displaced by Hidroituango," "EPM has kicked us out of the territory."

By the time the protesters arrived in Santa Rosa, the movement leaders had been released. Already halfway to Medellín, the group decided to continue to the big city, the site of EPM's headquarters. It took them ten days to get there. Radical students sympathetic to their cause invited them to take up residence in the University of Antioquia coliseum, where they ended up staying for several months. Telling the story, Fabio and Angélica relive the triumph of the moment.

"One time [the police] came in to get rid of us," Angélica says. "But a fight started. Those students armed themselves with *papas bombas* [home-made potato-shaped bombs that shoot scraps of metal and have long been the weapon of choice of the University of Antioquia's radical student body]."

"So it was because of the support of the students?"

"Yes, they said, 'You're not going to touch our campesinos,' and they threw *papas bombas* at them."

Every day the protesters organized demonstrations against Hidroituango in different parts of Medellín and managed the logistics of providing for roughly four hundred people. Feeding everyone was particularly challenging. Local unions donated firewood for cooking, and the food committee visited wherever they could think of to ask for donations.

"One day we had five sacks of carrots," says Angélica. "Because we didn't have anything else, we started cooking carrots in a pot, and we just had carrot water—what a disgusting thing!"

The protesters lasted eight months in the coliseum, drawing attention to their cause and forming the basis for a broader movement. Ríos Vivos joined the international organization Vía Campesina, bringing together rural struggles that challenge the model of corporate agriculture and extraction. Fabio attended an international gathering in Guatemala of groups resisting megaprojects like Hidroituango, and both traveled to visit anti-mining and anti-dam struggles elsewhere in Colombia. Their meetings with other campesino and Indigenous activists helped them learn about alternatives, deepening their agroecological practice. They attended trainings on how to make organic fertilizer, and learned about the beneficial microorganisms in soil. They also participated in seed exchanges, through which they acquired varieties of hot peppers, nuts, and vegetables that still grow on their farm to this day.

Resistance to the dam continued. The community organized *paros* over specific grievances: a military control post to protect the dam that limited local mobility and exposed community members to harassment, a family whose land had been seized with compensation only to the parents and not their sixteen children and grandchildren who also lived on and from their farm, the closure of a road leading to a dock where many locals kept fishing boats. In each case they were able to pressure EPM to accede to their demands. Dam construction, however, continued.

Participation in the movement entailed significant risks, no great surprise in Colombia, the world's most dangerous place to be a social leader.[2] The first member of Ríos Vivos to be assassinated was Nelson Giraldo, during the 2013 occupation of the University of Antioquia. He had left his wife and two kids to return home to Ituango and pan for gold to raise some money. He was found on the beach, shot in his legs and chest and with his throat slit.

Fabio says that when the movement community heard the news, "we were filled with fear in the coliseum. We didn't even want to return to the territory, because we thought they were going to kill us. So you didn't know; you told yourself, if you keep doing this, you're going to die. However, we've continued." Five movement members have been murdered, with countless others threatened.

In 2015 the land mine removal program came to El Orejón, promising a future free from violence. Angélica initially worked for the program as a cook. However, she was fired when program officials accused her of providing information to Ríos Vivos. Her boss had overheard her telling Fabio by telephone about a soldier who had been killed when he stepped on a land mine.

By now seasoned activists, Fabio and Angélica had indeed been organizing to demand that the land mine removal program make investments in the community. They pushed their neighbors to organize a *paro*, the threat of which eventually resulted in a new school, community meeting house, soccer field, and bridge (see chapter 2). But they were souring on Ríos Vivos. While much of the community had participated in the movement to some degree, nearly all started pulling back, feeling that movement leaders were using them to advance their personal and economic goals. Fabio and Angélica, who considered Ríos Vivos central to their identity, hung on longer than most. However, the breaking point came in a meeting when Angélica asked the public face of the movement what had happened to money destined for a shared agroecological project. "And she said to me, 'You're out of the movement.'" Angélica's voice fills with hurt and indignation. While her and Fabio's activism has continued, it is now articulated with El Orejón and neighboring communities rather than with Ríos Vivos.

The dam is not the only megaproject threatening local livelihoods. In the early 2000s, the Canadian mining company Continental Gold acquired mining concessions in roughly 80 percent of Briceño. Because of the FARC's presence, the Canadian company was unable to enter the area; but when the FARC disarmed, Continental Gold immediately sent representatives to Briceño, developing a plan to drill into Briceño's mountains to access the rich gold veins that lie deep within the village's mountains. One of the proposed drill sites is just above Fabio and Angélica's farm. Angélica speculates on a future in which they're stuck between the mine and the dam: "We'd be penned in. We already lost the economy of going down to the Cauca to take out gold.

And now, if Continental Gold comes to box us in from above—look, the water will start to dry out . . . and how are we going to stay here without water?"

For the moment, however, their water is safe. In September 2018, the re-armed FARC guerrillas killed three geologists on Briceño's border who were working for Continental Gold, forcing the company to leave Briceño. Nonetheless, Fabio and Angélica fear that more violence is coming, and that it is only a matter of time until Continental Gold returns.

In April 2018, a few months before the dam was supposed to begin operating, a landslide just upriver from the project blocked a tunnel that diverted the river's flow while the dam was under construction. With no way to pass through the massive retention wall, the river below Fabio and Angélica's farm rose steadily, turning a narrow, swift-moving river into a placid—yet rising—lake. The impending catastrophe dominated the nightly news in Colombia. If the river swelled high enough, it could destroy the entire dam project. And if it forced its way through the dam, heavily populated areas downstream would flood. The problem was no surprise to anti-dam activists, who had warned as early as 2013 that construction was loosening the mountainsides' porous rocks. Fabio says, "We told them our mountains have fragile rocks, that water filters through. We warned them, in our campesino way of speaking, of what was going to happen with that megaproject. And they laughed at us."

On May 12, 2018, the river burst its confines. Entire downstream communities were destroyed, and twenty-five thousand people were displaced. But the massive reservoir initially created by the blocked diversion tunnel has become permanent. And the effects are tangible: more (and stagnant) water below means more evaporation. Not only does this manifest itself in the form of clouds that cover the river every morning, but the increased humidity has negative effects on the community's crops. The cacao is developing new kinds of fungi that never existed there before. The coffee beans often fall from the bush before they've matured.[3] Fruit production has dropped by more than half. And the increased humidity has also brought more insects, particularly mosquitoes. Most disturbingly, the dangerous mosquito-borne illness dengue, previously unknown in the region, has arrived in El Orejón. Fabio and Angélica have both contracted it, including Fabio twice. In one instance, Fabio's illness advanced to the life-threatening critical hemorrhagic stage. The fever and changes in the microclimate are now part of the territory's "new normal"—further elements of the community members' exclusion from valued practices of living on and from the land.

Just as the dam's reservoir was filling in, the community received the last of its bimonthly subsidy payments for the coca substitution program. With the payments ended, the coca gone, the river flooded, and the crops weakened, the region has emptied out. "More people have been displaced than at the worst moments of the war," Angélica says.

Fabio and Angélica's activism has shifted; while they were initially focused on stopping the dam project, they now organize their neighbors to push EPM to help them establish a place for themselves in a transformed territory. Fabio often leaves voice messages on the community's WhatsApp group suggesting a variety of ideas: getting EPM to hire locals to reforest jungle destroyed by the dam project, creating a tollbooth on the community's road to extract money for its community action board from passing vehicles, soliciting resources from EPM to improve the precarious road (see chapter 7), selling community agricultural production to EPM's cafeterias, or establishing a market to sell agricultural goods at the foot of the dam. Many of Fabio and Angélica's neighbors think they are crazy dreamers, but some of their schemes have borne fruit.

Many of these ideas come to Fabio as he does agricultural work. "You're so relaxed here with the wind, the silence," he says as he plants turmeric on a steep hillside. "And then, suddenly, an idea comes to you." He also draws inspiration from the animals that surround him in this natural sanctuary from the surrounding pastureland. "Look at the *gulungos*," he says, referring to a group of large tropical birds with bright yellow beaks and tails in a tree above us. The birds, maybe a dozen in all, work together to build their nests, woven pouches with round bottoms that hang from tree branches. "They build their houses in those trees all together," says Fabio. "Every bird in community. You won't see a nest on its own.

"But there's another bird that takes advantage," Fabio continues. "They throw out the eggs of the *gulungo*, and put their own eggs in the nest." He chuckles softly, letting the metaphor sink in. "Even in nature, you see exploitation."

Fabio turns back to planting as the *gulungos* continue building in the trees above. Stubbornly, they persist in the face of forces that threaten to dispossess them.

Introduction

September 2018, two in the morning: Eleven geologists working for Continental Gold sleep inside a wooden cabin in a rural zone of Yarumal, on the border with Briceño. Seven men carrying assault rifles arrive, forcing the geologists outside. The men identify themselves as members of the rearmed FARC guerrillas. The guerrillas tell the geologists they are going to execute them for not following their orders to leave the area. In desperation, one geologist lunges at a guerrilla. Shots ring out. In the scrum, three geologists are injured and three are killed, all Colombians in their twenties.

Continental Gold has owned mining concessions in Briceño and the surrounding region since an early 2000s boom in which state-awarded oil and mining concessions to multinational companies grew to cover 40 percent of Colombian territory (Paarlberg-Kvam 2021). With Briceño under guerrilla control, however, plans for the mine were put on hold. When the FARC disarmed through the peace process, the Canadian company saw its opportunity. It sent representatives to the area to begin exploration, and to convince the community of the benefits a mine could bring. In November 2017, however, the FARC guerrillas rearmed, reestablishing the local authority they had held for decades. They let it be known that Continental Gold had to leave the territory. When the original group of geologists left in fear, the company sent another. After this new group was attacked on a fateful September night, Continental Gold left the territory entirely. The company was subsequently acquired by the Chinese mining company Zijin in 2020.

Community members' efforts to make sense of the killing and its impact on local authority relations were varied and complex. On the one hand, by stopping a state-supported mine project that locals feared would force them out of the territory, the killing demonstrated the power of guerrilla violence to defend local lives and livelihoods. On the other, it occasioned a wave of retaliatory military attacks that stoked fears of a return to the worst days of conflict. But if it threatened the community's hopes for peace, it also dealt a blow to the ambitions of economic and political elites. Briceño's gold is but one example of the valuable resources that both national politicians and multinational corporations expected to be freed by the FARC's disarmament. If violence has long been central to attempts to pacify Colombian territories and enable megaprojects like Hidroituango, the hope was that peace would now fulfill the same function.

Throughout this book, I argue that Colombia's peace agreement has joined democratization in intensifying the distribution of public resources through which communities in places like Briceño have begun to pursue their livelihoods through the state. The flip side of increased state aid to impoverished rural communities, however, is state support of megaprojects like Hidroituango and the proposed gold mine that threaten traditional campesino livelihoods. Zooming out even further, while the rural poor find their labor and agricultural production excluded from the global capitalist economy, their land, minerals, and water have become increasingly central to processes of capital accumulation. Put simply, the exploitation of their crops and labor has been largely replaced by the exploitation of the natural resources within their territories—a double shift that further compromises their ability to maintain rural livelihoods.

Ethnographic observation shows how this fact influences local authority relations and the dynamics of peacebuilding. I argue that the case of Briceño illustrates how Colombia's peace process has become subject to a fundamental contradiction between distinct visions for the countryside, as a site of small-holder production or of megaproject extraction. The peace agreement's largely unfulfilled calls for rural development and coca substitution promise the transformation of the countryside into an area where campesinos can produce, access markets for their goods, and enjoy improved health care, education, and infrastructural development. These same campesinos, however, are often obstacles to the exploitation of valuable resources like Briceño's gold and water. These extractive projects intensify their economic exclusion by imperiling the earth, water, and traditional economies on which they depend. This contradiction has the potential to cause violence, to generate support for armed groups at the expense of the state, and ultimately to endanger the peace process itself.

But if megaprojects threaten traditional ways of making a living, they may also enable other livelihood strategies. Similar to how Global South states implement trade liberalization policies that intensify economic exclusion while simultaneously distributing goods to meet the basic needs of the excluded, the Hidroituango dam has closed off access to river-based economies, but has opened opportunities for communities to access resources from the hydroelectric dam company. And just as the former process creates the basis for state governance, newfound local dependence on EPM has allowed the dam company to establish a level of regional control that lets them operate in the territory.

The first section of this chapter zooms out, describing how Briceño's two megaprojects—the dam and the thwarted gold mine—fit within a broader context, beginning in the 1990s and accelerating in the 2000s, in which national elites sought to push the Colombian economy toward an extractive model. While megaprojects like Hidroituango were long enabled by paramilitary violence, the peace process has been harnessed by a shifting regime of dispossession that uses guerrilla demobilization to free natural resources for new extractive projects. The example of Briceño, however, shows that dispossession through peace may produce violence and undermine the construction of state authority. And moving beyond Colombia, it calls into question dominant peacebuilding narratives and practices that see the resources available through extractive projects as engines of peace.

Second, I zoom in on the community of El Orejón, analyzing its collective claims-making on the Hidroituango dam. Here I describe a different shift, from a politics of resistance to one of contentious accommodation. The community has been forced to accept a new territorial reality in which the dam has eliminated riverside economies. Its accommodation to this reality, however, represents neither cooptation nor demobilization. Instead, local farmers push EPM to help them establish a place in the territory through ongoing cycles of contention, negotiation, small concessions, disappointment, and a return to contention in the face of broken commitments. Frustrating as this cycle may be, the resources locals receive through it have become critical to their struggles to make a living. It also impacts local authority relations, allowing EPM to continue operating in the territory and representing another way in which communities are pursuing their livelihoods through the state.

Dispossession in War and Peace

Two opposing perspectives describe the connection between civil war and natural resources. On the one hand, resource curse theory describes how valuable natural resources—whether diamonds in Africa, oil in the Middle East, or land, minerals, and drug crops across the Global South—may actually retard a country's growth by providing both motive and opportunity for conflict (Auty 1993; Basedau and Lay 2009; Frankel 2011). On the other hand, many peacebuilding interventions, including in Colombia, are based on the idea that the profits of intensified resource extraction will serve as "engines for peace" by providing needed jobs, tax revenue, and development (Lujala, Rustad, and Kettenmann 2016). The experiences of Briceño, as we shall see, offer a significant challenge to the latter claim. However, behind this debate are contingent ground-level processes through which violence related to the capture of valuable resources emerges or dissipates in particular forms, at particular times, and with particular justifications. Briceño may be cursed by its valuable water and gold, but understanding the changing relationship between megaprojects, conflict, and peace—and the potential for overcoming violence—requires a more nuanced look into the processes through which violence and resource extraction emerge.

The central process I describe in this book explains (1) how broader political and economic transformations influence community livelihood strategies, and (2) how these strategies, when directed to the state or to armed groups, configure local authority relations and dynamics of conflict. While previous chapters of this book have focused on how the rise of corporate agriculture and the elimination of wage labor have left the Global South poor unable to make a living through legal markets, this section highlights another dimension of economic exclusion: extractive megaprojects that dispossess the rural poor of their land and traditional livelihoods.

This phenomenon is captured by the Marxist geographer David Harvey's theory of accumulation by dispossession. Harvey (2003) argues that the central force behind capital accumulation has shifted from the exploitation of workers to the capture of new assets—including land and natural resources, but also the privatization of public assets or the imposition of intellectual property rights to commodify knowledge. The theory makes reference to Marx's (1942) description of primitive accumulation, a crucial foundational moment of capitalism in which peasants were dispossessed of their land and were thus forced to sell their labor power as part of a new industrial workforce. The difference for most modern-day dispossessed peasants is that without manufacturing jobs to absorb their labor, their dispossession now produces exclusion rather than exploitation. Their territory and the valued resources it holds are of interest; their labor is not.

In this context, the dispossessed and excluded poor seek help from distinct authority figures to make a living. However, *where* they turn can also be influenced by *who* is dispossessing them. As I will explain, the fact that Briceño's communities see the state as supporting an unpopular gold mine and the guerrillas as opposing it impacts the legitimacy of each. And the means through which dispossession is carried out also matter. Briceño, home to a hydroelectric dam project enabled by paramilitary violence and a proposed gold mine that seemed as though it would be allowed by the peace process, is a strategic site for examining shifts in how people are physically separated from their land, the narratives used to justify dispossession, and the related violence.

To carry out this analysis, I draw on Michael Levien's (2013, 383) concept of "regimes of dispossession" to explain changing "socially and historically specific constellations of state structures, economic logics tied to particular class interests, and ideological justifications that generate a consistent pattern of dispossession." Beginning with Colombia's 1990 economic opening, and accelerating under the direction of the Uribe administration and the influence of Plan Colombia in the early 2000s, elites turned the country into an extractive powerhouse through a violence-based regime of dispossession. Paramilitary groups used threats and massacres to displace and pacify the resistance of the communities who occupied resource-rich territories. However, like Briceño's gold, a large portion of Colombia's natural resources remained unexploited, protected by the guerrillas' ongoing control of huge swaths of the countryside.

In the 2010s, the Santos administration bet that negotiating a FARC disarmament would free these resources for extraction, with increased revenues serving as an engine for peace. This peace-based regime of dispossession, however, threatens to intensify conflict, not least by opening spaces for armed groups to govern by establishing their legitimacy through opposing unpopular projects. It also undermines the peace process's stated goals of driving a profound transformation of the countryside to eliminate the rural inequality and poverty that have long been at the roots of Colombia's conflict.

HIDROITUANGO AND THE VIOLENCE-BASED REGIME OF DISPOSSESSION

It was during those nights in the University of Antioquia coliseum, Fabio and Angélica say, that they came to understand the violence behind Hidroituango. For eight months in 2013, the coliseum was filled with the tents and makeshift shelters of four hundred campesinos dedicated to protesting the dam project. As darkness fell each night, they shared their stories, heartbreakingly similar tales that described a regional outbreak of violence just as the Hidroituango dam project was being launched. A mother from San Andrés had lost both of her sons when paramilitaries shot them dead and threw them into the Cauca River. A woman had lived through the paramilitary massacre downstream in El Aro, Ituango; she had avoided the fate of the fifteen murdered that day, but had lost her unborn child. A man from the hamlet of Chirí spoke through tears of his two sons who had simply disappeared. Journalists investigating the links between paramilitary violence and the hydroelectric dam have attributed more than eight hundred deaths to the imperative to pacify the region for the dam project (Rico Reyes 2019).

While the direct connections are often hard to trace, one name comes up repeatedly in the shadowy relationships tying together paramilitary groups, Hidroituango, and the regional wave of violence behind the dam project: that of former President Álvaro Uribe. As governor of Antioquia from 1995 to 1997, Uribe publicly promoted the Convivir program, which provided for the creation of citizen militias to fight the guerrillas (Ballvé 2020). These groups, however, were often fronts for paramilitary structures that already existed. Even when the Convivir program was disbanded in 1998, many of these militias were absorbed into the Self-Defense Forces of Colombia (AUC), an umbrella organization that brought together all the country's paramilitary organizations—and which publicly supported Uribe as he began entering national politics (Civico 2016).

These paramilitary groups were responsible for fifteen massacres of innocent campesinos in the dam's area of influence from 1996 to 1998 (Verdad Abierta 2011). Uribe is still under investigation for his role in two of them, each across the river from Briceño in hamlets of Ituango: one in La Granja in 1996, which claimed five lives; and one in El Aro in 1997, in which paramilitaries slaughtered fifteen people as Colombian soldiers established a perimeter around the village and a helicopter from the governor's office flew overhead (Human Rights Watch 2000). Shortly thereafter, in his last act as governor of Antioquia, Uribe launched the partnership that would build the Hidroituango dam. Then, with the project stalled ten years later, Uribe, by then president, pushed it forward by facilitating both tax breaks and environmental licenses to allow construction to begin (Román et al. 2020).

In the 1990s and 2000s, paramilitary violence became a central element in a national regime of dispossession directed toward enabling multiple means of accumulation across Colombia: a sustained wave of violence that displaced hundreds of thousands of Afro-Colombians on the Pacific coast to seize their land for massive African Palm plantations (Grajales 2013; Oslender 2008); hundreds of massacres targeting communities standing in the way of mining or petroleum megaprojects (Ramírez Cuellar 2005); targeted killings of trade unionists and social leaders to repress social mobilization directed at these same megaprojects, banana plantations, or industrial factories (Ballvé 2020; Gill 2016; Hough 2022; Ramírez Cuellar 2005); and, arguably most commonly, gray areas in which paramilitary violence combined with economic and legal mechanisms of dispossession (Grajales 2021).

The Hidroituango project itself is representative of this gray area of dispossession. The Cauca River had long provided all canyon dwellers with access to gold and fish. When campesino activists like Fabio and Angélica insist that they are "displaced by Hidroituango," they refer not only to violence but to the loss of the collectively held space that once provided campesinos with the cash that allowed them to sustain their rural livelihoods. With the loss of their *Patrón Mono*, followed by the disappearance of coca, campesinos' very ability to continue living in the region is compromised (fig. 4.4).

As Rob Nixon (2011, 150–51) points out, physical displacement is often preceded by a process of imaginative displacement, in which populations that stand in the way of projects seen as central to national development become "unimagined communities" excised from shared understandings of the nation. The 1990s–2000s regime of dispossession drew ideological justification from discourses that presented targeted areas and the people who inhabited them as "the other side of the nation" (Serje 2005): savage, violent, and sympathetic to guerrillas, but home to tremendous untapped wealth (Ballvé 2020; Grajales 2013; Serje 2012). Documents created to promote Hidroituango said the canyon of the Cauca River was "an area forgotten by progress, beset by armed actors, stigmatized, and with paradoxical poverty even in the midst of its natural wealth" (Cardona et al. 2016, 313; translation mine).

Justifications for dam construction and paramilitary violence also drew

FIGURE 4.4. Traditional fishing practices like the use of an *atarraya*, a weighted net, have been lost.

on the narrative of state absence I have described in chapter 2, which pre-scribes state presence to overcome these regions' violence and savagery. The geographer Teo Ballvé (2020) has described how the paramilitaries pre-sented themselves as allowing the entry of the state by destabilizing guerrilla power—even as they simultaneously trafficked drugs, plundered land, and murdered innocent people. This logic took over the nation. The popularity of Álvaro Uribe as a heavy-handed law-and-order president only grew, even as his links to paramilitary groups became increasingly clear. After suffering from decades of violence and fear, many Colombians were ready to accept paramilitary violence against populations who, by virtue of living in areas with guerrilla influence, were themselves subject to suspicion.

In this context, the Hidroituango dam was presented as a means for the redemption of canyon dwellers and the enrichment of the country (Cardona et al. 2016). As the construction of the dam began, the governor of Antio-quia, Luis Alfredo Ramos, proudly announced: "The moment has arrived to launch a gigantic achievement that will change the life of Antioqueños . . . , the source of permanent income that will allow the Department to revive [*oxigenar*] its revenues—for 100 years—and as a result realize a generous and unprecedented social investment which will invariably lead to the peace we dream of" (quoted in Cardona, Pinilla, and Gálvez 2016, 306).

This regime of dispossession was also wrapped up in broader economic and political transformation. In the first chapter of this book, I have described how Colombia's economic opening beginning in 1990 compromised small-holder agriculture by slashing protectionist tariffs and state subsidies. The flip side of the undermining of rural agriculture was the promotion of extractive economies, as the Uribe (2002–10), Santos (2010–18), and then Duque (2018–22) administrations each focused on turning Colombia into an extractive powerhouse.[4] By 2014, mineral and petroleum extraction represented 70 percent of Colombia's total exports, seven times their 1970 share (Sankey 2020). And. like other elements of economic liberalization, the promotion of extraction in Colombia was carried out in large part through the War on Drugs, and particularly the US-funded Plan Colombia.

Evidence of these links is not hard to come by. In a 1999 visit to Cartagena, then-US Secretary of Energy Bill Richardson announced, in reference to Plan Colombia: "The United States and its allies will invest millions of dollars in two areas of the Colombian economy, in the areas of mining and energy, and to secure these investments we are tripling military aid to Colombia" (quoted in Ramírez Cuellar 2005, 32). Indeed, this matches long-standing US goals in Latin America. Julien Mercille (2011) has argued that the War on Drugs has effectively promoted the three major post–World War II US objectives in Latin America. These are, according to declassified national security planning documents: first, "adequate production in Latin America of, and access by the United States to, raw materials essential to US security"; second, the "standardization of Latin American military organization, training, doctrine and equipment along US lines"; and finally, the creation of "a political and economic climate conducive to private investment, of both domestic and foreign capital" (quoted in Mercille 2011, 1641).

If the War on Drugs has done little to stem drug use or trafficking (see chapter 1), the resulting violence has systematically cleared the way for resource extraction. The journalist Dawn Paley (2014, 19), has coined the term "drug war capitalism" to refer to militarized antidrug initiatives that use terror to enable "the expansion of the capitalist system into new or previously inaccessible territories and social spaces . . . [to] benefit transnational oil and gas and mining companies."

International investment in Colombian extractive industries was also driven by a series of legal changes impelled by IMF structural adjustment policies, the Uribe administration, and provisions of Plan Colombia. In 1999, foreign oil companies had to enter into a 50–50 percent partnership with the state oil company and pay a 20 percent tax on royalties. By 2004, national law allowed them to own oil fields outright and pay a tax of only 8 percent (Leech 2011).

Mineral extraction saw similar legal benefits, as a 2001 mining code removed entry barriers to foreign and private investment and dropped royalties taxes from 10 percent to 0.4 percent (Sankey 2020). From 2000 to 2010, the government awarded almost nine thousand mining concessions (including one to Continental Gold in Briceño), as the territory under mining concessions rose from 221,000 to 7.4 million hectares (Paarlberg-Kvam 2021; Sankey 2020). A gold investors' publication sums up the international buzz over Colombia's resources: "For over 500 years, the world has been enticed by Colombia's gold. But for several decades, the South American nation has been so weakened by drug cartels and Marxist revolutionaries that foreign miners stayed out . . . This [wealth of unexploited resources] makes for opportunity without parallel" (quoted in Paarlberg-Kvam 2021, 8).

However, this enthusiasm was premature. Briceño's experience is a good example of how guerrilla control over large swathes of territory restrained extractive projects. While the Uribe government had granted Continental Gold legal concessions to mine gold in Briceño, the FARC granted no such permission. Instead, campesinos panned for gold until Hidroituango barred access to the river, and small-scale artisanal gold mines tunneled into Briceño's mountainsides, controlled or taxed by the FARC. From 2008 to 2009, outside miners affiliated with paramilitaries also engaged in illegal and environmentally damaging dredge mining along the banks of Briceño's Espíritu Santo River.

On a national level, with gold concentrated in rural areas under the control of armed groups, these informal mining practices also predominated. In 2011, legal large-scale gold mining operations made up less than 12 percent of Colombia's gold production (Massé and Billon 2017). Access to petroleum, coal, and other valuable resources was equally limited. Thus, the violence-based regime of dispossession had failed to enable access to massive quantities of valuable resources still hidden within guerrilla territory. In this context, the Santos government began peace negotiations with the FARC.

GOLD AND THE DECEPTIVE PROMISE OF PEACEFUL DISPOSSESSION

"Peace is going to permit us to extract more oil from the zones that were prohibited by the war."

JUAN CARLOS ECHEVERRY, president of Ecopetrol, the Colombian state oil company, April 26, 2016 (quoted in Lyons 2020, 80)

"The exploitation of our natural resources is absolutely necessary for the future of the country, and for post-conflict . . . these are incomes that are required for the financing of the coming programs."

LUIS CARLOS VILLEGAS, Colombian minister of defense, September 27, 2016, one day after signing of the original peace agreement (quoted in Massé and Billon 2017, 125)

When President Santos was awarded the Nobel Peace Prize in December 2016 for his negotiation of the peace agreement, it came with a gold medal—minted, as news accounts were quick to point out, from two legally certified Colombian mines (Massé and Billon 2017). It is no accident that Colombian gold was thrust to center stage in the most consequential ceremony in the Santos administration's efforts to brand Colombia as a postconflict state newly safe for increased foreign investment (Fattal 2018). The medal symbolized the hopes of the administration and a bevy of multinational corporations for an era of peace in which natural resources hidden within guerrilla territory would become available for extraction. The Uribe-era objective of basing Colombia's economy on foreign-financed extractive megaprojects was preserved. But the means for pacifying territories like Briceño were now different. Santos and his supporters were betting that a new regime of dispossession based on the guerrillas' peaceful demobilization would both unlock new resources and attract more foreign investors, generating the profits needed to build a lasting peace.

Their hopes are typical of both international peacebuilders and domestic elites, who see intensified resource extraction as a critical element of expected peace dividends (Lujala et al. 2016; Selby 2008). Peace processes in countries as diverse as Peru, Sierra Leone, Guatemala, Liberia, and Afghanistan have counted on the jobs, improved infrastructure, and tax revenues enabled by extractive projects as "engines for peace" (Lujala et al. 2016; Paarlberg-Kvam 2021). The statements of high-ranking members of the Santos administration quoted above are but two examples of what Kate Paarlberg-Kvam (2021) has called "open-pit peace," to refer to the idea that increased revenues from mining and petroleum extraction enabled by the peace agreement would quell discontent and fund the peace process itself.

Paramilitary violence as a driver of dispossession has not disappeared. Nevertheless, the Santos government sought to drive a shift—partial and incomplete, but consequential nevertheless—to a new regime of dispossession in which the peace process would replace violence as the major means of pacifying new territories for resource extraction. The experience of Briceño, however, suggests that the intensified modes of capital accumulation that result are more likely to drive new cycles of violence than serve as engines for peace.

*　*　*

Two months before the murder of the geologists, I sit in Coffeebri with Ricardo and Alberto, who have just come back from a meeting with Continental Gold representatives touting the benefits of a gold mine. While neither man supports mining, they're worried about the community's ability to stop the project.

"We need the coca substitution projects to be executed as soon as possible so Continental Gold can't take away our land or our water, because there are state investments that need to be protected," Alberto says. He draws our attention to a map of Briceño's mining concessions on his phone, zooming in with his thumb and index finger to indicate a crucial area. "They want to make two-thousand-meter perforations here. What's going to happen to all the fertile land, which is supposedly for [crop substitution] projects?"

"Some people may support mining because of the failing economy," Ricardo says. "They see Continental Gold as a way to make money. They don't see the environmental damage."

Ana, sitting at a neighboring table with her nine-year-old daughter, weighs in: "Just look at Hidroituango. A lot of people made money gold panning. But now there aren't beaches. A source of work that they had, that now they can't do. If Continental Gold comes, we'll be left without water. Crime would go up. More overpopulation. It would be chaos." A few minutes later, she tells us about her recent experience in a Continental Gold–funded trip for local leaders to Buriticá, a municipality west of Briceño where the company has a gold mine. "They explain it very well [in meetings], but go to Buriticá. There are holes everywhere, crime, prostitution. Imagine that here. And the wealth being taken to other parts. Not for us."

"I just don't know what people are supposed to do without projects," Alberto says. "And they [Continental Gold] have all the [legal mining] titles, the lawyers, the politicians."

"Exactly," Ricardo responds. "They bring the peace process here for them [Continental Gold], so they can come here without worries."

"Maybe they want us to go," Ana responds. "So they can take all of the resources from Briceño."

Community members directly confronted the potential for a gold mine for only the first three months of my research, before Continental Gold left the region in the wake of guerrilla violence. In that time, I found that a clear majority of villagers opposed the mine, feeling that it would compromise their water, their agricultural projects, and their very place within the territory. Like Ana, many turned to their experiences with Hidroituango to make sense of this new megaproject, drawing three lessons hinted at in the conversation above. First, the peace process—and through it the state—had only come to Briceño to access the village's untapped resources. Second, local communities were an obstacle to megaprojects aimed at extracting these resources, and would have little place in a territory taken over by a gold mine. And third, just as they been unable to stop the Hidroituango project, they would have little chance of stopping a gold mine—at least through legal means.

This latter assumption was well-founded in changing national laws. In 2017, seven municipalities in Colombia held binding referenda on proposed mining projects; all the projects were rejected overwhelmingly (González 2019). The following year, the Constitutional Court did away with these referenda entirely, ruling that the resources of the soil and subsoil were the property of the state and that neither communities nor local authorities had a legal basis for preventing their exploitation (González 2019; Redacción Judicial 2019b). Thus, while the previous regime of dispossession had harnessed violence to extract resources from territories considered to be the "other side of the nation" (Serje 2005), the peace process promised unity and inclusion—but an inclusion that entailed legal dispossession of rural populations. The coming of the state, Briceño's campesinos feared, had made the mine inevitable.

Enter the rearmed guerrillas. In functional terms, the FARC's killing of the geologists posed a clear challenge to the development of state authority. While state power supported an unpopular mine project that threatened local livelihoods, the guerrillas stepped up to violently scuttle the project. In doing so, they provided powerful evidence that it was they, rather than the state, who were taking responsibility for protecting the public good.

Still, I do not want to suggest that the community supported the killings. When I asked locals directly, they understood guerrilla violence as the only reason plans for the mine weren't going forward. However, it is difficult to generalize about community evaluations of armed groups because of a "law of silence" that prevents collective sense-making of their actions (see chapter 5).

In private conversations, I heard a range of responses to the killings. Many emphasized that, as one man said, the only reason Continental Gold wasn't in the territory was "because of the killing of the geologists." Some focused on the geologists, Colombians in their twenties who were generally cast as innocent victims. People varied, however, in whether they blamed the guerrillas who performed the murders or the mining company for ignoring the threats. Others worried that Continental Gold's disappearance was only temporary, and that the project would only bring more violence. For at least some of these people, the guerrillas represented the community's only possibility for resistance.

Tomás's comments, made as we sat alone outside his rural home, provide particularly strong evidence for how the killing of the geologists caused many to see the guerrillas as a legitimate authority. He followed the local custom, as part of the law of silence, of using ambiguous pronouns like "them" or "they" (*ellos*) to refer to the guerrillas:

> [The gold mine] has the support of the government, the army. I imagine the army and police will advance to get "them" out. That violence is the product of two forces. On one side, the force of campesinos, supported or not by an armed group. And on the other side, the force of the state, of capitalism, who want to enter no matter what. . . . It's about who is on the side of the campesinos. The forces of the state have never been on the side of campesinos. *Ellos* help solve problems in the communities, which makes people feel they're on their side.

This statement is indicative of the pitfalls of policies that treat extractive projects as engines for peace. Throughout this book I have argued that local authority relations rest on communities' decisions to turn to state officials or competing authorities for help with their livelihood strategies and everyday problems. Briceño's gold mine was set to be enabled by a new regime of dispossession promising to use the peace agreement to pacify the region. In doing so, however, it only opened space for the rearmed FARC guerrillas to establish their authority as local problem solvers. And at the same time, it compromised the fragile authority of a state whose promotion of extraction endangered its promise to bring peace and progress.

The political scientist Jacobo Grajales (2021) warns against analyses that draw a clear distinction between the plunder of war and the legitimate accumulation of a postwar setting. We must not, he says, pretend "that relations of power produced and reproduced through violence can be magically laundered whenever inequalities are no longer imposed through the use of the rifle, but rather sustained by the title" (Grajales 2021, 4). The case of Briceño suggests taking his critique one step further. Not only is inequality reproduced within the shift to legal and "peaceful" dispossession, but violence itself is likely to resurge in response to a regime that leaves little other potential for resistance. With the peace process failing to fully supplant guerrilla authority, and a multinational corporation still seeking the gold hidden deep within Briceño's mountains, campesinos fear that more violence is to come when either the army or paramilitaries seek to wrest regional control away from the guerrillas.

The peace agreement promised a transformation of the countryside that would address the poverty and inequality at the roots of the conflict, establishing a place for campesinos to live and produce in peace. This was based on a vision of rural Colombia as a site of smallholder production where campesinos could access land, legal markets for their products, roads, education, and health care. It was at its heart a promise of inclusion. As I have described in chapter 2, both comprehensive rural reform and coca substitution have fallen far short of their promises. But this ideal has also been compromised by a distinct vision for rural Colombia, one that has animated two decades of national economic policy. This is a vision of a countryside dominated by megaproject extraction, of denuded landscapes dominated by mines, oil wells, and hydroelectric dams. In this view, progress and prosperity are functions of increased gross domestic product and foreign direct investment, rather than an equitable distribution of these resources or an inclusive economy that offers a place for all Colombians to make a dignified living.

The contradiction between these two visions—rural Colombia as area of smallholder production, or megaproject extraction—endangers the peace process. It establishes an existential threat to communities like Briceño, one directly tied to a state that is struggling to establish its authority. And it creates an opportunity for groups like the rearmed guerrillas to construct their own legitimacy at the expense of the state.

But the outcome of this existential threat also depends on the livelihood strategies that excluded populations employ in response. As I have described throughout this book, those strategies may further endanger the building of peace and state power, particularly if community members turn back to drug cultivation—or, worse, to the ranks of armed groups. But the struggle to establish new livelihoods in a transformed territory can also bring them to officials and organizations associated with the state, including the very hydroelectric dam that threatens to dispossess them.

The Struggle for a Place in the Territory

> We must begin in a less spectacular place, before the sun rises, as the blankets are thrown off in the cold morning and, in the dark, a man and a woman grope for hat and shawl to face the day. This daily task of piecing together a living influences the form a people's political struggle takes.
>
> GAVIN SMITH, *Livelihood and Resistance: Peasants and the Politics of Land in Peru* (1989, 13)

The means through which Briceño's campesinos seek to piece together a living have been dramatically altered in the context of the hydroelectric dam and the peace process. The cash incomes from coca and gold panning have disappeared, pushing communities to scramble to develop alternatives. At the same time, however, both the dam and the peace process have opened political opportunities for them to do so. Hidroituango destroyed local liveli-hoods, but also pays legally mandated royalties (*regalías*) to the local govern-ment. These payments have combined with peace process funds to greatly increase the municipal budget, contributing to the political practices around local elections I will describe in chapter 6. But, particularly for communities adjacent to the dam, demands for a variety of resources directly from EPM have become a central and ongoing element of their new livelihood strate-gies. And with EPM a public company owned by the city of Medellín, this represents—along with the substitution program (see chapter 2), a variety of municipal programs (see chapter 6), and roadbuilding and maintenance (see chapter 7)—yet another way in which state resources have become central to community livelihood strategies.

In this section I describe the community of El Orejón's engagement with EPM over two and a half years from 2020 to 2022, a time when its collective action shifted away from resistance against the dam. Instead, the community turned to what I call a politics of contentious accommodation, in which it pushed EPM for resources to help it establish new economies in the face of the disappearance of gold panning, fishing, and coca.

But before I dive into this description, two disclaimers. The first is that while both EPM and Hidroituango are located within the field of state power (EPM is controlled by the municipal government of Medellín, and Hidroitu-ango is a public-private partnership that has received both state and private financing), their place within local imaginations of "the state" is complex. Indeed, in their disputes with EPM, social leaders often turned to other state actors for support, primarily Briceño's 2020–23 municipal administration, which repeatedly took the community's side in contentious episodes. Addi-tionally, while EPM's general manager is appointed by the mayor of Medellín, it is also overseen by a board of directors that holds the company account-able for producing a profit. EPM's contributions to the community have thus operated more around the logic of corporate social responsibility—meant to redistribute the profits or mitigate the effects of an extractive project—than of the state's provision of resources for the public good.

There is nothing unique or surprising about the incongruity between EPM and other state agencies; sociologists have long understood that states are made up of "many hands" with distinct goals, who are often in direct com-petition (Bourdieu 1999; Morgan and Orloff 2017). Still, the illusion that these diverse actors make up a unified and coherent whole—"the state"—is critical to popular acceptance of state authority (Abrams 1988). It is important to note that while social leaders criticized "*el estado*" for its *incumplimiento* of the substitution program (see chapter 2), their critiques of the hydroelectric dam explicitly blamed EPM rather than "the state." Consequently, much as I have described in chapter 2 on the substitution program, collective claims-making on EPM—and the goods received through it—helped extend material dependence on state resources. However, the extent to which these goods and the claims-making contributed to the symbolically powerful conception of the state's rightful role and responsibility is more limited.

And second, just as we should not uncritically accept the category of "state," it is important to avoid oversimplifying "community." The anthropologist Sherry Ortner (1995, 177) has influentially criticized resistance studies for what she calls an ethnographic refusal that overlooks the internal conflicts of dominated groups: "If we are to recognize that resistors are doing more than simply opposing domination, more than simply producing a virtually mechanical re-action, then we must go the whole way. They have their own politics—not just between chiefs and commoners or landlords and peasants but within all the local categories of friction and tension."

One point of tension was between those who mobilized against the dam project and those who worked for Hidroituango—eight different community members from El Orejón alone. While some people simultaneously worked for and opposed Hidroituango ("working for the enemy," one dam employee was fond of saying), other employees conspicuously avoided mobilizations related to the dam. Tension also existed around differences between families in terms of the compensation they received from the dam company, which ranged from nothing to substantial sums. And finally, community members often disagreed about which tactics to use, particularly in the case of *paros*, which required them to leave their crops and animals untended and exposed them to personal risk and discomfort. "The community," therefore, was not a unitary actor—instead, any degree of unity visible in this account was a tenuous achievement, produced through negotiations to overcome internal disagreements. However, I was also often surprised to see enthusiastic collaboration between people who had been engaged in heated arguments days or hours earlier.

FROM RESISTANCE TO CONTENTIOUS ACCOMMODATION

James Scott (1977) begins his classic study of peasant rebellion with the image of a farmer standing in neck-deep water, one ripple—or drought, slump in crop prices, or bad harvest—away from drowning. Confronting this reality, he argues, peasants have developed a moral economy based on securing their subsistence. Their communal outrage and potential revolt emerge not so much from a sense that their labor or harvests are being exploited, but more from their exposure to the risk of falling below the basic level of subsistence. Within this moral economy, "the test for the peasant is more likely to be 'What is left?' than 'How much is taken?'" (Scott 1977, 7). While Scott's analysis focused on Vietnamese peasants' changing patronage relations with powerful landowners, Briceño has historically lacked a significant elite agricultural class on which campesinos could make claims in the face of calamity. Instead, riverside communities have turned to the Cauca River.

As they bemoaned the enclosure of the Cauca, campesinos were fond of repeating that their *Patrón Mono* had never left them empty-handed. No one got rich from fishing or gold panning, but when they were in need, the river was always there for them, guaranteeing a basic income—the cash that served as the base of other economic activities (Tubb 2020). Following Scott, it is not surprising that by leaving campesinos without this safety net, the dam project generated collective resistance.

However, the demands of collective action changed over time. As locals were forced to accept a new reality without their *Patrón Mono*, they sought a distinct patron. Rather than resisting the dam project, they adopted a claims-making that held EPM responsible for remaking the conditions that would help them establish a place within a transformed territory. This, in turn, allowed EPM to quell dissent enough to continue regional operations and dam construction.

I theorize campesinos' changing relations with EPM as a shift away from resistance and toward contentious accommodation, with accommodation conceptualized in three distinct ways. First, it is a process through which community claims-making is directed *within* rather than *against* a territory dominated by the dam. The sociologist Pablo Lapegna (2016) describes a similar transformation from oppositional politics to accommodation in an analysis of Argentinian social movements against genetically modified soybeans. He warns against removing agency from social movement participants by accusing them of being co-opted; instead, he shows how groups and individuals make strategic concessions to meet material needs. As James Scott (1985, 247) wrote in a different text, "Dissident intellectuals from the middle or upper classes may occasionally have the luxury of focusing exclusively on the prospects for long-term structural change, but the peasantry or the working class are granted no holiday from the mundane pressures of making a living."

Second, the term "accommodation" refers to a technology of power in which elites accommodate the pressing needs of subordinate groups to establish consent. In chapter 2, I have argued that the promise of access to material resources pushed campesino leaders to support rather than organize against political officials who acted against their interests by dismantling the peace process. In this sense, elite accommodation to subordinate groups is similar to what Gramsci (1991, 119) describes as a passive revolution, in which a dominant class offers "small doses, legally, in a reformist manner—in such a way that it [is] possible to preserve the political and economic positions of the [elite] classes."

Finally, Briceño's campesinos seek accommodation in a sense invoked more often by hotel advertisements than by studies of power and politics: a place to stay. Throughout this book I have argued that the political and economic behavior of campesinos is rooted in their struggle to maintain valued rural lifestyles in the face of forces that threaten to dispossess them. As I will show, campesinos' ongoing claims-making on dam officials explicitly draws on this logic, calling on EPM to establish a place where they can live and produce.

Critically, while the first two senses of accommodation I describe—a social movement's turn away from resistance, and a technology for the reproduction of power—seem to suggest movement demobilization, Briceño's riverside communities are anything but demobilized. Instead, theirs is a contentious accommodation, drawing as needed on a well-established repertoire of collective action developed during anti-dam activism. These actions are part of cycles of contention, negotiation, minor material victories, de-escalation, and disappointment that have continued for the better part of a decade.

✳   ✳   ✳

We pick up the story in early January 2020. After the 2018 flood that destroyed area bridges, EPM had established a ferry across the Cauca River. When it inaugurated a new bridge across the dam's retaining wall in late 2019, EPM closed the ferry and the road that led to it, cutting off access to the river for fishermen who had been storing their boats at the dock. The community organized a *paro* (the fifth since 2013), occupying the highway that led to the dam. Locals not only called for the reopening of the road but presented a laundry list of additional demands. That same day, EPM negotiated with them, reopening the road that led to the dock, and scheduling a meeting with the community to address its demands.

Two weeks later, I'm on my motorcycle, heading to the meeting. In my bag, I carry a letter that I've typed and printed based on the community's handwritten draft. It outlines its plan: ". . . for a dignified life and participatory development, seeking to stay in the territory and improve our life conditions. To meet these objectives, we enumerate these essential projects for the families of El Orejón and neighboring hamlets. The proposal is to obtain the funding in cooperation with EPM for all the damages caused by Hidroituango."

The document proposes twenty distinct projects, including:

1. Redoing the 2008 census to include the families that were not previously compensated for the loss of their economic activity. . . .

4. Equipment to help transform agricultural products like coffee, chocolate, and animal feed (transform refers to modifying products for consumption or preservation such as roasting and grinding coffee and chocolate). . . .

7. Improvement and maintenance of the El Orejón road . . .

16. Creation of a campesino market to sell the region's projects by the dam. . . .

20. A scientific study to determine the effects of microclimate change on local agricultural production and compensate local farmers accordingly.

The meeting takes place in El Orejón's new two-story school. The building is easily big enough to hold a hundred-plus students across four different classrooms; but with the community down to seven children, the meeting doesn't interfere with classes. Five EPM officials sit at a table in the front. Carolina, a woman in her mid- to late twenties employed by EPM as a social worker, leads the meeting, responding point by point to the community proposals. One point of disagreement comes up when Angélica refers to the people who have been displaced because of Hidroituango.

"Hidroituango doesn't displace," Carolina says.

"There are forty people who have left the region," Angélica says. "And why? If I lived from gold panning, and I can no longer pan for gold. Or if I lived from fishing, and I can no longer fish. So Hidroituango does displace. You should create a project for these people because they're suffering in the cities, going hungry. Because the city isn't their culture, it's not their life."

As I have argued throughout this text, locals attribute a great moral value to rural lifestyles, with many feeling out of place in cities. Angélica's argument is exemplary of an oft-expressed belief within the community: Having destroyed their ancestral *Patrón Mono*, EPM is now responsible for stepping in to establish alternative livelihoods that guarantee locals a place within the territory.

In response to their proposals, Carolina promises to talk with her bosses, telling the community that neither she nor anyone else at the meeting has decision-making power. On this day they cannot negotiate or promise anything. The community responds with frustration.

"This is a lack of respect," a local farmer responds forcefully. "It's the same thing as always. You never send anyone with decision-making power."

Another man picks up the point, saying that during the *paro*, EPM had agreed to send functionaries who could make decisions. He gives an analogy: "It's like when you go talk to the mayor. You don't just meet with the person who cleans the mayor's office."

Carolina is apologetic, but what can she do? "I don't want to make promises I can't keep," she says.

While the proposal for the campesino market is new, most community demands date back nearly a decade. Throughout this time, EPM has sent one social worker after another, always young women who are not empowered to direct resources or make consequential decisions. They listen sympathetically, transmit the community's demands to higher-ups, and return months later with counterproposals. Sometimes the process results in some resources entering the community, like agricultural projects that have provided chickens or avocado trees. Often the proposals get lost in the shuffle, or the social worker is replaced by another young woman, equally sympathetic, who begins from scratch.

The meeting breaks up after a little more than two hours, with Carolina agreeing to the community's demands to give them an official response within a month.

✴ ✴ ✴

Exactly one month later, with no response forthcoming, the community acts. Community members organize a day of communal labor to clear jungle for the construction of a new curve in the road to bypass two steep landslide-prone sections. Somehow, EPM, which owns the land, gets wind of the plan and tries to get the police to stop the work. However, due to guerrilla presence, the police cannot enter the community. So instead, an EPM official calls the community president. The official says that EPM is planning to invest in the road, but that if the community persists in illegally clearing brush for a new route, it can forget about any help. EPM schedules a meeting to discuss the road issue, and the community desists.

The next day, however, community members carry out another action, putting the campesino market by the dam into action. I meet Fabio and Angélica at the entrance to their farm, where they are loading up mandarin oranges, chocolate, and bags of coffee onto a borrowed truck. We travel down the steep and serpentine dirt road that leads from El Orejón to the Hidroituango highway. It's no mystery why they want to redirect the route; my motorcycle's rear wheel nearly slides out as I brake hard to avoid losing control down its steepest sections.

When we reach the highway, we meet up with campesinos from nearby communities. We take off in a caravan—four motorcycles and a heavily loaded truck—following the highway downriver to the newly inaugurated bridge on top of the dam wall. In contrast to the green valleys of the rest of Briceño, everything is a drab gray—the road, the reinforced concrete covering the valley walls by the project, and the large gravel parking lot at the end of the bridge. As we pull into the lot, we unload immediately, filling plastic tables with local products. Two men build an improvised cover, digging holes for wooden poles they use to support a blue tarp. We're going to need the shade. While the farms of El Orejón enjoy a temperate climate 1,400 to 2,000 meters above sea level, we have dipped down to 300 meters, and the sun, reflecting off the concrete and gravel, is blistering hot.

Uncomfortable though it may be, the heat is good for sales. The first customers are dam employees, friendly and curious about what we're doing. They buy large glasses of iced *guarapo*, a mixture of lime and sugarcane juice. Each purchase comes with fliers announcing this as the first campesino market, along with a promise to return to the dam every Sunday. The flyer ends: "We are campesino families, creating conditions of dignified lives in the communities affected by Hidroituango."

Within fifteen minutes, a security guard rides up on a motorcycle, asking if we have permission to be here.

"Permission?" Fabio says. "These are the lands where we fished and panned for gold, long before this dam was ever here."

The guard is sympathetic but explains that he has to call the police. Meanwhile, sales continue. Fabio stops buses that pass by to and from Ituango, giving each bus driver a free glass of mandarin orange juice to let campesino vendors enter the bus to hawk their goods to passengers. At one point, a group of fifty motorcyclists arrives to see the dam. They make quick work of the remaining *guarapo*.

Two hours in, six police officers carrying semiautomatic rifles pull into the parking lot on a white truck (fig. 4.5). Fabio takes a leading role in talking with them: "Gold panning was our culture; that gave money for people to sustain themselves, but now it doesn't exist. The coffee harvest this year—the microclimate changed in the region, and the production dropped."

Angelica interjects, "Let's put it this way; we can't let ourselves starve to death."

"So what did we say?" Fabio continues. "We're going to bring what little we have to sell here."

"I understand," the police officer who seems to be in charge tells him. "But you need permission to be here."

"We have spent ten years without solving our problems," Fabio says. "What did we do this time? We changed the way we related to EPM. Before, we had

FIGURE 4.5. Police officers monitor the market in front of a denuded and repressed jungle river.

protests, we closed off the road. But now we brought proposals for solutions from the community." Fabio explains that EPM officials have promised an answer within a month. "But there hasn't been a response. So that's why we're here."

For two hours, negotiations continue, including phone calls with the mayor and EPM higher-ups. Though many feared we would be forcibly removed, no such action is taken. By the time we leave, the campesinos have sold nearly everything. The community agrees to a meeting the next week to discuss establishing a formal market.

The meeting takes place the following Saturday. EPM agrees to form work groups with the community to evaluate the possibility of organizing a campesino market "under conditions of security and hygiene." In the meantime, it refuses the community's petition for permission to sell products in the dam's parking lot.

"They just want to drag out the process even more," Fabio tells me. The community, with a decade's worth of reasons to be skeptical of EPM's promises, resolves to continue the Sunday markets.

The next week we return to the parking lot. Word of the event's success has spread, and there are now more than fifty campesinos and a greater variety of local products like tamales, fruit salad, and *patacones* (plantains that are fried, crushed until they resemble pancakes, and fried again). The police stay away. Suso and Eugenia come from Medellín by motorcycle, excited to see the river again serving as a meeting place and economic driver of the community. Spirits are high, as many of the participants comment that the market has provided the highest prices they've ever received for their legal agricultural goods.

This turns out to be the final campesino market. One day later, a beloved community leader and a woman he is taking to the hospital perish on one of the most dangerous stretches of the El Orejón road (see chapter 7). The grieving community cancels the market for one week. By the following week, Covid-19 has spread throughout Colombia, and plans for the market are scuttled.

Nor do attempts to improve the road fare much better. In 2021, EPM officials meet with Briceño's mayor and community members, committing to a bigger investment to improve not only the eight kilometers of the El Orejón road but also the other roads that continue to Briceño's village center. However, by early 2022 when the project is set to begin, EPM officials say they no longer have the budget.

In March 2022 we return to the same stretch of road where the community began clearing an alternative route to bypass the most dangerous parts two years earlier. This time, we are accompanied by an excavator, paid for with funds provided by the mayor, to help open the road. The excavator begins leveling a new path while the men use machetes to clear away jungle brush and the women make *sancocho*, a large communal pot of meat stew, for lunch. However, as Fabio says, remembering EPM's previous reaction in making a deal with the community, "it's not really to improve the road, but to push EPM into action."

EPM does act. In a meeting two days later, EPM representatives threaten that if the community continues cutting into the jungle on EPM property, they will send the army to stop them. However, they promise to live up to their commitment to improve the road in two ways: first, by hiring local campesinos for three months to do basic road maintenance, and second, by following through with a more comprehensive project for the road once that contract ends.

Suso is one of the ten men EPM hires to fix up the road. Without access to heavy machinery, the repairs are limited to what the men can do with shovels and machetes. They are paid a full minimum salary, but work only one day a week. The improvements to the road are minimal. Still, in a region with little work available, the pay is welcome.

In June 2022, EPM sends an official letter to the El Orejón community action board, offering to extend the contracts of the ten men for an additional forty-five days and to provide the materials to pave forty-five meters of the road. It is significantly less than the promised comprehensive road repair project. The letter stipulates that if the board agrees to the terms, "the

Community Action Board of the Hamlet El Orejón exonerates EPM from all responsibility, and consequently will make no legal complaint about what is agreed to in this bilateral modification, nor for the events that have led to it."

The community meets, furious that EPM is again reneging on its promises. Fabio points out that the dam is scheduled to finally begin producing energy in July, four years behind schedule. A *paro* leading up to its inauguration would threaten EPM's plans, pushing it to make concessions. After years of broken commitments, it's now or never. The community settles on a *paro* for mid-July, a week before the dam's scheduled inauguration.

A little more than a week before the agreed upon date, however, multiple paramilitary squadrons enter Briceño in force. They occupy a large farm—itself seized years earlier by the guerrillas away from a wealthy landowner rumored to be a paramilitary sympathizer—not far from El Orejón, torturing and killing one of the men who has been living there. A different group of paramilitaries occupies El Orejón, politely informing campesinos that they are now in control and have come to put the communities in order. No one is sure what the paramilitaries are doing in Briceño. Some fear that this is the first step in finally establishing the gold mine. Others speculate that long-standing paramilitary-guerrilla conflicts in neighboring villages have simply spilled over.

After encountering twenty-five armed men in the mule path that leads to their farm, Fabio and Angélica go to Medellín to stay with their children. Eugenia and Suso go to their home in Bello. The *paro* never happens, nor does EPM's promised road improvement. In December, however, Fabio proposes a project in which EPM would pay 130 local families to conserve and restore natural areas that have been damaged by the dam project. The EPM social workers he meets with promise to take the proposal to their superiors.

∗ ∗ ∗

Many locals see in EPM's actions an articulated strategy of distraction, delay, and disappointment. Indeed, over a decade, community engagements with EPM have followed a predictable pattern. Contentious mobilization leads to negotiations, which are drawn out because EPM sends employees who are not empowered to make decisions. These negotiations eventually lead to material concessions, themselves scheduled for months down the road. When the time comes, EPM fails to fully live up to its commitments, sparking another cycle of contention. Wash, rinse, repeat.

In functional terms, this cycle has operated as a tool of power, enabling dam construction through pacifying contention. Nevertheless, it would be a mistake to understand it as the actions of a sinister genius behind the scenes at EPM, calculating how to quell unrest by tricking campesinos and disbursing the minimum amount of resources. Instead, scholarly work on corporate social responsibility (CSR) within extractive megaprojects suggests that this cycle emerges through struggles not only between EPM and the community, but also within EPM itself. In an ethnography of a US-owned Indonesian mine, Marina Welker (2014) argues that profit motives alone are insufficient to explain what corporations are and what they do. Just as an understanding of communities or states as unitary actors breaks down when exposed to ethnographic analysis, corporations are also fields of struggle in which distinct actors may push different goals with varying degrees of success (Bourdieu 1999; Morgan and Orloff 2017; Ortner 1995; Welker 2014). Welker finds that while the mine caused environmental devastation and social inequalities, it also included a CSR division that provided local development, employment, and small business initiatives. Against common critiques of CSR as simply a means of overcoming local resistance, Welker describes how CSR—though often marginalized by the profitable production-focused divisions of the company—at times succeeded in promoting community interests over profit-seeking (Welker 2014).

Struggles between different divisions of a corporation, of course, are highly unequal: the social worker who genuinely wants to help the community of El Orejón will have trouble getting her goals prioritized over those of the manager responsible for the project's profitability or the engineer who is trying to get the turbines up and running. But community members can also have an impact within this field of struggle, particularly when they throw a monkey wrench into dam operations by blocking the highway that leads to the dam, or by threatening EPM's public reputation. These actions may shift the balance, opening the way for several days of an excavator to improve the road, a contract to reforest dam property, or a place to sell local products at the foot of the dam. This is contentious accommodation: a politics that accepts Hidroituango out of necessity, but defiantly pushes the dam company to establish a place for campesinos within a transformed territory.

Conclusion

This chapter describes two shifts, both occurring within a national economic transformation toward megaproject extraction, and both related to broader questions about the relationship between peace, power, economic development, and collective action. The first shift is on a macro level, describing the changing regimes of dispossession used to enable extractive megaprojects. While paramilitary violence was long used to drive megaprojects like the

Hidroituango dam, by the 2010s the Santos administration was pushing a peace agreement it expected to pacify FARC-controlled territories and enable the exploitation of their valuable resources. The example of Briceño's gold, however, suggests that these projects may represent the downfall rather than the dividends of peace.

While the peace agreement promised to address the roots of conflict through a vision of transforming rural Colombia into a place of campesino production, extractive megaprojects endanger rural livelihoods and further the dynamics of economic exclusion I describe throughout this book. While this can push locals to turn to EPM or the state to forge new livelihood strategies, it may also lead them back to coca, or even to the ranks of armed groups (see chapters 3 and 5). State support over local objections to megaprojects also imperils state legitimacy in territories where it has long been lacking, opening a space for groups like the rearmed guerrillas in Briceño to serve as local (violent) problem solvers.

Beyond Colombia, this finding challenges dominant peacebuilding practices and discourse that sees extractive megaprojects as engines of peace (Lujala et al. 2016). Of course, the dispossession—whether imposed through violent or peaceful means—that is behind these projects is itself worthy of critique. However, it may be particularly problematic where a peace process seeks to simultaneously establish extraction alongside state authority in communities that have long lived under armed group authority. For these communities, dispossession may come to constitute the terms of their inclusion within the nation, a political inclusion that ironically only worsens their economic exclusion by destroying traditional economies like the gold panning that long guaranteed Briceño's campesinos a profitable entry point into global economies. This fact can make alternative authorities seem appealing and threaten the legitimacy of both the peace process and the state itself.

The second shift is on a micro level, related to changing campesino livelihoods and claims-making. I describe how local politics have shifted from resistance to accommodation, in which communities now struggle *within* rather than *against* a territory dominated by the dam. While sociologists of collective action describe accommodation as an element of demobilization (Lapegna 2016), an ethnographic description of El Orejón's engagement with EPM over two and a half years shows a community that is far from demobilized. Instead, its accommodation is contentious, drawing on transgressive actions to push EPM to help community members establish a place for themselves in a transformed territory. Academic studies often romanticize direct resistance to rapacious capitalism and other structures of oppression, or conversely describe how elites achieve quiescence by coercing, co-opting, or confusing marginalized communities (Abu-Lughod 1990; Gaventa 1982). The people of El Orejón—and, I suspect, many other communities like it— neither wholly resist nor acquiesce. Instead, their political activity turns on the daily struggle to piece together a living (Smith 1989). The very fact that they accept incremental material concessions makes this struggle possible to maintain. And in turn, it is the fact that these engagements produce some level of consent to state or elite authority that allows them to produce material gains.

While the resources that communities like El Orejón receive emerge from great effort, do not compensate for the cultural and economic loss of the river, and often fall short of EPM's commitments, they nevertheless have become an important part of campesino livelihoods. As such, they contribute to the broader transformation I describe throughout this book, in which communities have begun turning to the state in a way they never did before. However, as I will explore in the next chapter, the state is not the only claimant to local authority.

When Does a Peace Process Not Bring Peace?

Dideison, Act Two

The year 2022 starts poorly for Dideison. In the early morning hours of New Year's Day, he stands in Briceño's main square with his girlfriend and two other young women, exchanging wishes of "*¡Feliz año!*" with passersby. Another young woman, accompanied by her friends, comes up to accuse one of his companions of sleeping with her boyfriend. A fight breaks out. Dideison tries to break it up, grabbing his girlfriend away. The police quickly step in and Dideison goes home, thinking the matter is over.

At five in the morning, however, he receives a phone call. A friend tells him that a young woman who was hurt in the fight is convinced that Dideison punched her. Her boyfriend and a group of his friends are looking for Dideison, carrying knives. At 6 a.m. the group shows up at his house. He keeps the door locked. However, when Dideison's brother arrives at the house after a long night out, they attack him, leaving him with a black eye.

The next day, Dideison gets multiple phone calls from unfamiliar numbers. The callers accuse him of violence against a woman, ignoring his protestations that he had only been breaking up the fight. They threaten him, telling him to leave Briceño. In desperation, Dideison calls Rodrigo, a longtime FARC commander who has languished in a Medellín jail since 2018 for his leadership of the rearmed guerrillas.

✶　✶　✶

Dideison's turn to a FARC leader was the continuation of a long history in which the FARC served as local authority and problem solver. Thirteen years earlier, with Dideison's family staying in Medellín following their displacement by paramilitaries, it had been Rodrigo who gave them permission to return to Briceño, to a hamlet controlled by the guerrillas. Within this community, the FARC imposed law and order: "If you had a dispute with someone, they would come help, to see who was to blame," says Dideison, listing a number of established fines: two hundred dollars for fighting, four hundred dollars for attacking someone with a knife or machete, eight hundred dollars for using a gun. "And if someone was stealing, they would make them leave; or if it was a kid, they would say, 'Think of it like you have been born again, and we're not going to do anything to you, but don't fuck up again [*no la vuelva a cagar*].' And if they fucked up again, the guerrillas would give them one day to leave."

With Rodrigo and his family living nearby, Dideison and his neighbors also developed personal ties to the guerrillas. Rodrigo's younger brother Felipe became one of Dideison's closest friends. When they were around fifteen years old, they began doing favors for the FARC. "They told me they needed eyes and ears," Dideison says, describing how he would report on the people who moved through the community. "Or to go pick up a bag and take it to another area." The guerrillas paid him for each favor, and started talking to him about joining the organization.

One night at a party, Dideison was speaking with a young woman when a jealous young man pushed him to the floor. Felipe, already a member of the guerrillas, pulled out a pistol. Dideison's attacker backed off. "That way of generating respect," Dideison says, "not even respect, but fear—that makes you feel superior. That made me think about [joining]."

Dideison even agreed to join the FARC, but Felipe stepped in. "He didn't let me," Dideison says. "He said that he didn't want me to be like him. And I think now, I could have gone down a completely different path." Out of a group of four close friends, Dideison was the only one who stayed out of the FARC. One was killed by the guerrillas themselves in 2016, accused of giving information to paramilitaries. Felipe was killed in a military ambush in 2018. The other friend was captured by the military and imprisoned in 2019.

In early 2017, the FARC guerrillas disarmed through the peace process, going to live in a demobilization camp in the nearby village of Anorí. "It was catastrophic for the community," Dideison says. "Because people who had been controlled by fear [of the FARC] started to say, 'There's no control, I can do whatever I want.' Someone was killed at a party, in [my community] there was a fight and someone was stabbed, various businesses were robbed."

The authority vacuum lasted less than a year before some of the FARC guerrillas rearmed in November 2017, announcing their presence with messages spray-painted on the walls of local sheds (fig. 5.1). Just like local campesinos who grew to depend on the state after the disappearance of coca and gold panning, the rearmed guerrillas turned to the state for resources, funding

FIGURE 5.1. The FARC graffiti reads: "When injustice becomes law, rebellion is a right. FARC-EP, 57 years of struggle for the people." Sporadic revolutionary messaging notwithstanding, locals do not consider the rearmed guerrillas to be ideologically motivated.

themselves through extortion payments known as *vacunas* (literally, vaccines). The guerrillas demanded regular *vacunas* from the municipal administration in addition to their share of all public works projects, backed by threats of violence and property destruction. They also resumed violently imposing law and order.

But authority was not the only issue facing Briceño. Shortly after the guerrilla demobilization, the coca substitution program eliminated the economy that had sustained the community. Program beneficiaries who entered as coca cultivators or noncultivators received a yearlong monthly subsidy, softening the economic blow. However, those who had worked as *raspachines* were not so lucky. Like Dideison, those who entered as coca pickers experienced major delays due to lengthy contracting processes (see chapter 2). These were the lucky ones, however. Many of the *raspachines* were excluded entirely because they were under eighteen years of age. The result was a critical mass of young men with no land of their own, accustomed to earning a regular wage, who were left with nothing.

This population represented a fertile terrain of potential recruits for the newly rearmed FARC guerrillas, who not only offered status but began paying their troops—something they had never done before the peace process. In Dideison's community and in neighboring areas, far more young men joined the guerrillas in a shorter time than they ever had done before the peace process.

Dideison had no interest in joining. But with no jobs available in Briceño, he left for a year to work with his uncle assembling prefabricated homes around Colombia. By 2019 he was back, working in a municipal job, entering the world of local politics, and continuing to wait for substitution program benefits.

✳ ✳ ✳

Two days after Dideison calls Rodrigo, the jailed FARC commander, he receives another anonymous phone call. The caller identifies himself as a friend of the young men who were after Dideison. This time, however, the voice on the line isn't threatening. Instead, the man apologizes for the misunderstanding. He asks Dideison whether his friends are likely to face guerrilla recrimination. Is it safe, he wants to know, for them to stay in the village? Dideison says that as far as he's concerned, the matter is resolved.

Rodrigo texts Dideison to make sure he's had no further problems. Even from jail, Rodrigo has demonstrated the guerrillas' continuing authority. Nevertheless, he offers a further recommendation—one that may be surprising to political theorists who see in the guerrillas' problem-solving a means of consolidating their authority at the expense of the state. He tells Dideison to visit the police station to file a formal complaint for the threats and for the assault on his brother. Turn not only to us as the local authority, he seems to be saying, but to the formal state as well.

Introduction

MR. PRESIDENT, A CORDIAL GREETING FROM US. THIS MESSAGE IS FOR THE FOLLOWING. FROM TODAY ONWARD, EVERYONE OLDER THAN 14 HAS TO JOIN THE COMMUNITY ACTION BOARD. ANYONE WHO REFUSES CAN'T BE IN THE HAMLET. THIS IS AN ORDER. ALSO, THERE IS A PERIOD OF 15 DAYS FOR EVERYONE TO PAY OFF THEIR DEBTS TO THE COMMUNITY ACTION BOARD. ALSO, BEGINNING NOW, UNKNOWN PEOPLE AREN'T PERMITTED IN THE AREA. IF THEY COME, THEY MUST BRING THEIR RESUME SIGNED BY THE PRESIDENT CERTIFYING THAT THE PERSON DOESN'T HAVE BAD INTENTIONS, NOR IS AN ENEMY. IF THEY DON'T HAVE THIS LETTER THEY WILL BE PUT UNDER OUR DISPOSITION.

Eduardo laughs as I finish reading the all-caps message on his cell phone, sent by Cabuyo, the leader of the rearmed FARC guerrillas. "*Esa gente* [literally, "those people," an expression commonly used to refer to the guerrillas] really fix up the communities." After the FARC disarmed, Eduardo tells me, his job as community president got harder. Local participation in *convites*, communal work groups usually directed to fix their road, dropped off. Eduardo continued to charge fines to those who skipped out, but without the guerrillas going to collect, most people ignored them. The message represents a call to order as well as a claim to authority.

"Some people like them being involved, others don't," Eduardo says. "But the community is working better since they came back."

In a classic text, Phillip Corrigan and Derek Sayer (1985) describe the historical formation of state power as an "immensely long, complicated, laborious micro-construction and reconstruction of appropriate forms of power" (1985, 203) in which state actors extended their influence to new spheres of social life, determining how people went about getting married, transporting themselves, and educating their children. Corrigan and Sayer argue that this represented as much a cultural as a political revolution, as people gradually began living their lives in state-determined ways—and alternatives became unthinkable. Scholars like Mara Loveman (2005) have shown that this transformation often involved concrete struggles with other contenders for authority, in which state agents imitated, co-opted, or usurped the administrative practices of nonstate authorities such as religious officials.

In places like Briceño, these processes of state formation are unresolved, as alternatives to state authority are not only thinkable but in many cases common sense. For someone like Dideison, there was little question that he would turn to the FARC, as he and his community had done for his whole life, in the face of violence. But this is not to say that the guerrillas have vanquished the state as the local authority. As I will describe in the next chapter, campesinos draw on clientelist relationships with local politicians to access work, education, and resources for home improvement. Locals visit the public hospital, send their children to public schools, and vote for mayor. And communities like that of Eduardo rely on the guerrillas to enforce participation in communal road maintenance while simultaneously turning to state officials to send municipal machinery to fix periodic landslides on the same road.

As I've described throughout this book, the state has become increasingly consequential to local lives and livelihoods, assuming some of the functions originally performed by the guerrillas. However, this transformation, critical to the success of the peace process and to Colombia's prospects of overcoming decades of violence, is incomplete, ongoing, and contested. In this chapter I describe what it means to live between two competing authorities, and how the roles performed by each are worked out in everyday life. Ultimately, I show, each group's ability to govern rests on local communities' choices—driven by practical concerns and collective processes of meaning making—to turn to the state or to guerrillas to resolve their pressing problems and set the rules of everyday life.

The first section explains the historical context of FARC governance, still critical to the local collective memory of the guerrillas as a useful group for the community. I describe how the guerrillas historically established governance practices by controlling theft and violence in rural areas that had never had an authority figure. I then discuss how community relationships with the FARC changed with the era of violence occasioned by the entry of paramilitaries. Finally, I turn to the rearmed guerrillas, describing how local understandings of the group hold the state responsible for the economic collapse and military violence that push young men to join.

The second section asks how communities come to turn to either the FARC or the state to fulfill governance practices. In contrast to literature that describes competing claimants to authority as locked in a bloody zero-sum battle for territorial control, I describe the often surprising entanglements between FARC and state power. I then analyze the bare heads of Briceño's motorcyclists, explaining how guerrilla helmet prohibitions came to trump national state law, which requires helmet use.

Finally, I describe the silent and invisible manifestations of guerrilla authority: motorcycles passing in the night, the hidden threat of land mines, and even local linguistic customs that demonstrate the power of the guerrillas through the very fact that they cannot be named. I analyze local responses to the guerrillas' murder of two sisters to describe how people make sense of violence, and the consequences for local authority.

"A Useful Group": The Historical Production of Guerrilla Authority

Those old enough to remember the period before the FARC entered Briceño describe a Hobbesian state of nature in which the lack of an authority figure exposed local communities to theft and violence. In early 2020 I spend a day with Eladio, the unofficial village historian, who at seventy-seven has a detailed memory of events of decades past. "Before the guerrilla, this area was very complicated," he says as we sit on the patio of his home in El Orejón, looking out over the Cauca River. The theft of mules and cows was a major problem, he explains. With no police or armed group to turn to, people either had to accept the loss of their animals or go after the thieves themselves.

Another issue was violence arising from disputes between neighbors. Briceño even had its own version of the Hatfield-McCoy feud, beginning with a disagreement over corn. Eladio explains that in 1971, one farmer asked his neighbor to loan him corn kernels for planting. When harvest came around and the neighbor went to collect, the farmer who had borrowed the corn accused him of taking too much. An argument led to violence, and one murder led to spiraling cycles of retributive violence that spread through the two men's families. By the time they made peace two years later, sixty-two people were dead.

When the FARC came to Briceño around 1981, it conducted what is known in Colombia as a *limpieza social* (social cleansing), killing or displacing known criminals and troublemakers. The community, Eladio says, quickly embraced the FARC as the local authority: "For any problem, we would call the guerrillas to solve it. If a marriage went wrong, we called the guerrillas. If a kid was misbehaving and wouldn't let the teacher teach class, we called the guerrillas. They went to the school to get the kids to behave. So we looked at them as a useful group. Because they were the presence of the law in the face of state absence." At that time the municipality had a small police force, but it did not stray from the village center.

The FARC organized communities, pushing them to form community action boards and hold *convites*, days of collective labor that went to fixing the local paths or to agricultural work like harvesting a large crop of beans. If someone didn't participate, the guerrillas would visit them to impose a fine, giving the money to the community action board. They also established a minimum wage, forcing landowners to increase the salaries paid to agricultural laborers.

Though the guerrillas began as outsiders, local young men and women periodically joined the group, deepening ties between the FARC and the community. Though I have no systematic data about why, who, or how many people joined, campesinos I asked usually described these decisions as emerging from a lack of other opportunities, a desire for status, or a means of escaping difficult home situations. One example is a fifteen-year-old girl who joined to get away from her abusive father.

Finally, the FARC organized meetings in which the guerrillas discussed what Eladio refers to as their "social message: that the country has an affluent class that is seizing the labor of the worker, the campesino. They get rich while we stay poor. And that the work of the people will never be valued, we will never have nice homes, health, education. That the people have to wake up [*concientizarse*] and take control of the government through armed struggle."

Eladio says, however, that over time the group became less revolutionary and more oriented toward military and economic objectives. This transformation matched the FARC's depoliticization on a national level, and escalated locally with the entry of coca and the paramilitaries to Briceño in the late 1990s (see chapter 1). Calls to revolution were replaced by meetings in which the guerrillas warned campesinos against selling coca or giving information to paramilitaries. The FARC now killed and displaced not only criminals, but also those accused of being paramilitary collaborators or selling their coca to outside buyers. The guerrillas began laying land mines, resulting in multiple tragic accidents like the explosion in El Orejón, described in chapter 2, that killed one young woman and wounded ten community members. For a time, they would even take positions in the hillsides above the village center and shoot downward toward the police station in the main square—traditionally the center of village social life—multiple times a week.

A period of intense fighting between the FARC and paramilitaries settled around 2004 into an informal compromise in which the two groups split up the municipality through invisible and shifting borders. The paramilitaries were often supported by the military and the police, who referred to them as their "cousins" based on their common enemy, the FARC. In 2013 testimony before a tribunal, Briceño's paramilitary leaders confirmed that they had both coordinated actions with the military and paid a regular salary to police officers (Ramírez 2018, 217–21). Gañote, the former paramilitary commander in Briceño, testified: "For me, the authority [in Briceño] was me. The police commanders did whatever I said" (Ramírez 2018, 220; translation mine).

Even in this context of intensified violence, the FARC maintained and the paramilitaries established practices to make themselves useful to the community. Each group organized *convites* and controlled theft and violence within its territory. Both groups also regulated the coca economy, which grew to dominate the municipality. However, the ongoing war pushed locals away from the danger of associating too closely with either armed group. The paramilitaries were particularly violent, notorious for maintaining lists of people they would kill, engaging in sexual violence against local women, and driving around in a black truck they would force people to enter, never to be seen again. Nevertheless, unlike the guerrillas, they paid their troops—and attracted local recruits as a result.

The dynamics of paramilitary control changed following a massive state-sponsored paramilitary demobilization negotiated with the Uribe government from 2003 to 2006. As in many other areas, paramilitaries in Briceño quickly reorganized to maintain their violent territorial control and their participation in cocaine trafficking. Nevertheless, these residual groups saw their cash flow disrupted. Paramilitaries began buying coca with *vales*, handwritten IOUs that farmers often had to wait months to cash in. And though police and military collaboration with paramilitaries didn't disappear entirely, paramilitary groups were rebranded by the government as "criminal bands" subject to military attack. While earlier paramilitaries had brazenly purchased coca and carried their weapons in the village center, now they hid away in rural areas. The most high-profile example of their changing status—and further evidence that the impact of armed groups on community livelihoods is critical to their ability to establish territorial control—was an incident around 2012, when community members fed up with having to sell coca to paramilitaries for IOUs gave information about their location to the military. Taken by surprise, roughly a dozen paramilitaries were caught by a military troop. They raised their hands in surrender, but the soldiers opened fire, killing them all.

When the peace process came to Briceño, it found a local population that was tired of years of horrific violence and which deeply desired a state that promised peace and progress. But Briceño's rural communities also had decades of experience turning to armed groups, and particularly the guerrillas, as the local authorities and problem solvers. This set of collective habits and memories would inform community behavior toward the guerrilla force that rearmed in late 2017.

THE REARMED GUERRILLAS

Cabuyo is the nom de guerre of one of the men who represented the FARC in the land mine removal program in El Orejón. Formerly a middle-level officer and explosives expert, he helped disarm mines for two years until early 2017, when he went with other FARC fighters to live in the FARC demobilization camp in nearby Anorí, Antioquia. Less than a year later, he abandoned the peace process, returning to Briceño to found and head a rearmed FARC guerrilla front. One of that group's first actions was to kill three outsiders rumored to be paramilitaries in an outlying area. This action, like the subsequent killing of the gold mine employees I described in the previous chapter, was sometimes invoked by locals who understood the guerrillas as defending the community.

In Colombia, the FARC groups that continued to exist after the peace process are known as *la disidencia* (the dissidents). They include guerrillas who either never disarmed, rearmed after initially disarming, or joined after the peace process. By 2021 they included at least thirty distinct fronts, though they lack the strong central command structure that characterized the FARC before the peace agreement (CORE 2021). They eventually split into two distinct groups, the New Marquetalia and the Central General Staff, that have at times battled each other for territorial control. Military reports state that

Briceño's group began with only 30 men in late 2017, though by July 2018 its membership had risen to more than 285—reportedly the largest guerrilla front in the history of Antioquia (Monsalve Gaviria 2018). The group's presence spread to include not only Briceño but parts of neighboring villages.

While many accounts describe the rearmed FARC guerrillas as longtime combatants who soured on the peace process (e.g., Casey 2019), the group's rapid growth in Briceño was a function of fresh recruits, rather than one of longtime guerrillas who abandoned the peace process. Rural communities were thus dismayed not only at the guerrillas' reappearance, but also by the unprecedented numbers of youth who joined. Community members reported that these recruits were young men left desperate by the collapse of the coca economy, which had excluded them from any chance at paid labor. One man told me they were "kids from coca-producing families, so they would have been working in the coca, but not anymore. The group is fueling itself from that void, that crisis that families are experiencing. Families have four hungry kids. [The guerrillas] say, 'Come, we'll pay you, give you food.'"

In the introduction to this book, I explained that in the face of widespread death and desertion, Colombia's armed groups have sustained themselves only through a steady flow of new recruits—and further, that a large supply of desperate young men without better options is a precondition for internal conflict across the world. The sudden disappearance of Briceño's coca economy illuminates social processes linking economic exclusion to conflict that are usually more gradual—how exclusion from the possibility of making a living through either wage labor or agricultural markets can turn joining an armed group into a viable livelihood strategy. And just as electoral competition and a variety of peace projects established relationships between community members and state officials (see chapters 2, 6, and 7), local recruitment by the rearmed guerrillas created direct ties to communities who now had sons, daughters, and neighbors in the groups—ties they drew on to gather information, convey orders, and ultimately to govern.

Most community members were dismayed by the high recruitment rates, fearing the loss of loved ones. Yet it is critical to note that public narratives making sense of this phenomenon often held the state responsible—both for the economic collapse attributed to the broken commitments of coca substitution, and for the actions of soldiers who, in attempting to wrest control of Briceño from the guerrillas, repeatedly abused local young men. This situation came to a head in a tragic incident that occurred as I was beginning my first extended period of fieldwork in May 2018.

As dusk fell one evening, a thirty-nine-year-old campesino named Gabriel Ángel Rodriguez was returning home on a mule, accompanied by two friends. The three men had traveled to the village center to receive their final coca substitution program subsidy payment. They plodded along, talking, as the shadows lengthened along the rocky route. Shortly after six, they approached a group of soldiers armed with semiautomatic rifles. They greeted the soldiers; and in response, the soldiers opened fire. The mules took off running, throwing two of the men to the ground—probably saving their lives, they told me later. Gabriel Ángel was shot in the chest and died instantly.

The community was outraged, holding two demonstrations to demand accountability. The FARC guerrillas encouraged local participation—even, a local leader told me later, surreptitiously taking attendance. People talked about the murder in two ways: first, as only another example of military abuse and stigmatization, and evidence of how, as Eduardo said when he took the stage at one of the rallies, "all our lives we've been marked as guerrillas." Second, locals invoked the killing to explain why young men were joining the guerrillas.

Oscar, a thirty-four-year-old man with a wife and two children, says his family prevents him from joining the guerrillas, though under the prevailing conditions of military persecution and violence, he understands the choice others make to join: "We, because of our children, our families, [won't join], but another person, with this persecution—I would go off with [the guerrillas] if I didn't have my family. At least if we were in the guerrillas, we would have someone to protect us. Or be able to be shot fighting. What happened to Gabriel Ángel causes a lot of indignation." The killing was only the most visible incident in a series of military abuses that became common practice in areas of Briceño that were historically associated with the guerrillas.

On a sunny afternoon in July 2018, I sit on a porch in one such hamlet with four mothers and Jimmy, a young man from the community. Jimmy tells the story of a time he was taken to the police station because he had left his identification card at home. "They asked me where I worked," he says. "I told them I lived in Los Pinos, but there's no work there, so I travel wherever I can find anything. When they heard 'Los Pinos,' they said, You could be a guerrilla.' For them, everyone is a guerrilla. In the end, they're going to kill all of us."

Jimmy's story unleashes a flood of testimony from the mothers present. Luz talks about how her son was slapped in the face by soldiers who stopped him on his way home from a soccer game. Andrea says that soldiers have been visiting schools, offering kids lollipops for information about the guerrillas. Carolina tells a story of two young men who were traveling to a plot of land they owned in a nearby hamlet to vaccinate some calves. Soldiers stopped them, pointed their guns at them, and made them turn around. They couldn't return for three days until the army left.

"What can we do?" Andrea asks. Her tone is desperate. "Our boys are bored, they don't have work, they're angry, they're desperate."

"Three from this community have already joined [the rearmed guerrillas]," says Luz.

"I have good boys," says Carolina. "And *gracias a Dios* they can find a little work here and there. But I don't want to think about what would happen if they joined."

✳ ✳ ✳

The tense climate of military abuse and rapid recruitment to the rearmed guerrillas dissipated somewhat as my fieldwork continued. For one thing, most of the young men who were going to join the guerrillas in the wake of coca's disappearance did so relatively quickly. For another, the local military commander, by all accounts an unscrupulous tyrant, was replaced by a man who had more interest in building positive relationships with the community. The army and the guerrillas settled into a tense coexistence interrupted by occasional outbreaks of violence.

The very existence of the rearmed guerrillas is a black mark on the promises of peace, pointing to ongoing FARC control, a substitution program that has failed to develop legal economies and has undermined local faith in state power, and a military that terrorizes rather than protects community members. However, just as the rearmed guerrillas have preserved many of the practices that originally made them a useful group for the community, so too have state power and resources become necessary to people's lives. The FARC and the state, therefore, both perform authority functions. While this sometimes brings them into competition, their distinct authority practices are often intertwined in surprising ways. These entanglements, and the complex ways in which authority and governance are worked out in everyday life, are the subject of the next section.

Entangled Authorities

In 2022, the coordinator of the municipality's Office of Community Development visits El Orejón to help them update their bylaws. She asks those present to vote to establish several rules: how much discretionary budget to give the president to spend before requiring a community vote, whether attendance at meetings is mandatory, and what sanctions they will level against people who miss *convites*.

When they get to the last point, the meeting breaks down into accusations of who has been shirking their responsibilities to fix the road. While it continues organizing *convites*, the community has split the road into different sections, three families responsible for each. Some have been taking the task more seriously than others. "If they don't want to fix the road," says a man named Edgar, referring to a group that has left its section derelict, "let's call *esa gente* [those people, which everyone present knows is a reference to the guerrillas] to handle it."

In response, several community members start yelling over each other, some in favor of the idea, others offended. The municipal employee, eager to establish the bylaws and begin the two-hour trip back to the village center, interrupts. "So what do you want to put as the sanctions for missing a *convite*?" she asks.

Edgar speaks up again. "The only way to make that work is with the guerrillas."

As Estefanía Ciro (2019, 177) has pointed out, conflict-affected Colombian territories are more likely to suffer not from a lack of legality but from an excess of laws imposed by distinct actors. Along these lines, the El Orejón meeting seems to show the collision of two different rule-makers and enforcers: the state, with an employee seeking to establish bylaws for the organization of collective labor, and the guerrillas, invoked by Edgar as the only authority able to make people pull their weight. However, if we look a little closer into this and similar incidents, the collision begins to look a lot more like an entanglement. The maintenance of community roads, a pressing problem of rural communities, is resolved through collective campesino labor articulated with two distinct authorities: the guerrillas, who enforce participation, and state officials, who help set bylaws and provide tools and other resources.

There are many spheres of social life in which authority roles in Briceño are clearly demarcated; only the state provides education and health care, while in rural communities like El Orejón where the police are barred from entering, it is unquestionably the guerrillas who control theft and violence. However, guerrilla and state power are often entangled, with governance, provision of public goods, and even local politics taking place through the combination of guerrilla and state authority.

A few examples illustrate the point. The municipal office of child and family services (*comisaría de familia*), receives reports of a local man who has been sexually assaulting girls in an isolated rural hamlet. They provide psychological treatment to the victims, but tell inhabitants to report the problem to the FARC to deal with the sexual predator. When Covid-19 hits, the municipality establishes social distancing protocols. The guerrillas push the resistant community to follow the protocols. Community members periodically complain to the FARC that state officials or community presidents are stealing state funds or otherwise are not fulfilling their responsibilities. The guerrillas investigate and call the accused party to a meeting in the jungle, using the threat of violence to restrain state corruption.

The guerrillas' major funding source, in a village where coca has mostly disappeared, even represents an entanglement. Much as campesino livelihoods have become increasingly tied to state resources, so too does the re-armed FARC depend on extorting the lucrative public works projects that have begun to enter Briceño in the peace process era. As a result, it has become increasingly active in local politics. During the 2023 mayoral election, it barred multiple mayoral hopefuls from participating, charged candidates money for the right to participate, and repeatedly called candidates to meetings in remote areas where it warned them against negative campaigning, among other things. Not only would it be dangerous to ignore the FARC's demands, but politicians know that effective governance depends on maintaining a working relationship with the guerrillas. "You need to have a relationship with that group," one mayoral candidate told me. "Not as an accomplice," he clarified. "But there's a thin line you have to walk, to stay out of legal trouble but also stay on the good side of the guerrillas, so you can govern."

In many cases, the guerrillas also push people to treat the state as an authority figure. In the story above, the jailed FARC commander resolves the dangerous misunderstanding faced by Dideison, but then tells him to file a police report. After seeing soldiers camped out at the local school and in the corridors of campesinos' homes, the guerrillas send a handwritten letter to the president of the community. They inform her that the soldiers are legally required to camp at least one hundred meters away from communities, telling her to turn to the local ombudsman (*personero*, a state official) for help in making the soldiers leave. Their call for state-sponsored legal means, however, ends with a veiled threat: "Don't forget that we are still at war and you as community decide if you want [the soldiers] close or far away. Don't say afterward that you weren't warned."

Finally, the guerrillas also push community members to organize and participate in demonstrations that make claims on the state around a variety of issues: in response to the military killing of an innocent campesino, as detailed above; to demand the substitution program's promised resources; and against coca eradication, as described in chapter 1. Indeed, when Alberto, as described in chapter 2, scuttled local plans for a road blockage against the failings of coca substitution, the FARC called him to a jungle meeting to hold him accountable. In some cases, these protests may help the guerrillas meet their own goals, like getting rid of coca eradicators. However, they are also efforts to help the community struggle for a *better* state, one that fulfills local needs without abusing campesinos—a state, presumably, that would more effectively establish its authority.

As the political scientist Paul Staniland (2012) has pointed out, most work on areas with opposing armed actors assumes that these groups are locked in a direct zero-sum struggle for the monopoly of violence (see, for example, Kalyvas 2006; Kernaghan 2009; Stoll 1993). These accounts treat contested territory as a giant game of Risk: competing violent actors seek to destroy each other and establish their own unquestioned authority within a given region. Ana Arjona (2016), writing about the context of Colombia, has described how governance practices fit into these struggles. She argues that groups like the FARC seek to elicit civilian cooperation and consolidate territorial control through establishing what she calls rebelocracy, a series of statelike practices including resolving disputes, regulating economic activity, and providing security and public goods. When multiple groups try to establish these practices, we may expect, as Winifred Tate (2015, 133) has written of southern Colombia, a situation of "multiple projects of rule vying openly with one another" in seeking to establish their own "competing norms and policies."

While this work explains why the FARC, state, and paramilitaries have long sought to perform governance functions in Briceño, it leaves little room for understanding the entanglements through which the rearmed guerrillas and the state do not compete but rather govern together. These entanglements, indeed, exist in many conflict-affected regions. María Clemencia Ramírez (2015, 43) argues that across Colombia, the FARC historically pivoted to seeking to establish not a counterstate but rather, in the words of longtime FARC commander Manuel Marulanda, a "government within the government" that opposed military actors while supervising local state officials to ensure that they provided for the population's needs (see also Peñaranda Currie et al. 2021 on the symbiotic relationships that developed between FARC, state, and community). And Staniland (2012, 244) has shown that in internal conflicts around the world, opposing armed groups often negotiate their coexistence on the basis of political interests beyond simply destroying the enemy: "States and insurgents are not simple-minded maximizers of monopoly but instead are optimizers of authority in complex, often counterintuitive, interaction with other armed actors."

However, there is still a missing piece of the puzzle, an additional party to this authority-determining interaction. Only rarely do state actors meet with guerrillas to determine who will do what in the task of governing Briceño. Instead, it is community members who choose which authority to turn to for help with a particular problem, or which set of rules to follow and which to disregard. Like most human behavior, these decisions are not deliberated on a day-to-day basis, but rather harden into collective habits that become common sense, like Edgar's assertion that the guerrillas are "the only way to make [collective labor] work." Following Corrigan and Sayer's (1985) description of state formation as a cultural revolution through which state actors insert themselves in all sorts of everyday behaviors, these commonsense habits are central to the establishment (or not) of state power. Thus, the question of how practices of turning to one authority or another are established and potentially transformed is critical. For an answer, I turn to local practices around motorcycle use.

HELMETS, PAPERS, AND THE EVERYDAY CONSTRUCTION OF AUTHORITY

In early June 2018, barely two weeks into my first extended fieldwork stint, I ride my motorcycle back to Briceño's village center from a meeting in a rural hamlet. I park in the main square and remove my helmet. Enrique, a city councilman with whom I've spoken about village politics, greets me warmly. "*Amigo*, where are you coming from?" he asks.

After I tell him, he gives me some advice: "When you travel to rural areas, don't wear a helmet." He explains that the guerrillas don't allow the use of helmets in Briceño; they want to be able to identify who is passing through the territory. The guerrillas' prohibition directly opposes national law, which requires helmets for all motorcycle riders and passengers. In Briceño, however, no one uses helmets. Nor, from this day on, do I.

Throughout this book, I have drawn on scholarly work that describes rule as achieved through people's everyday behaviors and livelihood strategies, based on the state's ability to insert itself in the "rituals and routines of daily life" (Corrigan and Sayer 1985, 197). Tellingly, when theorists of the formation and operation of state power in everyday life seek concrete examples, they turn to roads. The state's authority is expressed and created, these authors have argued, when its subjects stop at red lights (Bourdieu 2014, 166; Migdal 2001, 252) or use a driver's license (Sayer 1994). Roads may even provide the stage for one authority figure to assert its claims over another: an element of Argentine dictator Leopoldo Galtieri's ill-fated 1982 attempt to seize the Falkland Islands from the English was that of forcing motorists there to switch to driving on the right side of the road (Corrigan and Sayer 1985, 196). In similar terms, the bared heads of Briceño's motorcyclists emerge from a concrete struggle over the authority to determine everyday behavior.

A missing license plate gives me the opportunity to learn how helmets came to be excluded from the village's legal landscape. One day, I return to my apartment on my motorcycle to find that my plate has been jarred loose by Briceño's dirt roads. Getting a new license plate means riding the bike—an act illegal without the plate—five hours to the transit office where it was registered in Medellín, waiting in long lines to order a new plate, and waiting for it to come in before riding back. Friends suggest that I ask for help from Briceño's transit official, an affable man named Alfonso.

Sure enough, that same day I see Alfonso on the street. We sit and have a coffee as he explains what he can do for me: order a new license plate to be delivered to the village for twenty-five dollars. The process will take a month and seems dubiously legal, but will save me a lot of trouble. In the meantime, he tells me, I can ride around Briceño without problems—though if I'm caught outside the village, in regions with more clearly established state authority, the bike will be impounded. I agree, handing Alfonso the money.

Feeling positively elated to be free of the bureaucratic headache and united by our complicity in an extralegal transaction, I ask Alfonso about the nonenforcement of helmet laws. He tells me that when he came to Briceño in 2017, he was the village's first transit official. He immediately started enforcing the helmet law. "People complained that they had never used helmets," he tells me. The community went so far as to organize a protest, with sixty people riding their motorcycles in bareheaded protest. Still, many began wearing helmets as the military and police supported him in setting up checkpoints in the village center to ticket those who disobeyed the helmet law.

But then the guerrillas stepped in. They began stopping riders in rural areas, telling them to take their helmets off. People started wearing helmets in the village center and stashing them when they traveled to the countryside.

Dideison described his experience with a military checkpoint just outside the village center, where he was stopped for not wearing a helmet: "I told them, 'I'm not going to let myself get killed. You can give me a ticket if you want.' There were eight motorcycles stopped like this for more than a half hour. And we were all refusing to wear helmets. The commander was trying to figure out what was happening, but no one would tell him. Until finally, one man did. He said: 'Maybe they'll kill me for saying this, but the guerrillas aren't permitting helmets.'"

The conflict between authority figures was resolved, Alfonso tells me, when the guerrillas sought him out, taking him on motorcycle—with no helmets!—to a jungle meeting. "They said, '*Patrón*, we'll help you with the drunks, with accidents, with kids riding motorcycles, but not with helmets. We don't want infiltrators.'" The guerrillas told him that several men, their faces hidden under helmets with black-tinted visors, had recently ridden into the territory on motorcycles to execute three young men. The helmet prohibition was nonnegotiable. "We're in a territory where the guerrillas are in charge," Alfonso says, shrugging. "And besides, no one in the communities wants to wear helmets." He met with the mayor, police, and military, and together they decided to let the helmet issue go.

Helmet requirements, however, are not the only transit laws being flouted in Briceño. Most motorcycles in Briceño—80 percent, Alfonso tells me—don't have "papers": legally required accident insurance and certification that the motorcycle has passed a technical revision, which in 2021 had a combined annual price of roughly two hundred dollars.[1] And even if people had the money to get "papers," most of the village's motorcycles aren't even registered in their owners' names—instead, they've been passed along in a series of informal purchases that were never registered with the state.

"And what a stupid thing [*que chimbada*] for me to worry about all this," Alfonso says. "Think of a poor campesino with a sick child, and no public transport to the village. And he comes here for a medication. For me to take away his motorcycle [for lack of papers]. The mayor even told me, 'If you take people's motorcycles, you're going to earn yourself a problem.' It's just too expensive for the poor to do everything correctly."

I murmur my assent. Indeed, the yearly cost of motorcycle insurance and technical revision is roughly what a full-time worker in Briceño's stores makes in a month.

"You know," Alfonso continues, "if anyone here is organized with papers, it's *esos muchachos*" ["those boys," a reference to the FARC]. The rearmed guerrillas, he tells me, often solicit his help with their paperwork, just as I'm doing with the license plate. "They make sure to have their papers in order, to avoid problems."

✳ ✳ ✳

The nonenforcement of transit law in Briceño speaks to three elements of how rival claims for authority are worked out in daily life. First, the threat of violence lies behind any armed group command, giving it a weight that the dictates and tickets of state officials lack. While state power is always underpinned by coercion, the residents of Briceño all know multiple stories of people who have been killed for disobeying the guerrillas' orders. So long as the guerrillas have both the ability and willingness to exercise violence, even state officials like Alfonso—himself a member of the community—must fall in line.

Second, local decisions about how to relate to different authorities matter. The implied threat of guerrilla violence was clearly the determining factor in persuading the state actors to scuttle local enforcement of helmet laws, but local protests also influenced their willingness to do so. And even if Alfonso were inclined to check motorcycle "papers," a collective refusal to pay astronomical insurance and certification prices makes imposing this requirement impossible. As the mayor told him, attempting to enforce the rules would have earned Alfonso a personal problem; state officials have little hope of enforcing laws that local communities see as illegitimate. Recall Eduardo's story recounted in the introduction to this book, about when community members simply did not allow the military to arrest the FARC-supported coca buyer. And like the campesinos who betrayed cash-poor paramilitaries who forced them to sell their coca for IOUs, community members may even defy armed groups when they begin to see their rule as illegitimate.

Third, as different authority figures become entangled, state officials themselves are implicated in the recognition and reproduction of guerrilla power—and vice versa. The bare heads of Briceño's motorcyclists provide public evidence of the extent to which the guerrillas, and not the state, are able to set the rules of daily life and produce consent to their rule (Beetham 1991; Corrigan and Sayer 1985). This consent has eventually come even from state officials. And while the guerrillas pushed Alfonso to give up enforcement of helmet laws, they offered to help him enforce other legal prohibitions. They are also, paradoxically, among the few community members who actually follow state law in keeping their motorcycle papers in order.

An understanding of the state and the guerrillas as two opposing forces bent on destroying and undermining each other's authority is woefully inadequate for describing how authority is established in everyday life. Instead, authority emerges through the entangled decisions of community members, state officials, and guerrillas alike—decisions that are primarily rooted in such practical concerns as keeping roads passable, making a living, maintaining order, and avoiding violence.

Invisible and Silent Authority

At 9:30 on a pitch-black night, I sit with Eugenia, Suso, and their children watching a fictionalized TV series chronicling the life of the famed Colombian *vallenato* singer Diomedes Diaz. We hear motorcycles passing by outside. I follow Eugenia and her oldest son Adrián out to their patio and we see the lights of three bikes drive by on the road above.

"What a fright," Eugenia says. "*Esa gente* [the guerrillas] going back and forth."

"Why, Ma?" Adrián asks. "*Ellos* [they] are not going to do anything to us."

More than unusual, traffic at this time of night is dangerous. The rearmed FARC has prohibited traveling on the roads after 6 p.m., a prohibition it enforces by sporadically setting land mines on Briceño's roads at night, removing them by morning. Only the guerrillas themselves could know whether the roads are safe.

This relatively unremarkable experience offers a broader lesson about the production of guerrilla authority in Briceño. While state authority is often (re)produced through ultra-visible spectacle and pageantry (Hansen and Stepputat 2001), guerrilla rule is largely expressed through its *in*visibility and silence: motorcycles passing in the night, land mines hidden below the earth, and even common linguistic practices that refer to the guerrillas as *esa gente* or *ellos* rather than naming them directly.

Behind guerrilla rule is a violence that, despite being mostly invisible, marks everyday life. Over three years in Briceño, I witnessed not one act of physical violence. The specter of violence nevertheless influenced much of my fieldwork. I kept track of time to avoid being caught on the road past curfew, I checked in with communities I planned to visit to ensure that I could travel to them safely, I left my motorcycle helmet at home, and I learned to speak euphemistically and in low tones about the guerrillas. I learned what Nicolás Espinosa (2007) calls a social grammar created by violence: a series of implicit rules, configured and reproduced through campesinos' daily practices, that over time become common sense.

However, the relationship between silence and violence is paradoxical. On the one hand, violence is profoundly silencing and erasing. On the other, the force of violence depends on the narratives through which people collectively interpret it and experience both pain and terror (Aretxaga 2003; Das 1996). As Timothy Mitchell (2002, 153) has written: "A violence that erased every sign of itself would be remarkably inefficient. . . . To acquire its usefulness in the play of domination, violence must be whispered about, recalled by its victims, and hinted at in future threats. The disappearance or the hidden act of terror gains its force as an absence that is continually made present."

The presence of this absence only deepens with the linguistic custom of not directly naming the guerrillas, part of a more generalized "law of silence" that prohibits discussing armed groups. This was not something anyone explained to me directly. Instead, I quickly noticed that everyone was reluctant to talk about armed groups, and particularly about the rearmed guerrillas. In public settings, my questions about the guerrillas would sometimes make research subjects uncomfortable, and even in private, they would drop their voices and use one of several euphemisms to refer to armed groups: *esa gente* (those people), *los muchachos* (the boys), or simply *ellos* (they or them). While early on in my research I honored these linguistic customs to set my interlocutors at ease, I began to internalize them. Talking about the guerrillas in a public place began to make me uncomfortable.

This and other customs that make up the violence-created social grammar also affect how communities make sense of violence. For an example, I turn again to New Year's Eve, exactly a year before Dideison would turn to the guerrillas for help, in the first hours of 2021. At 4 a.m., several guerrillas carrying assault rifles entered a party in a rural area of Briceño, forcing two sisters, twenty-two and seventeen years old, to leave with them. The guerrillas took the women down the road before shooting them dead. The older sister was a FARC ex-combatant who had demobilized with the peace process.

I observed no public discussions of the murders. However, everyone I asked in private had heard different explanations for the killing, rumors that circulated throughout the village in private and hushed tones. In one version, the older sister had briefly joined a different rearmed FARC group north of Briceño. The killing was her punishment for deserting. In another, the younger sister had previously dated Cabuyo, the guerrilla leader, and was collaborating with the military to help them catch him. A similar story held that the military had tracked her cell phone to set a trap for Cabuyo, even knocking him off his motorcycle before he escaped into the jungle.

Violence destabilizes truth, making a "mockery of sense-making" (Taussig 1986, 132; see also Aretxaga 2005; Kernaghan 2009). However, in explaining the effects of violence, the truth behind violent acts matters less than how they are represented (Aretxaga 2005). Local rumors justified the killing by drawing on the collective memory of the guerrillas as a useful group that used violence to establish law and order. The logic that "it must have been for something" was repeatedly invoked by campesinos to understand guerrilla violence. This opinion was not consensus, as many locals denounced guerrilla violence in all its forms. However, it is noteworthy that similar justifications did not circulate for either paramilitary or state violence—the military's senseless killing of Gabriel Ángel Rodriguez being a prime example.

Even as hushed rumors and accounts of the killing circulated freely within the village, silence was complete in relation to state authorities. Police investigators attempted to interview community members, but everyone feigned ignorance. Dozens of people had been at the party and could have identified the guerrillas who were responsible. And within days, seemingly *everyone* knew secondhand who had been behind the killings. But they also knew enough to stay quiet—whatever their personal opinions on the violence.

The facts behind the killing became a public secret, which Michael Taussig (1999) has defined as a secret that draws power in equal measure from the twin facts that it is generally known and yet cannot be stated. Excluded from this secret, importantly, were state authorities; the police got nowhere in their investigation, and official accounts of the crime had obvious factual errors and omissions. Not only did the violence provide a chilling reminder of what had happened to those who had presumably crossed the guerrillas, but it also provided clear and public evidence of the limits of the state officials' ability to gather information, protect citizens, and monopolize violence within the territory.

Conclusion

Peacebuilding professionals and popular discourse alike commonly assume a clear-cut distinction between conflict and peace, in which peace agreements represent a return to a normal order with unchallenged state authority (Grajales 2021). This paradigm offers no guarantee of the endurance of "normality"; an oft-repeated statistic holds that nearly half of peace agreements end in a return to violence within five years (Högbladh 2012). But even this figure highlights the beguiling simplicity of efforts to evaluate peace agreements: Peace either fails or succeeds; Colombia is either in conflict or at war; Briceño is under the control of either armed groups or the state.

This paradigm breaks down, however, in the face of the lived experiences of real people. Normal, for Briceño's campesinos, has long been guerrilla governance. The peace process has objectively reduced levels of victimization in the village, yet the specter of guerrilla violence continues to influence many elements of daily life. State officials and resources have become newly important to local lives, but without supplanting the guerrillas' authority. There is an understandable temptation to characterize Briceño as undergoing a finite transformation that, when the dust settles, will establish either violence or peace, either guerrilla control or state control. The reality, like much of social life, is messier.

On a national level, rearmed FARC guerrilla groups have been blasted by the Colombian right as evidence of the illegitimacy of the peace agreement and the guerrillas' lack of interest in embracing peace. As in Briceño, however, most of what I've called the "rearmed" guerrillas aren't actually re-armed at all. Of the 5,200 to 5,500 members of the thirty rearmed FARC fronts in 2021, only 795 were estimated to have gone through the demobilization process before rearming, while an additional 800 longtime guerrillas never demobilized (González Perafán et al. 2021; Isacson 2021). The rest—70 percent at minimum—were new recruits. Of the 13,104 FARC members who formally demobilized in 2017, only around 5 percent have joined rearmed groups (González Perafán et al. 2021). As of 2023, most demobilized ex-FARC combatants continue receiving a monthly stipend of 90 percent of the national minimum wage, while more than half have received projects designed to help them develop agricultural livelihoods (Isacson 2021). Given the option, they have chosen to avoid violence.

The issue, then, is to understand why the guerrillas represent a viable career option for rural youth, and why communities continue turning to guerrilla authority. To the first question, economists applying opportunity cost theories of crime have long understood that delinquent behavior is motivated not only by potential rewards, but by a lack of alternatives (Becker 1974). These economists find that a mass of unemployed young men—the direct result of the widespread economic exclusion that has become a central feature of global capitalism—is an excellent predictor of conflict (Collier 2008; Hintjens and Zarkov 2014). Just as plummeting legal agricultural prices driven by changing economic policy drove campesinos to begin cultivating coca, the disappearance of coca and gold panning pushed jobless young men to the ranks of the guerrillas.

But why do rural communities tired of decades of violence keep drawing on the guerrillas as local authorities? The peace process has not only failed to establish profitable legal rural economies to replace coca, but has also failed to establish state authority to replace the FARC. The FARC's 2017 disarmament marked a special opportunity for building state power, as hundreds of municipalities were left without armed groups after decades of guerrilla control. However, as in Briceño, state entities failed to fill the authority void. In part this is a cultural issue: rural populations have years of evidence for why they should not trust state authorities, and particularly the police and military. However, as both Dideison and Eduardo described, state actors were unable to assume the governance functions that had long made the FARC a "useful group" for the community: controlling crime, resolving disputes, and organizing collective labor. On a national level, both rearmed guerrillas and a variety of other armed groups have stepped in to fill this void—particularly when FARC disarmament also left profitable illegal economies like coca and mining up for grabs. These groups' threat of violence establishes a silent and invisible authority that configures the rules of daily life.

The result is a situation of fragmented sovereignty, in which authority and stateness are shared between state officials and armed groups (Staniland 2012). Rather than being locked into a zero-sum struggle for local control, these "opposing" claimants to authority are entangled in unexpected ways, each consenting to and even supporting the authority of the other. While this phenomenon has been observed in conflict-affected regions around the world, the literature has not described how it is established or how it may be transformed. The missing piece, I argue, is an understanding of local livelihood strategies: the everyday actions and preoccupations of communities as they seek to put food on their tables, keep their roads passable, stay safe, and build a better future for their families. Their decisions—to turn to one claimant to authority or another in the face of different problems—reconfigure local dynamics of authority. They provide the basis for evaluating peace- and state-building initiatives like coca substitution or negotiated disarmament. And they offer the possibility for building more peaceful communities whether or not state authority reigns unchallenged.

6

Politics in the Peace Laboratory

Eduardo, Act Two

June 2019: Four months before the vote to determine the village's next mayor, Briceño's social life has been taken over by the election. As I ride my motorcycle to Eduardo's farm, I pass dozens of pasted-on fliers, spray-painted messages, and banners supporting one of the village's two candidates: Wilmar, a charismatic man in his mid-thirties who ran the successful electoral campaign for Cenizo, the current mayor, before a public falling-out; and Pacho, Cenizo's handpicked successor, a slightly older and more reserved man trained in veterinary medicine who has led the municipal office for agricultural technical assistance for more than a decade. Along with political propaganda, I also see progress on the road down to Eduardo's farm, where less than a year ago I fell off my motorcycle. Where before there was slippery loose gravel, a compacter has packed rock and dirt together. The steepest five-hundred-meter section has even been paved. I arrive without incident.

While Eduardo fertilizes his coffee plants in the far corner of his farm, I sit and drink mango juice with his wife, Flor. Our conversation turns to the election. She tells me she supports Wilmar; she likes his proposals and the fact that he's a campesino like them.

"And if he wins," she adds, "he said he'll give me a little house in the village center so our children can study." Their hamlet has only a primary school, meaning that of their three children, the two who have already graduated from fifth grade must leave the house at 6 a.m. and walk an hour uphill to catch a truck at 7 a.m. that takes them to a school in another hamlet. That school, however, only goes through the ninth grade. A home in the village center would allow the children to live there with Flor as they finish their high school education. Eduardo would stay behind on the farm to tend the coffee crops.

When Eduardo arrives, he laughs at our conversation: "Talking about Wilmar again?" He launches into a defense of Pacho, saying that the recently paved section of road is an example of the development Cenizo has brought to the municipality—and, he adds, their hamlet specifically. This wasn't originally the case, he tells me. In the first years of Cenizo's four-year term, he was supposed to execute a project to fix up their community's elementary school, which had fallen into disrepair.

"I don't remember which entity came, because a lot of entities came here," Eduardo says. "But they donated 150 million pesos [fifty thousand dollars] to fix the school." I am not surprised that he can't remember. The peace process has brought dozens of state agencies, NGOs, and international organizations that have funded a range of different programs. In many cases, like this one, the entities funnel money through the municipal administration. The school, however, was not adequately repaired. Rubén, the community president at the time, tried to hold the mayor responsible.

"There was a dispute between them," Eduardo says, "and the hamlet was being neglected [by the municipal government]. I had a good relationship with the mayor, so one time I was there and he said to me, 'If you want, take over [as community president]; I can work well with you, but I can't work with Rubén.' So I came to the community, I made the proposal, and they said, 'Ahh no, Rubén isn't getting anything [from the mayor's office]. We're going to support you.' "

When Eduardo took over as community president, he was able to leverage his relationship with Cenizo to access municipal resources: machinery to maintain the road, the road paving project, and a number of "home improvement" projects (*mejoramientos de viviendas*) in the hamlet. One of these projects added another room to Eduardo and Flor's home. Eduardo feels personally grateful to Cenizo for his help, and knows that Cenizo expects his political support. But like his wife, he also sees his political support as a bet on future resources.

"This is our culture here in Colombia," he says, showing me a video on his phone that has been circulating on WhatsApp. The video explains how corruption works in Colombia: wealthy people come together, choose a political candidate, and invest in their campaign; and when the candidate wins, they bleed the municipality through inflated contracts to recoup their investment. In this context, Eduardo says, the poor also offer political support during elections to guarantee their own share of public resources: "This is how it works. People contribute to the campaign, and the candidate writes it down in a notebook. The person who donated a pig or gave money for alcohol [for campaign events]. After the candidate wins, people go back to him, and they ask for a job or for a project to fix their roof. But the candidates end up prom-ising the same position to fifteen or twenty people. Those are the mayor's offices."

"Are Wilmar and Pacho doing this?" I ask.

"Of course," he says. "Everyone looks for how to make it. The poor have to look [*El pobre tiene que buscar*]."

"Have you spoken with Pacho about what he'll do for you?"

"Up to now, no."

"But will you?"

"The truth is, you have to look," Eduardo replies. "It's the culture of each citizen. I'll support you, but what can I get out of it? Yeah, I'll talk with him, of course."

"And what would you ask for?"

"To have a home in the village center to let my children study."

Eduardo and Flor themselves only studied a few years of elementary school. But even if they don't agree on the candidates, they share a common goal for their children. When their livelihoods depended on coca and gold panning, their lack of formal education was less of a handicap. In this new era, parents like Eduardo and Flor see education as essential to their chil-dren's future. And they depend on relationships with local politicians to ac-cess this education, among a host of other resources.

✶ ✶ ✶

As campaigning continues, it becomes increasingly clear that Wilmar will win. His rallies draw thousands of people, the exterior walls of local homes are covered with images of his face, and his campaign's social media pages share photo after photo of Wilmar posing triumphantly with voters who have newly pledged their support.

Roughly a week before the election, Eduardo himself is publicly tagged as a supporter. The Facebook page of Wilmar's campaign uploads a three-minute video with the caption, "Welcome leader Eduardo! God Bless all the campesinos who are thriving and striving for big dreams!" In the video, Edu-ardo films himself in his coffee fields with one of his neighbors behind him, declaring that he and the rest of his hamlet are now behind Wilmar: "We're here in the hamlet Arboledas and we're going to fully support our candidate Wilmar. He has very good thoughts, good plans, and he's going to transform the countryside. . . . So, Wilmar, from now on, I reaffirm for you that with my community, the hamlet Arboledas, we're 100 percent with you."

I ask Eduardo why he changed his support. His response, in a Whats-App voice message, highlights his responsibility as community president: "I wanted to stay with Pacho until the end, until we lost or won. . . . But if I stay with Pacho, the truth, *hermano*, is that I would have done harm to this community. . . . Wilmar has more people, he's going to win. If I go against him, then on the one hand this hamlet will be more abandoned, and on the other, the community will be mad at me because honestly, I wouldn't have helped them. So for that, *hermanito*, I had to support Wilmar."

Cenizo sends Eduardo a message calling him an ungrateful son-of-a-bitch. But Eduardo's calculation is correct. Wilmar wins in a landslide, and begins his four-year term in January 2020.

* * *

Eduardo's last-second effort to get in the new mayor's good graces, however, is insufficient. In November 2020, he asks me to use my Facebook page to publicize his community's struggles to get help from the local administration. "It's been more than a year since they've sent heavy machinery to do maintenance on our road," he tells me in a WhatsApp voice message. "We've been working on it, holding *convites* to cover holes and creating channels to divert water beside the road. But now it's out of our hands."

Eduardo asks me to post two videos he sends me that show community members attempting to help pull a *chiva* up their steep and muddy road. Brightly painted and built on heavy-duty truck chassis, *chivas* are motorized vehicles with wooden benches inside to seat dozens of people (fig. 6.1). But the most practical feature of a *chiva* is around the border of its roof, where a metal grating rises up more than a foot to let it carry large quantities of goods. The *chiva* only goes to Eduardo's community on Sundays, but the trip is crucial for community members, allowing them to transport agricultural goods for sale, visit the village center, and bring groceries and other products—from heavy bags of fertilizer to washing machines—back to their farms.

However, Eduardo's videos show that even the *chiva* couldn't handle his hamlet's poorly maintained road. In one video, five men pull on a rope attached to the front of the *chiva*. The vehicle belches black smoke as it lurches forward before its wheels spin in the mud and it slides back. In the other, the camera pans left to show that the tow rope is attached to another *chiva* that has gone down the road to try to help pull the first one out.

Eduardo tells me that the publication is directed to Wilmar, who repeatedly publishes Facebook photos taking credit for fixing the municipality's roads: "He likes to show off that the roads are in perfect condition, when it's not true at all. . . . I want to publish [the videos] so people see that it's not like he says. So that he gets to work. Because if we don't have roads, we might as well give up and leave the territory."

FIGURE 6.1. Chivas are the motorized workhorses of rural Colombia.

Eduardo sends me a message to include with the videos, which I post in his name: "Friends and neighbors, this is the daily reality of our roads, a struggle for drivers and farmers who have to risk our lives. We need governmental entities and the municipal administration to send us machines for our road. It's beyond our capacity to fix it, we've already done what we can." I don't ask Eduardo why he wants me to publish the videos for him. It's likely he thinks they will have a greater impact if posted by me, the municipality's lone foreigner, who often publishes articles documenting and analyzing local experiences.

The videos create controversy. One woman comments: "And where are the mayor's machines? He often posts about improving and maintaining the roads. So what happened?"

A man who works in the administration responds: "Every rainy season the same thing happens, the roads get destroyed and the mayor gets blamed."

Then Eduardo: "Of course, but it's because of the little interest he puts into the roads."

Less than two weeks later, Eduardo calls me to say the strategy worked. For the first time in his year in office, the mayor has sent machines to fix the road. The next day, the administration's Facebook page publishes photos of the work. Within two months, however, Eduardo steps down as community president. He tells me that after we posted the videos, multiple people from the administration told him the mayor was unhappy with him over the publication. "He told them he couldn't work with me," he says. "So I started thinking one night that if I'm going to be a stumbling block [*una piedra en la zapata*] for the community, I should resign."

Eduardo knows he has lost any chance of getting a home in the village for his children to study, at least until the next mayor takes over.

✳ ✳ ✳

A few months later, I sit in Coffeebri with Eduardo and Dideison, who are both on the outs with Wilmar and excluded from state resources. They marvel at how important local politics has become. Only a few years ago, Eduardo says, no one paid attention to the mayoral elections: "In that time, campesinos didn't turn to the mayor's office for anything. Coca moved everything, and we had money; we didn't need the mayor."

"No one even voted," Dideison adds. He says that previously, mayors won elections with as few as 900 votes. (In comparison, 2,744 people voted for Wilmar in 2019.) And when they took office, mayors struggled to find people interested in working for the municipal administration, and would have to bring their staff from outside Briceño. "No one cared, because they made more money with coca," says Dideison.

Eduardo agrees. "It's not like now, that everyone is looking for jobs."

Dideison himself had worked for Cenizo's administration in 2019, the only over-the-table, minimum-wage-or-higher job available. Campaigning for Pacho was his primary job responsibility. Upon entering office in 2020, however, Wilmar summarily fired the entire administration, replacing them with his own political supporters, who were themselves desperate for jobs.

Before the disappearance of coca and gold panning, municipal politics was of little importance to campesinos like Eduardo and Dideison. Now, however, political competition is fierce: to win an election to gain control of municipal resources, to secure one of the precious few jobs available, and to gain the favor of a mayor who can fix a precarious stretch of road or repair a leaky roof.

Introduction

On a sunny Saturday afternoon, we take off in a caravan, five motorcycles and a Jeep Montero filled with six passengers. Nearly everyone wears black hats with white script that says *Movilizando Ideas*—"Mobilizing Ideas"—Wilmar's campaign slogan. It's three months before the election. The candidate himself rides shotgun in the Jeep. We drive slowly on the municipality's steep dirt roads, honk enthusiastically at everyone we see, and stop often along the two-hour journey to greet people who live in the houses we pass.

Night is falling when we arrive at the campaign event. While some of his campaign staff distribute lollipops, Wilmar immediately starts making the rounds. Men he greets with a firm handshake; women he hugs and kisses on the cheek. He seems to know everyone's name—later he tells me that of the eight thousand people in the territory, he probably knows five thousand.

As I walk down to the open-air community house where the event will take place, I meet Leo, a forty-five-year-old man who excitedly predicts a victory for Wilmar. I ask what this victory would mean for the community. Leo responds with benefits he hopes to receive individually: "that he'll help me with work and improvements to my house." Leo is upset that the current mayor hasn't lived up to similar promises.

Down the street, four women tend to a massive pot of *sancocho*, a hearty stew of meat, potatoes, and plantains that will comfortably feed the roughly two hundred people at the event. A large stack of wood nearby feeds the fire. Leo tells me the community has donated all the food for the party, including two pigs. They expect that this support will be rewarded when Wilmar wins. Leo tells me that when he asked Cenizo for help in fixing an area in the road that had washed out in a heavy rain, the mayor, who supports the other candidate, brushed him off.

"He told me to ask Wilmar," Leo says. Wilmar has no access to the two machines the municipality owns for fixing roads, but the mayor's implication was clear. Demand for the machines is high in the municipality, where torrential rains frequently wash loose hillsides down onto dirt roads precariously carved into the steep terrain. He wasn't going to waste the municipality's resources on someone who supported Wilmar.

"But how did he know you're with Wilmar?" I ask.

"He caught me [*me pilló*] on Facebook," Leo says, laughing. "They're not going to give us anything until Wilmar enters."

While everyone eats *sancocho*, Wilmar gives a ten-minute speech in which he denounces the current administration for its *politiquería*—which he later defines for me privately as the practice of politics for individual rather than collective gain. He thanks the people of the community for supporting today's event, saying that because of them, he won't be beholden to wealthy donors who would expect their support to be paid back tenfold when he enters office.

After Wilmar's speech ends, a local band takes the stage. Dancing and drinking begin in earnest. I meet Diana, the bandleader's wife, as she serves me fried pork belly. She tells me the band normally gets around three hundred dollars to play at an event like this, but that tonight they're doing it for

free, in the expectation that when Wilmar wins, he'll help fix their instru-
ments and direct municipal funds to hire them for public events. She says
they've already played at six campaign events, all free of charge.

✶ ✶ ✶

Over the last few years, the source of the resources that sustain Briceño has
transformed. With the departure of economies that eluded state intervention, such as coca and gold, came a tidal wave of state resources that swelled
the city coffers. In 2008 the annual municipal budget was three billion pesos (US$1.5 million, based on the 2008 exchange rate). By 2018, it had more
than sextupled to nineteen billion pesos (then about $6.6 million, based on a
devalued peso), due in large degree to royalties from Hidroituango. By 2021
it was thirty-one billion pesos ($8.3 million). However, even these numbers
undersell the difference. In 2018, fully forty-five billion pesos in state funds
($15 million) entered the municipality, with the difference accounted for by
departmental funds like road paving projects, and peace process programs
like coca substitution.

As a result, community members who are excluded from making a living
through the market have thrust the state front and center in their livelihood
strategies. Municipal jobs are essentially the only work available that pays at
or above minimum wage. Former coca farmers who must now ship heavy
legal goods to purchase points depend on municipal machinery to fix their
precarious roads (see chapter 7). They also draw on resources from a range of
agricultural programs to plant and fertilize their crops. Those who don't have
homes seek their inclusion in state programs to provide them with housing.
Homeowners use state home improvement programs to build indoor kitch-
ens or bathrooms, or call on the mayor's office for roofing materials, gutters,
or cement. State funds have also come to constitute a large portion of local
businesses' profits. Restaurants cater public events, hardware stores provide
supplies for municipal works projects, for-profit swimming pools host public
celebrations, and motorcycle repair shops compete for the contract to fix the
motorcycles of the mayor's office.

But these resources are not equally available to all. They are largely distributed at the discretion of the mayor, who uses them to reward political
supporters (the coca substitution program is a notable exception). In this
context, mayoral elections have become a crucial time for locals across social
classes to put themselves in the position to access state resources. Mayoral
candidates use promises of the jobs and goods they will control when they
win to mobilize votes. And, as Eduardo described, community members
use their political support, money, pigs, and time to make specific deals and

develop ties of reciprocity they can invoke later. Those who fail to develop a positive relationship with the mayor or who back the losing candidate are condemned to four years with little hope of accessing state resources.

Clientelism, broadly defined as politicians' exchange of resources for political support, is essential to the politics and survival strategies of the poor in a variety of contexts around the world. While political scientists tend to understand these exchanges in stark instrumental terms where the behavior of clients and patrons is driven by rational calculations (Kitschelt and Wilkinson 2007), sociologists and anthropologists have focused on their moral character, as exchanges rooted in affective ties and norms of reciprocity that produce political support (Auyero 2001). In Briceño, these exchanges and the relationships that develop around them are simultaneously instrumental and moral. They are rationally calculated to help patrons to acquire political support and the poor to acquire jobs and resources, yet they are embedded within (1) a moral universe based on norms of reciprocity that assigns meaning to their actions and dictates what they can expect in return, and (2) a broader transformation through which state resources have become essential to their lives.

As I have explained in the introduction to this book, these practices fit within a broader shift in which states in the Global South have taken an increasingly active role in distributing goods to their poorest citizens. The primary driver behind this transformation, I argued, was a wave of democratization that granted the poor leverage, in the form of their vote, to negotiate access to state resources. Colombia, celebrated within the nation's high school social studies curriculum as the continent's oldest democracy, is an awkward fit within this global shift. In 1977, just as the democratizing wave began, it was one of only four Latin American countries not classified as autocratic; by 2017, only one autocracy remained (DeSilver 2019). However, the political practices described here were dependent on shifts *within* Colombian democracy that decentralized state power and allowed rural communities to compete for state resources through local elections.

The first reform was the institution of competitive mayoral elections in 1988; mayors had previously been appointed by governors, themselves appointed by the presidential administration. The functions of these municipal governments also expanded, as they were given national funding to deliver education and health services. Finally, in 1994 Colombia established a system of mining royalties that directed even more funds to municipal governments, to be spent at their discretion (Gutiérrez Sanín 2019a, 304).

These decentralizing reforms helped loosen the long-standing domination of the Liberal and Conservative parties, which had previously counted on voting blocs with strong unchanging political loyalties and had mediated their territorial control through wealthy landowners who demanded the allegiance of their rural laborers (Escobar 1994; Negretto 2013). As the central leadership of traditional parties lost their stranglehold on state resources, local elections were instituted, and the labor needs of rural patrons decreased (part of the shift to technologically advanced agricultural production I have described in chapter 1), the poor stopped simply voting the party line and began using their vote as a bargaining chip to negotiate needed state resources—a transformation that Colombian scholars have described with the term "market clientelism" (Dávila Ladrón de Guevara 1999; Gutiérrez Sanín 1998).

The political practices around these constantly renegotiated exchanges of political support for state resources—given weight by the disappearance of alternative income sources like coca and gold panning—are a primary means through which the state has become important to local lives. In this chapter, I use an ethnography of the 2019 mayoral election to describe the clientelist practices that have emerged from Briceño's transformation, the way those practices determine local experiences of the state, and their consequences for the ongoing project of establishing state authority.

In the first section I describe clientelism in Briceño through a typology of three forms of clientelist relationships: those of high-intensity supporters, who leverage their political support for the municipal jobs that represent the only middle-class work available in the village; those of low-intensity supporters, who seek informal favors, inclusion in public home improvement or agricultural programs, and low-paying temporary jobs; and finally, relationships mediated through community action board presidents, who not only seek individual benefits, but must ensure their communities' access to collective public goods.

I then discuss how these clientelist practices contribute to state formation. I show that the state's newfound importance to local livelihoods has made campaign participation something that must be done even by people who are unenthusiastic about the candidate they support. These widespread practices have established a new understanding of and role for the state in community life.

"The Commitments That Are Made": Three Forms of Clientelist Relationships

I began chapter 2 with the promise of the state's arrival at Briceño by no less distinguished a figure than the Colombian president. Still, the peace process notwithstanding, the effects of national institutions on people's everyday experiences of the state are often hidden. Instead, as is typical on the margins of state power, local experiences of the state are dominated by encounters and relationships with personally known officials (Aretxaga 2005; Das and Poole 2004; Gupta 1995)—none more important than the mayor, who controls most of the state resources that enter Briceño. Elections have become a crucial time for people to cultivate a relationship with this mayor to guarantee their access to individual and collective goods. However, the kinds of relationships people develop with the mayor, their participation in campaigns, the benefits they expect, and the moral dimensions of these exchanges vary.

HIGH-INTENSITY SUPPORTERS

I sit in Briceño's main square with Eliana and Luisa; we eat hamburgers as we celebrate Luisa's twenty-fifth birthday. I've gotten to know the two women through hanging around Wilmar's campaign. They are enthusiastic and dedicated participants, holding semiofficial positions, participating in planning meetings, and often traveling to campaign events. They ask me how easy it is to get permission to go to the United States to work. Eliana, who at forty-two is a single mother of two, has a degree in environmental administration. She tells Luisa, who doesn't have children, that she should figure out how to go to the United States. "There just aren't any opportunities in Colombia," she says. "There are only two ways to make money in Colombia: politics or drug trafficking."

Eliana has worked for the mayor's office off and on for the last twenty years, in positions including secretary of education and coordinator of the system that keeps track of families eligible for public assistance. She says she's gotten all her jobs through *rosca*, which translates literally as the thread on a screw which gives it purchase as it bores into a surface. In Colombia the word is used to refer to connections with powerful people that can be harnessed for individual benefit. All of Eliana's jobs have come from supporting victorious mayoral candidates. She's currently volunteering for Wilmar's campaign, leading a group that reaches out to the women of Briceño. If Wilmar wins, she expects a high-ranking position within his administration.

Luisa tells me she worked as an administrative aid for the school until a couple of months ago. When her contract ended, rather than continuing with the school, she went to work for Wilmar as campaign secretary. Like Eliana, she isn't being paid, but she expects Wilmar to reward her with a position in the new government. She's also hoping that he will use municipal resources for repairs on her parents' house, where she lives. Luisa says that if Wilmar doesn't win, she'll have to move to Medellín to look for work. There just aren't any other jobs available in Briceño.

For high-intensity supporters, mayoral campaigns are essentially a full-time job they must repeat every four-year election cycle. Without access to municipal funds, Wilmar cannot pay Luisa, Eliana, and the rest of his team. However, many supporters of Pacho—Wilmar's opponent, who is backed by the mayor—already hold municipal jobs. Dideison is one. He was offered his job in early 2019, the election year, by one of the mayor's trusted advisors. His major responsibility, the advisor made clear, would be to campaign; it is illegal for current municipal employees to participate in campaigns, but the practice is widespread. For months, rather than performing his official job functions, he has traveled around Briceño's rural areas, helping set up political rallies and visiting people's farms to convince them to vote for Pacho.

High-intensity supporters on each side expect their participation to result in paid public positions if and when their candidate wins. In many cases this is something they discuss explicitly with the candidate, with expectations generated by both sides. While some told me they sought out the candidate to ask for a job, others were recruited with the promise of a position. Of note is that high-intensity supporters are highly educated in comparison with the village norm: they have all completed high school, and most have some form of postsecondary education. But that education, rather than generating job opportunities, has left them frustrated. Like Luisa and Eliana, they complain of the lack of jobs that take advantage of their education and provide appropriate financial compensation. The few that exist are controlled by the mayor's office. Thus, the decision of whom to support in the election is critical.

Carlos, an outgoing young man studying public accounting, gave up a municipal job to support Wilmar. While this decision means going six months without a paycheck, he expects it to ultimately set him up for another four years of public employment. He travels to Medellín every weekend for his classes while working full-time during the week—first for the mayor's office, coordinating youth programs, and, beginning in June 2019, for Wilmar's campaign. His municipal job came from his lifelong relationship with Cenizo, a distant relative. In February 2019, however, he told the mayor he was going to support Wilmar.

Carlos says, "2019 is a political year. It was known that if you weren't with the mayor's candidate, you had to leave." He adds that all the public municipal contracts in 2019 were limited to five months rather than the standard full year, "to make sure the contracted workers were going to support Pacho. To have them under pressure."

But it was not just Carlos's vote Pacho was after. Because of his charisma and work with the community, Carlos was seen as someone who could persuade voters.

"What did they want from you?" I ask him.

"That I would use my influence for them, to get support. At one time, after I had already said no, someone from the same team proposed something economic. To change my decision."

"How much?" I ask.

Carlos laughs, evading the question. "That's not something you can say. I'm not interested in the position as such. More the work with the community. Actually, I'm not going to have a position there, with Wilmar. What I'm going to do is, how do I explain it? He's going to give me the freedom to keep working on all those programs with the youth."

"And with a salary?" I ask.

"Yes, of course."

"And did you talk about this with Wilmar before joining his campaign?"

"You're worse than the SIJIN [a unit of the national police dedicated to criminal investigation]," Carlos says, laughing. He changes the subject, saying that while these clientelist practices have always existed, the current mayor has been particularly brazen. "Politics has always been run like this; those public positions are used for campaigning. But previously, it was more secretive."

After Carlos reflects a little more on the mayor, I ask again about the conversations he had with Wilmar as he was joining the campaign.

"First, it was the responsibility he gave me," he says. "Because I lead the youth outreach, communications. So I started to feel more committed to the campaign. And afterward, obviously, the commitments that are made, for after you win."

Turid Hagene (2015, 141, 157) writes that ethnography on the perspective of clients is crucial because it permits analysis of "what they do and do not talk about, their silences and moral evaluations, . . . tracing questions of moral universes, forms of rationality, . . . [and] the 'taken-for-grantedness' of that which 'goes without saying.'" At two points in the conversation reproduced above, Carlos resists precise explanation of what happened, signaling a degree of moral discomfort and preferring to leave commonly understood—but rarely explicitly described—arrangements unsaid. First, he describes the money he was offered to support Pacho rather than Wilmar, saying that someone from Pacho's team "proposed something economic" for his support, and then refusing to tell me how much they offered: "That's not something you can say." Then, when I ask about conversations he had with Wilmar as he was joining the campaign, he is comfortable talking about the fact that he would be paid a salary, while describing it not as a position, but as the freedom to continue working with youth. However, when I try to understand whether this was a deal Carlos made with Wilmar before joining the campaign, his reply indicates some moral discomfort, revealed by his joke about being under criminal investigation: "You're worse than the SIJIN." When I later return to the topic, he uses vague terms that present his support and his position not as a negotiated arrangement, but as fitting into a customary web of reciprocal relations that go without saying: "obviously, afterward, the commitments that are made, for after you win."

Javier Auyero (1999, 309) writes that clientelist exchanges become habitual knowledge, "part of a universe in which everyday favors imply some return as the rule of the game." In similar terms, high-intensity supporters take for granted that their significant support for the campaign will lead to a job down the road. To borrow Carlos's words, he and other supporters, like Luisa, who have given up paying jobs to work unpaid full-time for Wilmar's campaign, "obviously" and "of course" expect to receive jobs. Nonetheless, the contingent nature of this exchange makes Carlos uncomfortable. He prefers to highlight the work he expects to continue with the community. This is not a smokescreen; Carlos is passionately committed to his projects with Briceño's youth. But he is also fully aware that doing good work is not enough. He must strategically leverage his support during election time to position himself to maintain that work, and to ensure himself a paid job he can use to support himself and continue his education. The point is not to parse whether Carlos supports Wilmar because he thinks Wilmar would be a better mayor, because he sees an opportunity to guarantee himself a salary for the next four years, or because that support will put him in a position to continue helping the community. The point is that given the political culture, the structure of politics, and the moral universe of Briceño, his participation in clientelist politics lets him do all three of those things simultaneously.

When Wilmar wins, he replaces nearly the entire municipal administration, filling the jobs with his supporters along with outsiders recommended by his political godparents, powerful figures in the Liberal Party. Carlos, Eliana, and Luisa all get the positions they expect. Many others, however, do not. Wilmar expands the municipal workforce from 70 to 120 people, but is still unable to find jobs for all the people who need and expect them. Widespread local complaints of his broken commitments support Eduardo's point that "the candidates end up promising the same position to fifteen or twenty people" in order to win the election.

Those on the losing end, of course, have no shot at a job. On a January morning in 2020, shortly after Wilmar takes office, I sit across from Dideison and Duván, another young man who, like Dideison, supported Pacho. Duván pretends to wet his index finger against his lips and touches it to Dideison's shoulder. He makes the hissing sound of water falling on a heated pot. "*Te quemaste* [You got burned]," he says.

Dideison has been left unemployed. "You, even more," he says to Duván as he playfully knocks his hand away. Duván, twenty-three, ran unsuccessfully for city council on Pacho's ticket. Within a month he'll leave the village and a newborn son behind, chasing a job opportunity in southern Colombia. Indeed, many of Pacho's high-intensity supporters, including most of the municipal administration, will leave Briceño. Even though Dideison has been burned, Dideison uses his political connections to get a job working for a business owned by Pacho's campaign manager. Like people who work in other nonmunicipal jobs in the village center, he's paid under the table, makes significantly less than minimum wage, and does not receive benefits.

Neither Dideison nor Duván is bitter, however. Within local commonsense understandings, the state and its attendant resources represent a winner-takes-all prize. They know they have lost. "That's politics," says Dideison, shrugging.

Still, their experience is instructive for local youth. Young people repeatedly complain that the only decent jobs in Briceño are highly precarious, linked to political alliances rather than to merit or credentials. The result is a brain drain, in which the youth who do manage to get postsecondary education usually seek more stable employment in cities rather than throwing in their lot with local village politics, and municipal administrations are robbed of both continuity and some of their best potential civil servants.

LOW-INTENSITY SUPPORTERS

Eugenia supported Cenizo in the 2015 mayoral campaign, just as the land mine removal program began increasing the state resources entering Briceño. While campaigning, Cenizo promised to give her a home improvement project, providing materials to fix her kitchen's leaky roof. Cenizo's term began well, Eugenia says. As community president, she asked him for help in building Briceño's road (see chapter 7); he sent her $6,500 of municipal funds. After Wilmar and Cenizo fell out, however, Wilmar included Eugenia in a WhatsApp group he formed for local leaders to support his own political aspirations. She did not know that Cenizo had a spy in the group, reporting everything that went on in it.

"In the group, I would send thumbs up emojis, or 'Let's do it!' ['*¡Vamos con toda!*'], just to encourage people," Eugenia says. Cenizo interpreted her actions as support for Wilmar, his political rival. "He called me *torcida*" (literally, "crooked," in reference to traitorous behavior). Eugenia never received the home improvement project. Already with designs on the mayor's office, Wilmar told her not to worry, that he would get her the project when he was in charge.

During the 2019 campaign, Eugenia invited Wilmar to El Orejón, speaking on his behalf there and in neighboring communities. When his term began, he slotted her for a nationally funded home improvement project designed to build indoor bathrooms for homes that lacked them. Though her house already had an indoor bathroom, she planned to use the project to modernize it. However, the program stalled. Wilmar did send the excavator to turn the dirt entrance to Eugenia's farm into a proper gravel driveway that allows trucks to bring supplies all the way down to her home. Also at Eugenia's request, he gave funding to the community to hire its own excavator to fix the road. Without the home improvement program, however, Eugenia feels that Wilmar has broken his commitment to her.

Eugenia expresses her frustration one day after unsuccessfully calling Wilmar to check on the project: "We hoped this one [Wilmar] might be different, but it seems like it's more of the same. There are so many programs that come to Briceño. But it's like spreading seeds down a slope: they pass through the governor's office, the municipality, contractors, sometimes even the community action board. By the time the seeds reach the beneficiaries at the bottom, very few are left."

Her metaphor is appropriate for a community accustomed to farming on Briceño's impossibly steep hillsides. It is also typical of how locals draw on a logic of corruption to explain the inadequacies of state programs. Indeed, narratives of corruption are central to people's understandings of the state across the Global South (Diamond 2023; Diamond and Gold, forthcoming; Gupta 1995)—though increasing calls to "drain the swamp" of Washington suggest that such narratives have become politically consequential in the United States as well. Briceño's rapid transformation adds a particular immediacy to campesinos' efforts to understand a newly consequential state.

Low-intensity supporters like Eugenia do not treat electoral campaigns as a full-time job. Instead, they attend campaign rallies, donate small amounts of money or goods, and publicly demonstrate their support with signs, in social media, and by wearing hats and T-shirts. Nevertheless, they depend on successfully harnessing their political support to secure their access to state resources that are important to their lives and livelihoods: a watertight roof, several bags of fertilizer, or a few months of employment.

The kinds of resources expected by low-intensity supporters take three forms: informal favors, inclusion in formal agricultural or home improvement programs, and jobs. Informal favors are usually requested after the election, directly of the mayor. These include Eugenia getting access to the municipal excavator to fix up a driveway, a few bags of cement for a construction project, or even the transportation and logistics for selling agricultural goods in a campesino market in the village center. They are also a safety net in the face of disaster: the mayor uses municipal resources to cover rent for families whose homes are washed away by landslides, to provide groceries for those suffering economic hardship, to donate materials to rebuild a home damaged by fire, and to help with medical expenses, including medication and transportation to appointments outside Briceño. The mayor's office maintains accounts with local stores—owned, of course, by supporters—that it uses to distribute many of these resources.

Additionally, formal projects transform local homes and farms. I was surprised to find that the majority of rural homes had received some form of public investment: a roof, a kitchen, gutters, or even the entire home itself. In similar terms, agricultural projects are critical to farmers' cultivation strategies, whether in providing fertilizer for coffee, chickens to lay eggs, or the seeds and agricultural goods required to establish avocado, passion fruit, lime, or cacao crops. Like the home improvement projects, these are usually funded by departmental or national programs, or even by NGOs and religious or international organizations. Nevertheless, they depend on the municipal government to identify beneficiaries. Thus, mayors use them to reward supporters, and beneficiaries usually interpret them as personal favors from the mayor.

Finally, many low-intensity supporters seek to leverage their political support for jobs—usually lower-paying and shorter-term jobs than those expected by high-intensity supporters, but consequential nevertheless. The most common examples are jobs in construction of roads, bridges, and municipal buildings like schools and community meeting houses, as well as work in home improvement projects.

Roberto, a man in his fifties with decades of local experience in construction, tells me that during the coca era, work was easy to come by. "I couldn't finish one job before people would call me for another—to build a house, pave a patio, or add a new room to their home. I rested on Sundays, but otherwise there was work every day." In the cash-poor era of the peace process, however, these private projects have mostly disappeared, and most construction is funded by the mayor's office. During the 2019 election, Roberto promises his own vote and those of his family members to Wilmar's campaign in exchange for future work in public construction. But it is not only experienced construction workers who seek this work. Municipal construction jobs have become increasingly important components in campesinos' patchwork livelihoods. As a result, the demand for jobs far outstrips supply. Within a few months of Wilmar taking office in January 2020, complaints begin that he is failing to deliver promised jobs to many of his supporters (the onset of Covid-19, which puts many projects on hold, doesn't help). Roberto himself only ends up with a few months of work—a needed cash injection, but short of what he expected. He plants coffee and subsistence crops on a family farm, and in the 2023 election he again seeks to exchange political support for a needed job.

Electoral politics has become so central to the social life of the village that private jobs often depend on the alliances formed during campaigns. As a result, even support for a losing candidate can bear fruit, as it did for Dideison, who ended up working for the manager of the failed campaign.

Eliana explains to me one day in Wilmar's campaign headquarters that the only thing community members can't be is neutral: "You have to align yourself with one of the candidates, or you'll be unable to get a job."

"Even if you lose?" I ask.

"Lose, win, whatever," she says. "Let's say Wilmar wins. He only controls so many jobs: in the mayor's office, hospital. But there are so many people tied to the campaign expecting positions, so it's really not that many jobs." She gives an example. "Say you want to get a job in the hardware store, even if it's only for sixty dollars. They'll say, 'You were with Wilmar.' And they won't give you a job."

"What if you weren't with either side?" I ask.

"Ah no," she says, laughing. "That's the worst of all. Then you have no one to help you."

MEDIATED CLIENTELIST RELATIONS:
THE COMMUNITY PRESIDENT

While a surprising number of individuals within Briceño establish personal relationships with the mayor through which they make direct claims on municipal resources, many also access resources through relationships mediated through their community action board president. As I've described through Eduardo and Eugenia's struggles to improve their communities' roads, hamlets depend on municipal resources for geographically bounded public goods. Other than roads, these may include aqueducts, milk tanks to collect the community's dairy production, tools that the community action board can use for *convites*, repairs to the local school, and, more recently, satellite internet service, installed at the school but available to all community members.

And just as low-intensity supporters call on the mayor for help in the face of individual calamity, community presidents draw on their relationships with the mayor for help with collective disasters, most notably landslides that periodically cover local roads.

The importance of community presidents' relationship with the mayor is best illustrated by an established practice in which a hamlet will change its president if the mayoral candidate it supports loses an election. Jaime first describes this practice to me when I visit his home in 2018. He is president of one of the hamlets of Briceño that has seen the greatest level of investment during Cenizo's administration, including home improvements and a new road, library, and aqueduct. He directly attributes a large part of this investment to his positive relationship with Cenizo, whom he supported in the 2015 election. But Jaime wasn't president before the election. While campaigning, he told the people of his hamlet that if Cenizo's campaign was successful, he would assume the presidency of the hamlet to ensure that the new mayor would direct resources to it. Most tellingly, when Cenizo won his race, the hamlet's president, who had supported a different candidate, stepped down voluntarily, recognizing that Jaime's relationship with the new mayor would bring more resources to the community.

"The community action board has to be renovated with the terms of each mayor," Jaime explains to me one evening. "There are hamlets that weren't on the mayor's side, and they're in very bad shape. The community is conscious of this, that it needs to work with a president from the same side. Because the mayors are sometimes very jealous. The mayor says that while so-and-so is president, I won't help you."

"He's said this directly?" I ask.

"Yes. The mayor works like a godfather. I got the mayor 104 votes."

"And how did you get the votes?"

"I make a campaign, I speak with people," he says. "They tell me, 'You're the one who says which direction we're going, who we have to support.'"

Jaime says his calculation to support Cenizo has paid off: "I was on [Cenizo's] side, I worked with him a lot, and I can't complain, because if I come to the mayor with a problem, he fixes it for me. On the other hand, in many hamlets it's the opposite."

In poor rural areas like Briceño, the struggle for public resources is a zero-sum game. The flip side of the high level of municipal investment in Jaime's hamlet from 2016 to 2019 is that other hamlets were, as Eduardo put it, abandoned. If Jaime could call on Cenizo to send an excavator to fix a landslide after a torrential rain, several other communities with washed-out roads had to wait their turn.

Elections, therefore, are a time of high stakes for community presidents. They must ensure their hamlet's access to needed public resources for the next four years. At the same time, like Eduardo and Eugenia, community presidents have their own personal needs which they hope to meet through their political support. They also know that if they support the wrong candidate, they may be replaced, like Eduardo, for the good of the community.

In a point I will develop in the next chapter, municipal employees must also cultivate relationships with community presidents, and not only to enlist their help in mobilizing votes. Even after they are in office, these employees draw on relationships rooted in campaign allegiances for help in implementing state projects and making sense of complex social and property relations in the territory. Thus, the clientelist relationships developed through elections are central not only to citizens' attempts to access state resources, but to state officials' ability to govern.

Despite bringing significant resources to Briceño, the state has failed to fulfill its promises of progress and prosperity. It has, however, made locals dependent on personal relationships with the state, whether embodied in the figure of the mayor or mediated through community presidents. These relationships have become central to people's livelihoods, future goals, and efforts to shield themselves from the precarity of rural lives marked by their exclusion from agricultural markets. And, as I describe in the next section, they are critical to ongoing processes of state formation.

Clientelist Relationships and State Formation: The Things That Must Be Done

> The manager of a fruit-and-vegetable shop places in his window, among the onions and carrots, the slogan: 'Workers of the world, unite!' Why does he do it? What is he trying to communicate to the world? Is he genuinely enthusiastic about the idea of unity among the workers of the world? . . . I think it can safely be assumed that the overwhelming majority of shopkeepers never think about the slogans they put in their windows, nor do they use them to express their real opinions. That poster was delivered to our greengrocer from the enterprise headquarters along with the onions and carrots. He put them all into the window simply because it has been done that way for years, because everyone does it, and because that is the way it has to be. . . . He does it because these things must be done if one is to get along in life."
>
> VACLAV HAVEL, *The Power of the Powerless*, pp. 5–6

Vaclav Havel's (2009) reflection on the nature of power under the Czech communist regime takes off from the story of a shop manager who displays the regime's slogan in his window. In Havel's analysis, the meaning of the slogan has nothing to do with its content; nor does it matter that the manager doesn't

believe in it. Instead, what matters is that he is "accepting the prescribed rit-
ual, by accepting appearances as reality, by accepting the given rules of the
game" (Havel 2009, 10). His silent participation shows the exercise of power,
and allows the game to continue uninterrupted.

In the months leading up to the 2019 mayoral election, Briceño's physical
landscape fills with campaign propaganda. People hang banners across village thoroughfares, put up posters on the walls of their businesses and homes,
and decorate their bodies with campaign hats and T-shirts. Briceño's social
media landscape is similarly transformed. Supporters share posts from each
campaign's Facebook page, post videos and photos of campaign events, and
pose with their candidate's hat or T-shirt prominently displayed. Why do they
do it? What are they trying to communicate to the world? And how do these
practices help determine who can govern the excluded?

In the previous chapter I described how guerrilla authority is marked by a
silence and invisibility that, rooted in the threat of violence, nevertheless establishes a social grammar that determines daily practice. In contrast, state authority is established through its visibility, including electoral practices that publicly
communicate enthusiastic support for a given candidate. These practices are
encouraged by campaign strategies intended to make their candidates seem
popular. In participating, locals provide public evidence of consent to power
(Beetham 1991). Thus, efforts to demonstrate the strength of a particular candidate end up expressing the power of the state itself—albeit a highly personal-
ized state that must be accessed through relationships with local politicians.

On the day of Wilmar's campaign launch, a huge party featuring nationally famous singers, Eliana explains this strategy. I sit with her in a corner
of Wilmar's campaign headquarters, facing the main square. As we eat from
Styrofoam bowls of *sancocho*, she points at the masses of people filling the
plaza. Most wear red shirts the campaign has given out that bear an image of
Wilmar with a triumphant smile, a clenched fist raised high, and the slogan
"Mobilizing Ideas."

"More than one person will see this strength, and will choose to support
Wilmar," Eliana says. Around three thousand people are at the event, including many who have been brought here on trucks and buses from outlying
hamlets and even from Medellín. Transportation and the event itself are
funded by shadowy donors who expect their support to be rewarded with
lucrative municipal contracts.

Eliana tells me about a training Wilmar's staff has received from outside
consultants on why people vote. The consultants say that 15 percent of people
will compare the candidates' proposals and vote based on ideas. Another
40 percent vote on emotion. And 45 percent analyze the situation and vote for

whom they think the winner will be, just to be associated with that person. "I nearly had a heart attack when they said that," Eliana says.

Caught up in the excitement, I mention that I would like to get a T-shirt.

"Don't put on that shirt," she says forcefully. She refers to my research. "There are many people you will want to work with on the other side. It's best to keep your doors open on both sides. Everyone sees you as a researcher. . . . Don't mark yourself with that shirt."

Forrest Stuart (2018, 213) writes that ethnographers should treat their own transgressive "presence in the field as a kind of breaching exercise that allows them to reveal and make sense of the invisible social orders and norms that guide action and pattern behaviors." Eliana's reaction to the idea that I would put on a T-shirt in support of Wilmar is particularly telling, because at the moment she expresses it, she is herself wearing a campaign shirt. Multiple times a week, she posts WhatsApp statuses supporting Wilmar's campaign. She understands this, along with the countless hours of volunteer time she puts in, as something she must do to secure a future job in the administration. However, in speaking with an outsider who does not have that same necessity, she leaves little doubt that she would prefer not to mark herself in this way— and not least because for her it shuts the door to the other side, which may itself end up controlling municipal resources.

As I argued in my account of the coca substitution's broken promises in chapter 2 of this book, even when state programs and officials don't make good on their commitments, public complaints about their failings and attempts to access resources help spread commonsense conceptions of the state's rightful role and responsibility as provider of the common good. People like Eliana, Eugenia, and Eduardo are often frustrated and disappointed by the clientelist political practices they must use to access state resources. Nevertheless, since they are left with little option other than to play the game, their participation in political campaigns has become critical to their livelihood strategies. Clientelist practices have become things that "must be done if one is to get along in life" (Havel 2009, 6)—perhaps the most important driving force and compelling evidence of the state's growing influence in Briceño.

Conclusion

As my fieldwork for this book is ending, my mother visits me in Briceño. After I describe the exchanges and relationships that characterize local elections, she asks, "Does *anyone* vote based on politics?"

Just a week later, I meet with Eugenia, who, even after receiving some resources, continues to be frustrated with the broken promises of home improvement programs. "This is why we're trying to give our children an education," she says. "So that they can get out of the countryside, and not depend on *la política*."

La política, or politics, has a very specific meaning in rural Colombia. Contra my mother's interpretation, it does not refer to different visions for state intervention in the economy, territory, and society. Instead, it is a competition to control municipal resources that have taken on an outsized importance to people's livelihoods. It is an ongoing struggle, intensifying during elections, to maintain the relationships with state officials who can grant needed resources, protection against life's insecurities, and even the possibility of an improved quality of life. It is, in the words of Julieta Lemaitre (2018, 79; translation mine), "a continuous activity . . . that is part of daily life and another way to survive with outside aid. Understood in this way, *la política* is based on a tacit, or at times explicit, agreement, between the vulnerable and those who can offer them protection. . . . It is about protection in the face of hunger, a life on the street, the lack of schools, medical attention, and shelter, or the constant threat of suddenly losing everything because of sickness, disaster, or bad luck."

The importance of *la política* to local livelihoods is a central element in Briceño's transformation, impossible to understand outside the disappearance of coca and gold panning economies that had little need for state resources. But even beyond these elements specific to the experience of Briceño, clientelist practices are enabled by broader political and economic transformation: the exclusion of massive populations from making a living through legal markets, and the institution of the popular vote as a leverage point that allows the poor to access state resources. In the late 1990s it was coca, organized by armed groups, that allowed farmers to preserve their valued rural lifestyles in the face of exclusion from legal agricultural economies (see chapter 1). Now, with coca mostly gone, locals instead pursue their livelihoods through state resources—a condition that has spread to characterize the lives of an increasing number of the marginalized poor.

It is not a new insight that poor people's politics across the Global South are based on accessing limited state resources to meet everyday survival needs (Auyero 2001). The case of Briceño, however, pushes us to understand how these practices impact the ongoing and contested formation of state power. While classic accounts focus on states' ability to defeat competitors by extracting taxes and military conscripts from their subjects (Tilly 1990), modern states largely extend their power by distributing resources to their citizens, monopolizing problem-solving rather than, or in addition to, violence. In the absence of alternatives, these resources have pushed Briceño's campesinos to pursue their livelihoods through the state, and have flipped the role of the state in community life.

However, as I have argued in chapter 2 of this book, on the outsourcing of the coca substitution program, the way in which state resources are delivered matters. On the one hand, resources distributed through clientelist practices are usually understood either as compensation for political support or as personal favors from the mayor—not as proof of the privileged role of "the state" as the guarantor of order and provider of the public good. Therefore, these practices may compromise the establishment of the state's symbolic power. On the other hand, these same clientelist practices also establish concrete state/society ties that both make the state accessible and enable officials to intervene in communities. As I will describe in the next chapter, this has unlocked a distinct process of state formation based on relations of dependence on state officials and resources.

7

Paving the Way for the State?
The Material and Symbolic Dimensions of State Formation Through Rural Roads

Ocaris Areiza, in Memory

Early on a Tuesday morning, just as sunlight begins to peek in through the curtains, Enrique speaks to me from outside his family's guest room. "Alex, are you awake? Get ready to go, there's been an accident."

I'm in the first days of a weeklong stay with Enrique's family in the hamlet Altos de Chirí, perched above Hidroituango's reservoir just upstream of El Orejón. Enrique's wife, Lina, has left before dawn with a delegation of locals traveling to meet with the mayor, Wilmar. After supporting him in the election, they're hoping they can get him to reverse a decision to cut one of the community's three teachers in the face of a decreasing student population. Not long after taking off, however, Lina calls her husband to tell him they've encountered an accident on a stretch of road in the neighboring hamlet of El Orejón known for its repeated landslides. Ocaris Areiza, a respected community leader who has hosted my field visits many times, was driving the wrecked vehicle.

I quickly get dressed and we leave, taking our motorcycles down Chirí's dirt road to the modern highway that leads to the hydroelectric dam. As the sun crests the valley walls to reach the river's repressed waters on our left, we pick up speed on the highway's banked curves. After ten minutes of smooth riding, we reach the entrance to El Orejón: an unsigned dirt road that climbs up the valley walls to our right. Enrique and I both circle out into the incoming lane to make the sharp turn and pick up the momentum we need to coax our motorcycles up the steep hill.

The turnoff is literally jarring, each rut and rock a perilous reminder that we have left a smooth modern highway for a road used only by the inhabitants of a remote village. If the challenge of highway motorcycle riding is that of overcoming the engine's soothing hum in order to stay alert to any

FIGURE 7.1. Briceño's motorcyclists feel the limitations of state investment through potholes, landslides, and the resulting injuries.

potential danger, Briceño's dirt roads do not let the rider relax for even a second. Instead, reaching the destination is a feat of sustained concentration; you must constantly scan the road ahead to avoid the loose gravel, slick mud, and larger rocks that can unceremoniously steal your equilibrium and send you knee-, elbow-, or wrist-first to the ground. Just before beginning field-work in earnest in May 2018, I purchased a motorcycle and learned how to ride it within the space of two days. That summer I fell from my moto four times. I began to have dreams about riding in which I would suddenly awake with the unsettling feeling of having lost control; and I still have vivid memo-ries of picking bits of gravel out of my bleeding elbow under a hot shower. Such everyday scrapes and perils, not limited to the novice rider, become important elements through which rural Colombians feel the state (fig. 7.1).

By March 2020, however, when Enrique and I are traveling to the scene of the accident, I am a more experienced rider, and we arrive without incident. But the road has already claimed its victims. We stop when we reach a crowd of thirty people. As we dismount, we see a group of six men clambering up the steep hill that falls away from the road, carrying Ocaris on an improvised stretcher. He has deep gashes on his head, and one of his hands hangs limply at an unnatural angle, ripped nearly free of his arm, forearm bone protruding. From the way his body nearly slides off the stretcher, from the way the men gently put him down by the side of the road, from the way the surrounding crowd glances at him before looking away uncomfortably, it's clear that Ocaris is dead. Laid out on a stretcher just up the road, an older woman is also lifeless, her body covered by a poncho. The crash has two survivors: a boy around six years old and his mother, a young woman who appears to have injured her chest.

I walk up to a woman I know who was with the delegation, and I give her a hug. While crying softly, she explains what has happened. The previous night, a local woman fell grievously ill. With the sick woman, her niece, and her niece's young son riding in his white truck, Ocaris set out on a three-hour journey to the relatively modern hospital in neighboring Yarumal, taking the El Orejón road down to the Hidroituango highway.

They never made it to the highway. A short distance below the newly built school, soccer field, and community meeting house that mark the center of El Orejón, the truck reached one of several sections of road that, cut out of steep hillsides and passing over streams that swell with the region's torrential rainfalls, are often covered by landslides. On this night the road was passable. However, Ocaris made a slight miscalculation on a section where the road dipped before curving suddenly to the left. With only its headlights illuminating the way, the vehicle's right wheels slipped over the edge. He and the sick woman were thrown from the vehicle as it went over the precipice and began to roll down the steep embankment. Both were killed instantly. Miraculously, the younger woman and her son survived, crawling out of the truck after it came to a stop against a tree trunk two hundred meters below. They spent a cold night huddled together by the side of the creek.

Ocaris' wife arrives, breathing heavily and looking frantically from side to side. By now, someone has covered the dead man's face. An onlooker touches her elbow, directing her gently to her husband's body. She kneels beside him, placing her right hand on his chest. The first thing she says, looking up at the semicircle of people that has formed around her: "Was this an assassination [*atentado*]?" Someone assures her that no, this was an accident. Her question, revealing of how repeated tragedies emerge from the combination of armed group violence, the dangers of social leadership in Colombia, and the perils of everyday rural life, is, years later, my most poignant memory of the accident.

By now the crowd has swelled to a hundred people. Briceño's volunteer firefighters load the dead into the municipality's ambulance. Paramedics in blue vests bearing the logo of EPM, the public utilities company that owns the Hidroituango dam, take the young woman and her son the opposite way, down the El Orejón road to the same hospital they set out for last night. The modern highway below, itself built by the dam company, will allow the EPM ambulance to transport the survivors to needed care relatively quickly.

However, locals grumble at the sight of the EPM paramedics. Though their reaction is partly a function of a general animosity toward a hydroelectric dam that has disturbed local ways of life, they have a very specific reason for blaming EPM for this tragedy. As described in chapter 4r, just ten days before this accident the community of El Orejón organized a *convite*, where it worked to reroute the road to avoid some of the steepest, most dangerous, and most landslide-prone areas. The area of the road it sought to improve, while not the site of ythis accident, was on EPM property. EPM officials discovered that people from the community were working on the company's land, and they called the police to stop them. The day before the accident, as we prepared to head down to a campesino market in the dam parking lot, I video-recorded Fabio explaining why the community was seeking to change the road's path. Watching the video later, with the knowledge of what would shortly happen, is eerie. "The rainy season is coming, and it gets very hard to take out agricultural products [to sell]," says Fabio, looking into the camera. "The road as it stands now is very problematic. It has parts so steep that it destroys cars and motos, but most important is the danger to our lives."

With the dead and injured taken away, people break up into circles of conversation, trying to make sense of what has just happened. Many draw connections between the tragedy and their dispute with EPM over the road. I scribble some of their comments in my notebook:

> "We knew this road was dangerous and those sons of bitches call the
> police on us."
> "They talk about licenses and permissions, and people are dying."
> "Maybe this had to happen for us to get our road."

Introduction

Following the tragic accident, Eugenia sends me a WhatsApp voice message.

> After, with so many difficulties, we were able to open our road, seeing the death of Ocaris, my partner in leadership, is such a serious loss. We see that the crisis we're living is deepening every day. That road is all we have, but after EPM didn't let us continue [rerouting it], we can't do anything else. I've told you a lot of the story. We held raffles, we organized festivals, one way or another I found some money, and we managed to open that road. . . . One way or another, here we are, trying to get ahead on our own because we have no support from the government, especially after we lived up [to the coca substitution agreement] and the government hasn't.

Eugenia's words illustrate a surprising complexity around the formation of state power through Briceño's roads. Indeed, most scholarly accounts treat roadbuilding as a relatively straightforward technology of state power. Theorists of historical state formation have described how it allowed the state to penetrate social relations throughout the entirety of its territory (Mann 1984; Soifer 2008), to make isolated areas legible and accessible to centralized state authority (Scott 1998; Uribe 2019), to establish its symbolically powerful privileged role as the provider of public goods (Guldi 2012), and to culturally and economically integrate far-flung communities into the national territory (Weber 1976). In similar terms, policy literature on conflict-affected states has described roads, among other public goods, as a core function that lets the state make its advantages tangible to its citizens, inspire legitimacy from subject populations, and eliminate competing authorities (OECD 2011; Van de Walle and Scott 2011). Building roads should allow the state to unlock what the literature describes as a virtuous cycle. The provision of needed goods creates a sense of loyalty, legitimacy, and obligation; citizens therefore comply with state demands, increasing state capacity; and the higher-capacity state is able to improve its provision of goods and generate more legitimacy (Levi et al. 2009; OECD 2011).

Eugenia's message, however, illustrates the shortcomings of these analyses when applied to Briceño's roads. First, her repeated use of "we" underscores the fact that Briceño's rural communities have led the building of their own roads, and see them as the fruit of their own labor more than that of state power. Second, Briceño's roads may even serve as indictments of the state; her account of the lack of "support from the government" and EPM's prohibitions hold the state responsible for the roads' poor condition and, by extension, Ocaris' death. Finally, her comment that their road "is all we have" illuminates how roads—and through them, the state—have become newly important to struggles to develop new livelihoods in the face of coca's disappearance and an exclusionary global food production regime that establishes razor-thin profit margins for legal agricultural goods.

I argue that these roads do contribute to the formation of state power—just not in the way the literature has described. Even as local communities lead road construction, the need for resources to build, maintain, and improve these roads binds them into relations of dependence on state officials, establishing the state as a useful material and symbolic force in their lives. While we often think of dependence as a loss of agency, this newfound reliance on state resources is itself a product of community agency in two respects: campesinos' collective decision, in the face of economic change, to pursue their livelihoods through roads; and the significant community effort to establish and maintain the relationships through which resources flow. As James Ferguson (2015, 97) has written, "Material dependence on others is not a passive condition—it is a valued outcome of long, hard social labor. . . . While 'dependency' is obsessively decried as a problem or a trap in social policy discourse, an ethnographic view suggests that it is really only via relations of 'dependence' that most of the population survives at all. Dependence is, in this respect, not the name of the problem; it is the name of the solution."

This dependence, when established through shared resources like roads, becomes a collective rather than individual condition. And as such, its implications for state formation hinge not only on public goods but on publics themselves, in John Dewey's (1927) classic sense of political collectivities called into being by issues that create shared interests. Goods like roads are not necessarily built for already constituted communities (Collier et al. 2016). Instead, what Noortje Marres (2012) has called "communities of the affected" come together to advocate for collectively needed roads, aqueducts, or sewage or electrical lines. As I will describe, these communities become infrastructural publics (Collier et al. 2016; Kingsbury and Maisley 2021) through the daily stuff of politics: informal conversations about shared needs, public meetings to unite diverse perspectives into communally acceptable plans of action, negotiations with powerful others, and the coalescing spirit of collective struggle.

There is no guarantee that these publics will address their concerns to the state. In Briceño, rural communities have long drawn on the authority of the FARC guerrillas to help them organize collective labor to maintain first mule paths and now roads. However, when economic transformation drives people to reconfigure their livelihood strategies, these publics allow desire for the state to itself become public—not an internal individual feeling, but a collectively determined orientation to action. As discussed in chapter 2, this contributes to belief in "the state" by spreading commonsense ideas of the state's rightful role and responsibility. But these publics also enable the state's influence to spread by providing an "in" for state formation as organized collectivities appoint representatives who can interface directly with state officials. As I describe here, relationships with those who are credibly understood as representing communities are key both to officials' ability to implement state initiatives and to the broader project of establishing state authority in areas where it is still an open question.

In what follows, I develop this argument through an ethnographic description of five moments in state formation through rural roads. First is the moment of not needing roads, which describes how isolation was acceptable and even desirable for coca-cultivating communities who maintained their mule paths with the aid of armed group authority. Second is the moment of needing roads, which details how the local demand for roads emerged from farmers' collective decision to replace coca with heavy and perishable legal agriculture. Third is the moment of building roads, which reconstructs the community of Orejón's efforts to build their road to show how turning repeatedly to state officials for needed resources established relationships through which the state became a useful force in their lives. Fourth is the moment of maintaining roads, which describes how the ongoing need to fix their roads extends these relationships and allows officials to enlist community presidents' help in implementing a variety of state projects. Fifth is the moment of improving roads, which shows that paving projects express the state's promise of progress and modernity but also provide an arena for the exercise (and funding) of guerrilla authority.

Moment One: Not Needing Roads

In 2008, roads reached only five of Briceño's thirty-eight hamlets. For most of the municipality's eight thousand inhabitants, leaving Briceño or even traveling to the village center meant a daylong journey along mule paths cut into the region's steep mountain hillsides. Ten years later, the village had 230 kilometers of rural dirt roads that connected all but two of its hamlets to the village center. The new road infrastructure has greatly improved the quality of life in rural communities, facilitating access to groceries, health care, education, and social life, whether by motorcycle or by public transportation routes that travel to most rural hamlets. Campesinos also depend on roads to get their goods—coffee harvests, perishable milk, and fragile food crops—to market.

Nevertheless, when the municipal economy was based on coca and gold panning, rural communities did not need roads. Gold is particularly light; campesinos would put it in their pockets and bring it to sell on their infrequent trips into the village to buy groceries. A large coca harvest, which weighed only ten pounds, was easy to transport on foot or by mule to nearby rural guerrilla or paramilitary purchase points. Coca did present farmers with a transportation challenge: that of bringing back to their farms gasoline and the other goods needed for transforming coca leaves into coca paste. The military often attempted to intercept those chemicals, either seizing them or charging coca farmers money to let them pass. So while roads theoretically could have made transportation easier for coca farmers, in practice they would have facilitated military interdiction.

Even worse than military confiscation of the supplies to process coca were military eradicators who either destroyed their crops or extorted money from coca farmers (see chapter 1). Coca farms that were easier to access were targeted more often, particularly by corrupt soldiers in search of easy paydays. As a result, coca farmers saw roads as not only unnecessary, but a liability. Eduardo, for example, said his community didn't seek to build a road until 2015, when the FARC warned them of the upcoming substitution program. "Building a road would have made it easier for the government to enter," he says, referring to military eradicators. "When we knew coca was ending, only then did we want the road."

While locals did not need roads to get their lightweight coca paste to market, they did depend on mule paths—to travel to nearby coca purchase points, to buy groceries and agricultural supplies, and to visit friends and family. But just as the shared need for roads would later tie local livelihoods to the state, these mule paths pushed locals to depend on armed groups. As described in chapter 4, communities maintained their paths with the use of communal workdays called *convites*. Both the FARC and paramilitaries ensured widespread participation in areas under their control, working in collaboration with community action boards. They visited community meetings to announce that everyone had to participate, followed up with community presidents to ask who had been absent, visited those who shirked their responsibilities, and imposed steep fines, turning the money over to the community action board.

Just as they do now, therefore, community action boards have long established a representational face (the community president) who allows claimants to authority, whether armed groups or the state, to interface with communities to both impose social control and organize service delivery. Then, as now, a shared interest in maintaining transportation infrastructures is the primary element molding groups of individuals into territorialized publics. But in the era of coca, with coca eradication incentivizing isolation, mule paths were sufficient and even preferable to roads. In this context, communities needing to enforce *convite* participation to maintain these paths turned for help to the FARC guerrillas—and away from the state. This situation would begin to change, however, with the village's economic transformation.

Moment Two: Needing Roads

The collective and ongoing project of replacing gold panning and particularly coca economies with legal agriculture like cattle and coffee has pushed locals to pursue their livelihoods through roads—and through them, the state. And while it wasn't until 2017 that the substitution program mostly eliminated coca, this process began earlier. As I have described in chapter 2, the area under coca cultivation in Briceño dropped from 2,400 hectares to 504 hectares between 2008 and 2016 for three reasons: a dip in production due to ecological factors like the worms that ate coca leaves and a fungus that dried them out, military eradication campaigns that cut into farmers' bottom line, and a major increase in the cost of growing and processing coca due to military disruption of supply chains. Most roadbuilding took place over this same period, as communities began seeking alternatives to coca.

The most common alternative is cattle farming, for three reasons: both meat and milk have relatively stable prices, cows are understood as a safe investment not subject to the blights of crops, and milk provides a daily income rather than periodic harvests. Because farmers must be able to reach the milk trucks that take their product to market, roads are a precondition of dairy economies. Each new meter of road built means another meter down which the milk truck can travel. Even today, the localized production of milk is an excellent predictor of road quality. Dairy-farming communities are quick to fix damage to their roads, as each day the truck can't enter is a day their production goes to waste.

Next to cattle, coffee is the most prominent alternative to coca. And while Briceño's farmers historically produced coffee without access to roads, the elimination of economic protections like the International Coffee Agreement has exposed coffee to market forces and has driven profit margins perilously low (see chapter 1). In this economic context, roads have become essential to coffee's potential profitability. Though coffee has only one yearly harvest, that harvest is massive. Suso, for example, produces roughly five tons of coffee every year—a harvest he must ship to purchase points in a nearby village. He calculates that with the El Orejón road, his freight charges have dropped from $800 to $250. This can easily mark the difference between a successful crop and one operating at a loss.

In addition, roads make rural life much easier. Previously, taking mule paths to buy groceries and agricultural goods entailed a three-day odyssey for Suso. The community's new road not only allows him to reach the closest stores in half an hour by motorcycle, but also improves access to health care and his children's education. While these advantages are less tied to the disappearance of coca, it is important to note that now they are no longer counterbalanced by a desire to be out of the reach of military eradicators.

Thus, as farmers began turning away from coca cultivation in the early 2010s, they debated in their community action board meetings the idea of building roads. Those meetings were often contentious, and represented nothing less than a collective debate over the future economy and authority structure of their communities: whether to continue isolating themselves to avoid state power and protect coca economies, or pursue legal agriculture and turn to the state for help with roads. Unsurprisingly, areas with higher levels of coca cultivation were more resistant to building roads, while early roads were built by communities where many farmers already had cattle and wanted to be able to commercialize milk. But even if some communities, like Eduardo's, initially voted against roadbuilding, and even if some individual farmers maintained their opposition, the decision-making process eventually established public support for roadbuilding in nearly all of Briceño's hamlets.

Together, the region's farmers reached the conclusion that isolation would no longer be an advantage, that getting crops to market would no longer be a matter of carrying a few pounds of coca paste to a nearby buyer, and that mule paths would no longer be sufficient. They began to need roads—and, through them, the state. Thus, when community presidents reached out to state officials for help with roadbuilding, they acted as representatives of an infrastructural public that, dissenters notwithstanding, had collectively chosen to pursue its livelihoods through the state.

Moment Three: Building Roads

Eugenia's response to Ocaris's death included a short and telling statement of how the community built the road on which he perished. "We held raffles, we organized festivals, one way or another I found some money, and we managed to open that road." Notably, her records of how they financed the road might lead to a different conclusion. Of the road's cost of sixty-five thousand dollars in total, fifty thousand dollars came from an international NGO through a state official, seven thousand came from the mayor's office, nearby businesses and hamlets donated four thousand, and the community itself contributed only four thousand dollars with its festivals and raffles. The seeming disjuncture between Eugenia's statement and her bookkeeping reveals two broader points about Briceño's roads. First, as she says, they have been built by local effort, and thus are understood within communities as products of their own labor. Second, community initiative notwithstanding, the roads are financed with state resources, thus establishing relations of dependence on state officials.

As we chat during her brief mid-morning respite between cleaning up after breakfast and making lunch, Eugenia tells me that the El Orejón road began when a group of local women got together in late 2015 to begin clearing a route *a pica y pala* (with picks and shovels). Like Eduardo's community, they had just learned that coca substitution was coming to the community, and they faced the challenge of developing legal economies. Fortuitously, they

FIGURE 7.2. Eugenia used this picture, in which she is carrying a gasoline-powered generator, to solicit road funding.

also had newfound access to state officials who they hoped could help them finance the road. Their community was home to the headquarters of the land mine removal program that represented the first collaboration between the FARC and the Colombian government through ongoing peace negotiations. State officials from a variety of agencies flocked to the community.

On the first day when women began to clear the path, Eugenia took photos of their labor with her phone (fig. 7.2). "It was with those photos that I started to *gestionar* resources," she says. The word *gestionar* normally translates as "manage" or "operate," but in this case it refers to the ability to procure resources from powerful others. This concept of *gestión* (the noun form) is key to understanding the insistence of Eugenia and other local leaders that roads were products of their own initiative. Roads were not simply built for them by officials seeking to extend the state's reach. Local leaders had to struggle at each step of the way to *gestionar* the resources they needed to continue the projects. Eugenia sent the photos of women working on the road construction to all the state officials she had met—"as evidence of our necessity," she says.

"With women," Suso adds, looking up from sharpening his machete. "So they could more easily see how much we needed it." The photos implicitly scolded a state that had failed to live up to its paternal responsibilities to such an extent that women were forced to take up picks and shovels to build a road.

Eugenia's *gestión* began to work. Most important was a contact with the Ministry of Foreign Affairs (*Cancillería*), who visited El Orejón many times to coordinate international aid that entered in the land mine removal program. He arranged for the Pan American Development Foundation (FUPAD), an international NGO, to send the El Orejón community action board an initial donation, and in late 2016, the community used the money to hire an excavator to begin breaking the road, from the highway upward (fig. 7.3).

Even as the excavator did the heavy lifting, significant community labor was still required. At least once a week, men and women gathered in *convites* to clear away vegetation so that the machine could work. They had to house and feed the machine operator as well as give him an assistant; these duties rotated among community members, sometimes becoming the subject of arguments over who wasn't doing their share.

Continuing to pay for the excavator as it slowly made its way up the valley walls was also a matter of community labor and initiative. Three times the

FIGURE 7.3. The need for these excavators ties local livelihoods to the state.

community ran out of money, the excavator left, and the project stalled. The people organized festivals, soccer tournaments, and raffles—fifteen events over two and a half years—to raise money to ensure that the work could continue. Eugenia describes these as exhausting affairs in which she and other community members prepared huge pots of meat stew, fried *empanadas*, and sold chips and alcohol. These periodic events, along with the physical labor to support roadbuilding and even arguments over who wasn't doing their share, reinforced membership in an infrastructural public—not just a group of people who happened to live near each other, but a community that was collectively devoting significant labor to its shared interest in a road.

The money from state officials also required ongoing *gestión*, with Eugenia repeatedly calling on the mayor and, most importantly, her contact at the Ministry of Foreign Affairs for help. In the end, her contact got FUPAD to make six distinct donations, each of which required Eugenia and another woman to make an arduous trip to Medellín. The fact that an NGO rather than the state itself funded the road may seem, alongside the community's leadership in roadbuilding, to challenge the symbolically important image of the state as provider of public good. But this situation was atypical: most community roadbuilding efforts, occurring before the El Orejón road and without the same access to national state officials through the land mine removal program, drew on the mayor for resources. Further, I found that locals often lumped state and NGO programs together under the same banner of institutional strucure (*institucionalidad*; for other work on how NGOs produce state effects through assuming governance functions, see Ferguson and Gupta 2002). More important than the money's source, however, were the patterned relations generated through the donations, as Eugenia repeatedly turned to state officials for needed help. And just as critically, while it was Eugenia who developed personal relatioships with these officials, she did so as representative of a public that was highly invested in the outcome of these relationships. She reported back to the community through its WhatsApp group and in monthly meetings where the members debated next steps.

The road was finally finished in mid-2018. "We're living in glory now," Eugenia says. "Never in our dreams did we think that we would have a road going to our house. But we suffered a lot for that road."

Rather than seeing their new roads as evidence of the state's ability to bring modernity and progress, unlocking a virtuous cycle that might inspire obedience and consolidate state power by establishing the state as the guarantor of the public good, Briceño's farmers see them as a product of their own effort, suffering, and initiative. It is pragmatic concerns—the resources and machinery needed to build roads, which exceed community labor power, budgets, and shovels—that push community leaders like Eugenia to turn to state officials again and again for needed resources. Still, these patterned actions form relations of dependence through which the state becomes a useful force in the life of the community, essential to local livelihoods and aspirations. But the need for state resources doesn't end with a road's inauguration. As I describe in the next section, the ongoing struggle to maintain precarious roads strengthens collective membership within an infrastructural public. It ensures that the relationships with state officials persist, and allows those officials to draw on relationships with community presidents for help in implementing state projects.

Moment Four: Maintaining Roads

If the oft-repeated point that roads and other infrastructural projects are invisible until they break down (Star and Ruhleder 1996) is true, it is equally important to note that from the moment they are built, infrastructures begin a process of constant decay (Gupta 2018). This is particularly true in Briceño, an exceptionally hilly place where roads are cut into steep terrain, and where they traverse swift streams and face periodic torrential downpours. The region's economic transformation is also a factor; the growth of the cattle economy has driven massive deforestation, which only further destabilizes the hillsides. Particularly during rainy season, landslides around the municipality occur on a weekly basis, with roads either washed away or covered by deposits of rock and mud from above (fig. 7.4).

In this context, the state of local roads has become a matter of daily collective interest. Locals wake up after a heavy rainfall to check their roads. Those who need to travel to the village center or visit another farm call friends in the communities they will pass through to inquire about the state of the roads. When a section is damaged, people share photos on their community action board's WhatsApp group, debating what to do about the problem. Though clearing landslides often requires access to municipal heavy machinery, when they can fix the damage with picks, shovels, and elbow grease, the community gathers in *convites*.

These *convites* to maintain roads represent an important means by which communities enact their shared interests. Clearing mud and rocks is backbreaking work, but the *convites* are also social affairs—people share delicious stews prepared in massive pots with meat bought by the community action board, and plantains and yuca from their farms. Particularly during the rainy season, many communities devote at least a full day of labor to their roads every month. Road maintenance is thus by far the major public issue that brings

FIGURE 7.4. Community members drag a motorcycle across a landslide on the Orejón road. This space is notorious for landslides; the community once gathered to reopen their road to motorcycles on a Saturday, only for a landslide to again cover it on Tuesday. They organized another *convite* for the following Saturday. Opening the road to larger vehicles requires the municipal government's heavy machinery.

communities together, materializing their shared interests to constitute them as collective political actors.

This was also true, of course, even when communities only had mule paths. In this case, however, they turned instead to FARC guerrillas who helped organize work groups to maintain the paths and imposed fines on individuals who didn't participate. Indeed, this is an important part of the history behind local conceptions of transportation infrastructure as a public matter. Now that communities have roads, however, *convites* and guerrilla governance are often insufficient. When entire sections of road are washed away or are covered by large landslides, or when it periodically becomes necessary to pack down the roads' dirt surfaces, communities depend on the municipality's heavy machinery: one of two excavators; a road grader, used to create a flat surface; and a road roller, used to compact dirt. With Briceño's 230 kilometers of rural roads in a process of constant decay, demand for these machines is high, pushing communities into direct competition with each other.

A range of ethnographic and historical work has shown that roads and other infrastructures are a terrain of power, politics, and contestation in which communities struggle for limited resources. In directing their struggles to the state, the communities establish its power and authority (Anand et al. 2018; Guldi 2012). Nikhil Anand (2017) describes how in Mumbai, residents' struggles to access water bring them together to make claims on the state as "communities of the affected" (Marres 2012). Through ongoing political advocacy in defense of their water needs—protests, public meetings, and "intimately known and negotiated relations" (Anand 2017, 149) with city officials—they constitute themselves as "hydraulic publics," and the state itself as the subject of their claims.

Much like the shared demand for water in Mumbai, the communal need to maintain their roads brings Briceño's rural inhabitants together as political collectives that make claims on the state. It is largely through this claims-making that locals come to recognize the state as provider of public goods, an essential element to the formation of its symbolic power. If roadbuilding established patterned relations through which leaders like Eugenia turned repeatedly to state actors for needed aid, road maintenance provides the basis for a set of political practices that ensure the persistence of these relations of dependence.

On a Sunday morning I attend the monthly meeting of the association of community presidents. Cenizo, the village mayor, stands in front of the room of forty chairs mostly filled by men who have traveled to the village center to represent their hamlets' interests. "This space is for you," he says, referring to the presidents. This leads me to believe that he'll cede the floor quickly. I'm mistaken. He talks for half an hour, mostly about how hard he's working and how no one appreciates him. But he also gives the presidents direction for how they should relate to him and the municipal administration.

"I want you to be like small mayor's offices," he says. "If there's a problem in your hamlet, you should be the one who brings it to me." He draws on a metaphor. "The mayor's office is like getting a girlfriend. You try to get her to be with you. She says no. You keep saying yes, insisting. Eventually she gives in. It doesn't matter if you're black or white, ugly or attractive." His joking metaphor, received with knowing chuckles, establishes the insiders' trust of an old boys' club in this male-dominated space. This is how you need to court the mayor and get the state resources under his control, he means to say. Though I'm still an outsider, his tasteless joke is indicative of how being a man has helped facilitate my access to the sphere of local politics.

After Cenizo finishes, he sits down to be wooed. The first man who speaks thanks him for his hard work, and for recently sending the road grader to his community. He says Cenizo's help has been crucial. The crowd applauds. Then he asks the mayor if he can send the excavator; they've had a landslide on a particularly steep section that is preventing them from leaving the community, and the milk truck from entering. Their milk production is in danger of spoiling. The mayor puffs out his chest as he stands up. He promises to send the machine next week. The man thanks him profusely and comes up to shake his hand, bowing slightly. The crowd applauds.

Nearly all speakers follow the same pattern. First, they thank Cenizo for some project he has implemented, complimenting his hard work. Then they raise something they would like support for. All but two of their requests have to do with fixing roads. Often Cenizo grants it, and they shake hands as the crowd applauds. In a few cases he refuses. "It's easier to build a road then to maintain it," he remarks, while explaining to one man that because it's rainy season, the section he wants fixed would quickly be washed away again.

I later realize that mayors' discretionary decisions of which communities will receive the municipal machinery have a great deal to do with the clientelist relationships described in chapter 6 of this book. Unsurprisingly, like Eduardo, who used my Facebook page to criticize Wilmar for not sending machines to help maintain his community's road, people often complain about the mayor's use of limited resources. However, these periodic complaints do not challenge state authority. Instead, in expressing a baseline assumption that the state is responsible for roads, rural communities' most important public good, they both establish and affirm the state's rightful role and responsibility.

In a setting where the state's symbolic power is well established, where subject populations believe in "the state," the authority of the mayor is guaranteed by the office itself and its place within the state (Bourdieu 2014). In Briceño, however, the figure of the mayor—and, by extension, the state— long existed with little authority. Community presidents say they were more likely to turn to guerrilla commanders for help with collective problems like controlling criminality, organizing the coca economy, and maintaining mule paths. They often did not even bother to attend meetings with the mayor. But now they must establish positive relationships with the mayor or face being replaced, like Eduardo, by new presidents better positioned to obtain municipal resources.

These relationships are also critical to state officials' ability to effectively implement projects in the territory. The municipal Office of Community Development, for example, regularly calls on community presidents to identify beneficiaries of home improvement programs that use state funds to pave dirt floors, build indoor bathrooms, and fix leaky roofs. When Covid-19 struck, these same presidents coordinated the delivery of groceries to needy families.

The substitution program also drew on community presidents to organize goods delivery and ensure community attendance at agricultural trainings.

While state programs like these, which meet local needs, simultaneously depend on and incentivize relationships with community presidents, the relationships also help officials access needed information about social and property relations that are otherwise illegible to the state. The municipal government's most effective population census comes from membership lists shared by community presidents. With state records of property deeds hopelessly out of date, officials also depend on community presidents to identify the owners of land where they plan to build electrical lines or aqueducts. Most tellingly, one day while I met with a municipal employee, a representative of the departmental government (the equivalent of a US state) called him to ask about an anonymous tip that the guerrillas had been obliging communities to organize *convites* in areas known to have land mines. The employee called the presidents of the affected communities and verified the information within minutes. In a context where providing information about armed groups can be a death sentence, this is remarkable—and it would have been completely unimaginable outside those presidents' relationship with him.

Thus, the ability of state officials to meet their objectives depends on relationships with community presidents that allow the state to interface with communities. Community presidents' deference toward the mayor and cooperation with other state officials are inspired more by a practical need for resources under their control than by a suddenly developing belief in their authority. And the fact that community presidents who support the wrong candidate may struggle to persuade the mayor to send municipal machinery to their communities may challenge rather than reinforce the ideal conception of the state as the impartial provider of the public good. Nevertheless, frustrating as they may be, the state/society relations that unfold through the ongoing struggle to maintain precarious roads are critical to state effectiveness and authority.

Moment Five: Improving Roads

In May 2019, after nine months away at graduate school, I return to Colombia for my second extended fieldwork stint. With all my worldly possessions for the next three months strapped precariously to the back of my motorcycle, I turn onto Briceño's dirt access road, still a bumpy hour and a half from the village center. But shortly, a pleasant surprise: a stretch of road that had once turned into slippery mud with any rainfall is newly paved! I accelerate,

FIGURE 7.5. The entrance road to Briceño has been paved section by section.

enjoying the views of the village center far across the Espiritu Santo River valley, as my moto rolls smoothly over the new concrete surface (fig. 7.5). Within a kilometer, the paving ends, and I return to picking my way through mud and rough rock. However, two other sections of the road have also been paved, reducing my travel time considerably. Is this proof, I wonder, of the modernity and development promised by the coming of the state, one stretch of pavement at a time?

Progress is also notable on the roads to Briceño's more isolated communities. The municipality is executing multiple projects to improve particularly steep and landslide-prone sections of isolated roads. These use *placahuellas*, a cheaper form of paving common for low-use rural roads in Colombia, in which only two narrow tracks corresponding to where you would expect a vehicle's tires to go are fully paved, and the rest of the road is filled in with a mixture of rocks and concrete (fig. 7.6). These projects make a tangible impact. Not only is it easier to get around the territory, but the targeted roads are much less likely to be rendered impassable, and communities do not need to dedicate as much time to *convites*.

Two separate projects are also underway to pave the first stretch of road that connects the village center with most of the municipality's rural hamlets. However, these projects seem to be stalled. At one point, where newly paved surface suddenly gives way to muddy gravel, a large concrete mixer sits abandoned by the side of the road, marked black by an apparent fire. Within a couple of weeks, the burned mixer is signed with the spray-painted tag of the guerrillas: "FARC 36th Front."

I try to figure out what has happened. By the time I sit down with Guillermo, a clean-cut and friendly man in his mid-thirties who works as a manager of the paving projects, construction has resumed. "The problem started with a *vacuna*," he tells me. The term *vacuna* is used in Colombia to refer to the payments that business owners, contractors, and occasionally private citizens pay to armed groups who operate protection rackets. Guillermo tells me that the rearmed guerrillas reached out to the contractor in charge of the paving project, demanding he pay a *vacuna* of $40,000. The contract itself was for a total of $1.67 million, Guillermo adds, implying that the *vacuna* was relatively small. "But the man played dumb [*se hizo el loco*] and didn't pay."

Construction went on for three months until one night, under cover of darkness, the guerrillas torched the concrete mixer, rendering it inoperable. The construction work then stopped for nearly six months. Finally, the contractor paid the *vacuna* and work resumed. The guerrillas, however, added another condition. "After burning the first one," Guillermo explains, "they prohibited bringing in another machine."

"Why would they do that?" I ask.

FIGURE 7.6. Before the *placahuellas* project, this steep stretch of road was prone to landslides.

"With all the unemployment in the municipality, they made it known that it's to generate more jobs. And now everyone knows that in any construction job, you can't use that kind of machine." Before the guerrillas burned the large motorized mixer, a team of ten workers had used it to process and lay down roughly 280 bags of cement each day, mixing them with the sand, gravel, and water that goes into making concrete. Now, Guillermo tells me, twenty men using two small manual concrete mixers can handle 260 bags per day. With nearly the same output, they are providing twice as many jobs.

The disadvantage, Guillermo tells me, is for the contractor, whose costs increase by roughly 20 percent because of the extra workers. "But he's already making enough," Guillermo says. "Without even mentioning the mayor and the guerrillas. Why not give a little work to people who really need it?"

Though I don't ask him if he's aware of the exact deal between the mayor and the contractor, Guillermo's cryptic mention of the mayor is a reference to a customary arrangement in which would-be contractors support mayoral candidates in exchange for no-bid access to lucrative municipal contracts, eventually kicking back a significant sum to the mayor. As described in chapter 6, the mayor also uses these jobs to reward political supporters.

But Guillermo says that while the guerrillas' extortion ended up creating jobs in the project he is working on, a different paving project just up the road is currently stalled by their demand for a *vacuna*, leaving thirty-five men who had been working there temporarily unemployed. I ask Guillermo how the men working on his project interpreted the guerrillas' actions.

"They have jobs, which isn't nothing," Guillermo says. "But I guess the guerrillas never would have burned the machine in the first place if the contractor had just paid the *vacuna*. And now the other project is stopped. So that's thirty-five people. If it doesn't continue, what are they going to do? This problem didn't exist when there was coca. There was always work for coca pickers. But now, people are desperate. What's going to happen when these construction projects stop?"

✳ ✳ ✳

These road improvement projects illuminate the complexity of the construction of state authority in Briceño. On the one hand, roads provide a meeting space for the symbolic and material, where ideas about the state encounter its literally concrete instantiation (Harvey 2005). Paving projects represent a marker of inclusion within the protective and prosperous reach of the state, while also providing needed jobs that deepen the state's increasing importance to local livelihoods (fig. 7.7). They represent one of the most tangible ways in which the state has brought progress to the village, challenging

FIGURE 7.7. Road paving provides jobs and tangible evidence of the state as carrier of progress and modernity.

widespread understandings of state abandonment (see chapter 2). Locals feel the state's concrete contributions through smooth roads and decreased transportation times—though they also feel the painful shortcomings of state power through tragedies like Ocaris's death, and from the gravel they pull from their skinned elbows after a motorcycle accident.

Paving projects also highlight the self-interest that seems to be behind much of state power. The jobs and projects are distributed on the basis of clientelist logic, meaning that many needy communities and individuals are excluded. And they are haunted by the ever-present suspicion of corruption, contributing to a sense that they always fall short of the progress they *should* bring to the municipality.

Finally, these projects establish another arena for the entanglement of guerrillas with state authority (see chapter 5). Road paving and other public works projects represent significant investments in the community, but they also provide the primary source of guerrilla funding. And like the state, guerrilla intervention in road paving establishes a tension between self-interest and collective good. The guerrillas extort large sums of money from these projects, bringing them to a halt when contractors or state officials don't pay. At the same time, they intervene to ensure that the projects provide sorely needed additional jobs—evidence that even state actors must accede to their threat of violence, and that this threat continues to fulfill useful functions for the community.

Conclusion

Over ten years, while a hydroelectric dam and a landmark peace process brought Briceño under the gaze of state power, the village's transportation infrastructure went from rudimentary mule paths to a network of 230 kilometers of dirt roads that connected its rural hamlets to the outside world. Political theorists and policymakers have long understood roadbuilding as a central means by which the state extends its power, allowing it to penetrate social relations throughout its territory, culturally and economically integrate isolated communities, and create legitimacy and consent by establishing itself as the provider of the public good (Guldi 2012; OECD 2011; Scott 1998; Weber 1976). Briceño's explosion of roadbuilding, however, occurred through not state but local leadership. While an awkward fit within common assumptions of state-led roadbuilding, a focus on community initiative reinforces this book's argument that collective decisions to pursue livelihoods through the state or through alternative governors are what determine who can govern the excluded. This chapter's ethnographic account of efforts to build, maintain, and improve these roads illuminates the processes through which livelihood strategies configure local authority relations.

A first step, and one way of understanding the relationship between state formation and economic transformation, is to explain why communities begin to enlist the state for help in meeting their everyday needs and future aspirations. Briceño's campesinos only began to need roads through the collective project of replacing coca and gold panning with legal agriculture. Multiple elements were behind their changing livelihood strategies: state initiatives like the dam project, the coca substitution program, and the military suppression of coca; ecological factors in the form of worms and fungus that ate away at coca profits; and a global food production regime, enabled by national economic policy, that drives down the prices of agricultural goods. This is not a sinister project to put campesinos at the mercy of officials who control state resources. Rather, these varied forces have articulated together as a "strategy without a strategist" (Dreyfus et al. 1983, 187), driving an economic transformation through which communities have come to depend on roads and on the state itself for their livelihoods.

And while the contribution of public goods provision to state formation is well documented, I argue for a focus on publics themselves—political collectivities brought together through shared needs for things like roads or water (Anand 2017; Collier et al. 2016; Dewey 1927). As I have described, it was through collective struggles around road construction and repair that communities came together as infrastructural publics capable of appointing representatives to engage state officials on their behalf. These publics are a precondition for the processes of state formation I describe here; their representatives build relationships with state officials that not only enable communities to access needed resources but allow officials to enlist collaboration in executing state projects. Over time, these collective efforts may lead to the development of a taken-for-granted belief in "the state" as provider of the public good. But particularly in its early stages, state formation depends less on embedding ideas and practices of the state within individual lives than on building mutually beneficial relationships between state officials and community leaders who credibly represent public interests.

A related finding is that local struggles over authority are carried out more through establishing relations with community representatives around the resolution of collective problems than through military confrontations (which were rare during my fieldwork). Theorists have long understood that areas where state authority is not well established tend to experience alternative systems of governance rather than an authority vacuum—and that convincing civilians to follow state over alternative systems of social control is critical to state formation (Arjona 2016; Migdal 1988). In chapter 5 I used the example of helmet use, required by state law but banned by guerrilla decree, to describe how tensions between competing systems of law and order are resolved in everyday life. But authority figures do not only give orders; on a global level, both states and alternative governors have taken an increasingly active role in promoting the livelihoods of their subjects (see the introduction to this book).

If building and fixing roads brings Colombian communities to the state, keeping law and order and enforcing participation in collective small-scale road maintenance—problems the state does not resolve—simultaneously provides the basis for a different set of ties with guerrilla commanders. And just like the state, the effectiveness of guerrilla governance practices depends on their ties to community representatives. The guerrillas in Briceño are only able to enforce *convite* participation, for example, because presidents identify free riders. The tensions between guerrilla and state systems of social control will be resolved largely on the strength of relationships, rooted in the resolution of collective problems, that communities build with each. Before the state can monopolize violence, therefore, it must monopolize community problem-solving.

Building state authority—like building the roads—is an imperfect, contested, and ongoing process involving a variety of actors motivated by a range of different interests. State power and authority are neither a guaranteed outcome nor necessarily the primary driving force behind this process. Nevertheless, the case of Briceño suggests that the best chance for establishing state authority may come through collaboration with local communities around the provision of roads and other needed goods. It is through those goods that locals began turning to the state for help with their everyday problems, and providing public authorization of state power. It is through those goods that the livelihoods of locals and their ambitions for the future become tied to the state. And finally, it is through the relations of dependence that unfold through goods provision that state officials can govern.

Conclusion: An Alternative Model?

During Colombia's 2022 presidential election I joined a small group in Briceño that was campaigning not to position themselves to access state resources, but to support a candidate promising a new vision for Colombia: Gustavo Petro, a former member of the M-19 guerrillas, who hoped to become the first left-wing president in the country's history. His running mate, Francia Marquez, was an Afro-Colombian woman who had gotten her political start opposing a hydroelectric dam project and a multinational gold mine that menaced her community. After years of accompanying Colombian political campaigns as an observer, I ditched any pretense of objectivity and for the first time actively tried to influence potential voters. Many of Petro's campaign promises spoke to my own sense of reforms that would benefit communities like Briceño: scaling back of extractive industries, subsidizing of campesino economies, renegotiation of free trade agreements to protect domestic agriculture, resumption of a peace process that had ground to a halt, and negotiation of new peace agreements with the country's remaining armed groups (fig. C.1).

Petro's landmark win created an opportunity not only for meaningful reform, but for evaluating the potential to counter many of the historical trends I have described in these pages. Could his administration reconfigure Colombia's place within global agricultural economies to open space for smallholder agricultural production? Could it put the brakes on a decades-long shift to extraction as the motor of rural economies? Could it dismantle coca economies, repressive coca eradication campaigns, and related violence? And finally, could it negotiate with or weaken the country's many armed groups to establish peace and state authority?

These are lofty goals for any four-year administration, and a comprehensive analysis of its performance is beyond the scope of this book. Nevertheless,

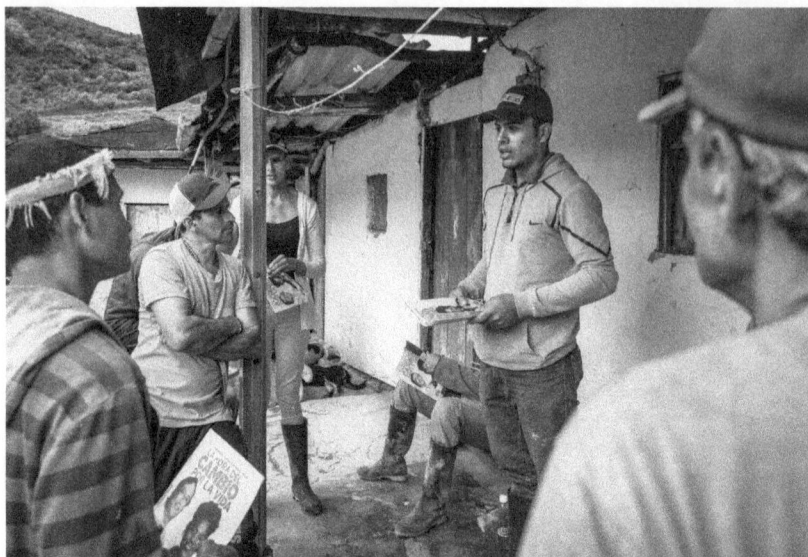

FIGURE C.1. Dideison campaigns for Petro.

the experiences of Briceño in the Petro administration's first two years offers clues to some of the challenges—but also opportunities—in the effort to push back against a globally dominant economic model and to rewrite local authority relations across Colombian territory.

For one thing, the administration's efforts to negotiate peace agreements with the country's remaining armed groups are falling flat. Even where groups like the National Liberation Army have ideologically motivated national leadership, the aging revolutionaries are out of touch with local commanders who are more concerned with maintaining their illicit incomes. Briceño's rearmed guerrillas belong to a national organization headed by Iván Mordisco, a longtime FARC commander who refused to join the 2016 agreement and is known for a propensity for violence and a hunger for power and illicit profits. Mordisco did briefly enter into peace negotiations; but in places like Briceño, the rearmed FARC guerrillas took advantage of a ceasefire to consolidate local control and intensify their extortion of local businesses, farmers, and state projects. While the guerrillas continue working with community action boards to resolve a range of collective problems, they seem to have abandoned any underlying revolutionary vision.

The best chance at supplanting guerrilla authority, unfortunately, has come from the Gulf Clan, a paramilitary group that began repeated incursions into the territory in June 2023, culminating in November of that year when a large troop entered in force, killing one civilian and confining hundreds of campesinos to their homes for days. The guerrillas, defeated, fled the area. The mayor went to Bogotá to plead for help, and eventually the military entered to drive the paramilitaries back. The guerrillas returned, but with their territorial control under attack, they intensified their recruitment of local youth.

The underlying uncomfortable truth is that for decades Colombia has been signing peace agreements that fail to establish peace. In these peace processes, aging commanders negotiate their retirements, many longtime troops take to civilian life, and structures of local control are disrupted. Yet the armed groups themselves have consistently reconfigured rather than disappeared. The usual pattern is that demobilization allows ambitious mid-level lieutenants to rise to the rank of commander: this is the history behind both the village's rearmed FARC group and the Gulf Clan, which emerged from the country's negotiated paramilitary demobilization in 2003–6. The effectiveness of any peace process will be highly limited as long as desperate youth lack better options than to take up arms, and illicit profits are up for grabs.

Colombia's most prominent illicit economy, however, has seen major dips in profitability. In 2022 it entered into crisis as coca cultivators across the country reported that no one was buying their production. Reports identified a number of causes: overproduction, disputes for territorial control, an increase in the cost of goods used to process coca, and the disruption of trafficking routes due in part to the retirements of corrupt police and military officials, in most cases forced by the Petro administration (Forero Rueda and Fukuda 2023; Isacson 2023). When I returned to Briceño in 2024, I learned that coca farmers there had gone nearly a year without finding buyers. With as many as four consecutive harvests worth of coca paste saved up and unpurchased, they were abandoning their illicit crops. It was the second time, after the 2017 launch of the substitution program, that local coca farmers had to refashion new livelihoods.

To replace coca, many campesinos and armed groups have turned back to gold. But while campesinos' traditional gold panning along the beaches of the Cauca River, now flooded by the dam reservoir, required no aid from either the state or armed groups, Briceño's newly established gold extraction economy is directly organized by the guerrillas. In early 2024 illicit entrepreneurs brought in heavy machinery to extract gold from the banks of the Espíritu Santo River, an illegal and environmentally damaging process that is highly destructive to local ecosystems (fig. C.2). As they did with coca, the rearmed guerrillas charge a 10 percent tax on all revenues. But they also ensure that campesinos can share in the profits.

FIGURE C.2. A photo Dideison sent me of Briceño's gold mine shows the environmental devastation—and economic opportunity—created by these mining practices.

In a customary practice long imposed across the region by different armed groups, including in a similar mine in Briceño from 2008 to 2009, the guerrillas make those who are running the mine grant space to locals to pull their own gold from the massive holes they dig along the riverbanks. Digging deep uncovers gold that has been trapped in the ground for decades. Dideison spent months there, working in concert with two other young men to use streams of water, a metal lattice, and the traditional bowl-shaped wooden gold pan (the *batea*) to separate flecks and pebbles of gold from the silt. On a bad day, they might find no gold at all. But on good days, Dideison took home as much as a hundred dollars—and some locals reported making twenty times as much.

There was so much demand, Dideison told me, that the guerrillas established three separate three-hour shifts, ensuring that everyone had a chance—
everyone, that is, except municipal employees. The guerrillas' reasoning in
barring state employees from taking a shift was that the mine should generate
an income for those who did not already have employment. But the decision
perfectly highlights the tension between local decisions about whether to
pursue livelihoods through the state or through alternative governors. Some
municipal employees even quit their jobs to pursue gold profits that, while
less secure, offered the promise of greater windfalls.

For a concrete example of how these livelihoods strengthen armed groups'
authority and endanger the Petro administration's efforts to govern, we need
only travel a few dozen kilometers downriver to a region called the Lower
Cauca, where the Gulf Clan paramilitaries use similar practices to organize
and profit from illicit gold mining. In 2023, acting on the president's orders
to protect the environment and attack the paramilitaries' finances, the Colombian military destroyed several illegal gold dredgers—boats that scrape
the sediment on the bottom of rivers to extract gold from it. In response,
the community carried out a *paro*, blocking traffic on the highway that leads
from Medellín to the Caribbean coast. The paramilitaries supported the *paro*,
forcing local businesses to close and community members to participate (IPC
2023). The region was paralyzed for a month.

Popular debate centered on whether the mobilization represented poor
communities' efforts to defend their livelihoods from state repression, or the
paramilitaries' instrumentalization of the community to protect their own
power and illicit incomes. But the critical point is that both those interpre-
tations were accurate. Like Eduardo's community's defense of the captured
FARC-supported coca buyer I described in chapter 1, local authority relations
turned on the fact that locals depended on an illicit economy run by armed
groups. This allowed the paramilitaries to enlist the community to recognize
and even defend their authority claims at the expense of the state.

But gold panning is not the only traditional livelihood strategy that has
experienced a resurgence in Briceño. Even as coca agriculture tanked, in late
2024 the price of coffee jumped to $3.50 a pound (compared with less than $1
five years earlier), a result of underproduction caused by drought, followed
by torrential rains in Brazil. Not only have Colombian coffee farmers cashed
in, but the boom created demand for coffee pickers during the three-month
end-of-year harvest—the kind of labor, traditionally performed by unedu-
cated young men, that can restrain armed group recruitment. And if the new
modality of gold panning provides the basis for guerrilla authority, coffee,

dependent on local roads and supported by countless state agricultural programs, ties local livelihoods to the state.

Coffee is labor-intensive, well suited to Briceño's volcanic soil and high-altitude slopes, and highly valued in both global consumption markets and campesinos' collective imaginaries. It is exactly the kind of crop that should offer the possibility of building a peaceful future. But the history and internal dynamics of coffee markets suggest that its prices will crater as worldwide shortages overcorrect. Briceño's coffee farmers are already responding to high prices by planting more; by the time those bushes bear fruit, the global market may be flooded. Perversely, the best shot at overcoming such market dynamics may come from climate change making extreme weather conditions—and the resulting shortages and price booms—more common, a development that would benefit Briceño's coffee farmers only until their own crops are destroyed.

Can Global South states give their smallholding farmers a better shot with policies designed to protect agricultural prices, preserve valued rural lifestyles, and, particularly in conflict zones where alternative governors organize illicit economies, ensure that communities pursue their livelihoods through the state? The Petro administration has tried; it has nearly tripled the federal budget for agriculture; halted new contracts for gas, coal, and petroleum exploration; and established programs to facilitate campesino access to credit and subsidized agricultural goods (Redacción Economía 2022; Sojo 2023). Nevertheless, other reforms have been blocked or watered down by an opposition congress. And just as the IMF used loans and the United States used military aid to persuade Colombia to open its economy to international investors (see chapters 1 and 4), efforts to close the national economy to multinational profiteers draw informal sanctions, not least through the devaluation of the Colombian currency.

We should not overestimate the ability of Global South governments to reconfigure national economies. The economic opportunities available to the poor shift through a complex conjuncture of factors including technological innovation, international pressure, state economic policy, local political competition, armed groups' income strategies, global market forces, and even non-human forces like weather and worms. While these forces have transformed the livelihood strategies from which Briceño's campesinos have to choose, the collective dilemma they share with conflict-affected communities across the world has been preserved: Will they pursue their livelihoods through armed groups, or through the state? How they resolve this dilemma will be decisive to local authority relations, the national government's ability to transform Colombian society, and the future of an embattled peace process.

A Final Elegy

I had planned to close this book with the story of Dideison. When I returned to Colombia in the summer of 2024, I found to my surprise that he had just moved to Medellín. This was Dideison, who had said city living made him miserable. Dideison, who in the six years I knew him had matured into one of Briceño's most capable and eloquent social leaders, president of the municipal youth council, dedicated to building a better future for the village. Dideison, who only a year earlier had begun his university studies online because he didn't want to relocate to the city.

I was going to explain how electoral defeat had quashed Dideison's chances at accessing the state resources that have become essential to local livelihoods. He had spent much of his adolescence picking coca before a short stint in the municipal administration in 2019, where he campaigned for the mayor's preferred candidate. After his side lost the election, he patched together a precarious living with gold panning, work on the family coffee farm, and sporadic support—including temporary low-wage jobs—from politicians who hoped to recruit him into future campaigns. By 2023 he was back on the campaign trail. But again, his candidate lost. And again, Dideison knew he had no shot at a municipal job.

I was going to describe how the local escalation in conflict pushed him to Medellín. In Briceño, under periodic military assault from the paramilitaries, the guerrillas had sought to increase their numbers, drawing in local youth with promises of status and money. With no other work to be had, many of Dideison's friends had joined. Dideison, working weekends at a local nightclub, had repeatedly encountered the guerrillas. They had asked him to hide their guns, had invited him to join the group (even offering to pay his university tuition), and had forced him to give a risky motorcycle ride to a high-ranking member who was wanted by the military. Without a stable income, and fearful of getting caught up in violence, Dideison had left for Medellín.

I was going to describe the neighborhood to which he moved, perched in the hillsides above the city and filled with nearly a hundred Briceño transplants who helped each other make ends meet. When I visited Dideison there only a week after his arrival, he was already working as a carpenter's assistant, and on weekend nights as security for a nightclub. Both the carpenter and the club owner were from Briceño. Dideison had regrets about leaving the village behind, but was happy to be working and living among friends and family (fig. C.3).

I was going to leave this vignette without a neat resolution, typical of the uncertain futures faced by the poor as they piece together a precarious living.

FIGURE C.3. Dideison gave up rural landscapes for city streets.

The carpentry position didn't last, and Dideison struggled to pay his bills. The last time I saw him, he was planning to seek help from political contacts. One idea was to drive for Uber, borrowing one politician's car and getting another to pay for his driver's license. I was going to suggest that Dideison— forced to leave the land he loved, caught between competing authority figures, casting a wide net to eke out a precarious living—stands in for billions of the excluded poor across the Global South.

But before I could write it up, Dideison's story came to a tragic end. On July 15, 2024, he was stabbed to death in a village north of Medellín. He was twenty-five. Days later, his grieving family received another blow: a police report that said he was killed while he and two other men were stealing four pigs. It is a story, in a country with a long history of murdering and stigmatizing poor and innocent young men,[1] that those who knew Dideison have rejected. It is also a story, in a country whose epidemic of social leader killings was once dismissed by the defense minister as "skirt troubles" (*líos de faldas*), that I do not believe—though I have been unable to figure out what really happened.

Still, for anyone who did not know Dideison, the story seems believable. Across the Global South, people excluded from the possibility of making a living through wage labor or agricultural production commit and are victimized by acts of crime and violence. Those who join armed groups, commit petty crime, and cultivate and traffic drug crops come overwhelmingly from the excluded poor—desperate people without better options.

Accompanying Dideison over the years as he shifted from picking coca through an economy organized by the FARC guerrillas to participating in electoral politics in the hopes of getting state resources allowed me to understand a broader, if incomplete, transformation. Briceño's communities have begun pursuing their livelihoods through the state rather than, or in addition to, armed groups. An ethnographic perspective shows that turning to the state in this way helps establish its authority by driving a growing belief in "the state" as ultimate political authority and by creating ties with community representatives that officials use to implement state projects.

Yet the state's new role is not exclusive, whether in Briceño or many other areas of the Global South. Just as Dideison drew on guerrilla authority to resolve a dangerous misunderstanding (see chapter 5), alternative governors resolve problems the state does not. And while the army and guerrillas periodically shoot at each other, the conflict between the FARC and state authority is often not conflictual at all. These purported rivals are instead entangled in surprising ways, sharing governance functions and at times even supporting each other's authority. More than exchanges of bullets, local dynamics of authority—determining who fulfills which function or who can enforce which law—are constituted by community members as they turn to armed groups to sell coca, to guerrilla commanders or the police to control crime, or to the mayor for a job or help with their roads.

Centering livelihood strategies does not mean focusing on agency at the expense of structural forces. Rather, ethnographic description of how people seek to make a living offers a window into understanding how broader economic and political forces play out on the ground. Most important is explaining the reasons why so many people across the Global South must turn to the state or to alternative governors to meet their basic needs: widespread economic exclusion driven by technological advances that slash labor needs for both manufacturing and agriculture, extractive projects that dispossess rural communities of land and traditional livelihoods, and trade liberalization that undermines local producers by dismantling barriers to the global circulation of cheap commodities.

But political shifts also open opportunities. Democratization has allowed people like Dideison to negotiate access to state resources, providing the basis for the intensified state resource distribution that I argue is now the primary driver of state formation in the Global South. On the other hand, prohibitionist drug policies have protected drug crops from the plummeting prices of legal agriculture, left drug economies to armed groups, and pushed drug cultivators to avoid state forces and eradication programs that attack their livelihoods. The strategies that people like Dideison, Eduardo, Suso, Eugenia, Fabio, and Angélica employ to meet their daily needs and build a better future in response to these changing opportunity structures will also determine who can govern the excluded.

Acknowledgments

The paradox of writing is that, while it is an inherently solitary act, it cannot be done well without support from others. This book has come about thanks to the many people who have supported, mentored, collaborated with, and critiqued my work since I began research for this project in 2018.

My greatest debt is to the community of Briceño, the village whose stories animate this book and the place where I lived for more than three years. In academic settings, people's most common reaction to the mention of this extended time period is a kind of impressed concern, based on the assumption that it represented years of suffering and self-sacrifice. But the truth, thanks to its inhabitants, is that I thoroughly enjoyed my years in Briceño. Ethnographic research *is* hard, from the discipline of willing tired fingers to type field notes after a long day of fieldwork to the need to jettison personal boundaries as you seek to inhabit other people's worlds. But thanks to its people, living in Briceño was also pleasurable. From the start, the village's inhabitants invited me into their lives and homes, embraced my research project, and treated me with warmth and generosity. I am particularly thankful to Alejandra, Anderson, Andrés, Aracelly, Arcadio, Beatriz, Camilo, Darío, Deivi, Deisson, Deris, Duván, Edgar, Guillermo, Genaro, Gloria, Ignacio, Isleny, Jader, Jhon Jairo, Julián, Julie, Leany, Luis, Mario, Mauricio, Ocaris, Omar, Patricia, Primo, Richard, Rosita, Rubén, Wilmar, Yaned, Yeison, Yeleny, Yofre, and Zancudo. This manuscript is filled with their insights, and I will forever be grateful for the trust and friendship they have offered me. I would also be remiss if I did not recognize my favorite baristas, Andrés and Juan, who made me delicious caffè lattes, let me turn their café into my "office" in Briceño, and always made me feel welcomed and cared about.

A central part of my day-to-day research was the filming of a documentary film, titled *An Uncomfortable Peace*, which focuses on two of the families whose stories I tell in this book. I thank Fabio Muñoz, Angélica Mazo, Bernardo Pelaéz, Suso Mazo, Eugenia Holguín, Adrián Mazo, Sebastián Mazo, Susana Mazo, and Dubian Mazo for not only allowing us to record their lives but enthusiastically participating in the filmmaking process. I also owe a great debt to Carlos Álvarez, Luis Carlos Gallego, Óscar Osorio, and Ricardo Venegas, my behind-the-camera collaborators on the film. All accompanied me on filming trips in Briceño, patiently tolerated my lack of filmmaking experience, and inspired me with their creative and political vision. Ricardo also supported my early forays into photography with needed advice on equipment, composition, and editing.

I carried out my research through generous support from various funding agencies: the National Science Foundation, the Harry Frank Guggenheim Foundation, the United States Institute of Peace, the American Philosophical Society, and the Urban Ethnography Lab and Rapoport Institute for Human Rights and Inequality at the University of Texas. Fragments of this book appeared in articles published in the *American Journal of Sociology*, *Contexts*, *Ethnographic Marginalia*, *Qualitative Sociology*, *Social Problems*, and *Sociological Forum*, and as a chapter in the book *Portraits of Persistence: Inequality and Hope in Latin America* (University of Texas Press, 2024). I am thankful for permission to reprint these passages, and to the journal editors and anonymous reviewers for helpful feedback on my work.

I began research for this book as a doctoral student at the University of Texas at Austin. I am grateful to Maya Charrad, Dani Fridman, Phillip Hough, and Harel Shapira for constructive criticism and needed help in navigating the choppy waters of political and economic sociology as I struggled to harness the stories in this book to make a broader theoretical argument. Javier Auyero was a generous and brilliant advisor, modeling a mix of concrete guidance, intellectual inspiration, and human kindness that I now try to reproduce with my students. I thank him for teaching me how to study politics through everyday observation, for responding to my emails within five minutes, and for embracing a Latin American approach to solving institutional problems. I am also thankful to Bill Bigelow and Jim Dyal (at Franklin High School) and Mary Ann Clawson and Rob Rosenthal (at Wesleyan University), who inspired the early stages of my academic journey. I finished this text as a member of the Oklahoma State University sociology faculty, with colleagues who have managed to establish a supportive and harmonious environment even as sociology departments across the country are under attack. I thank Danny Alvord, Jonathan

Coley, Jared Fitzgerald, Tammy Mix, Stephen Perkins, Corinne Schwarz, Kelley Sittner, and Monica Whitham for always having my back.

I was fortunate to share my formative years as a researcher with fellow students at the University of Texas and beyond, who even to this day continue pushing me to become a better scholar. For feedback, intellectual stimulation, and community, I thank Marta Ascherio, Nino Bariola, Ana Braconnier, Hyung Min Cha, Travis Cuvelier, Ilana Friedman, Tomás Gold, Maricarmen Hernández, Eldad Levy, Leslie MacColman, Sophie Morse, Francisco Sánchez, Patrick Sheehan, Ricardo Venegas, and Maro Youssef. The University of Texas Urban Ethnography Lab's weekly meetings taught me how to be a better colleague, and provided critique of early versions of some of these chapters. A collaborative book that came out of the lab, *Portraits of Persistence*, helped me find my voice as an ethnographic storyteller. I am honored to have a chapter in the book alongside those of Cynthia Ammerman, Javier Auyero, Allison Coffey, Jorge Derpic, Maricarmen Hernández, Katie Jensen, Eldad Levy, Marcos Pérez, Dennis Rodgers, Jennifer Scott, Sofía Servián, and Katie Sobering, and I am thankful for their comments on parts of chapter 4 in this book.

I also benefited from putting my work into conversation with a number of excellent scholars of Colombia like María Ximena Dávila, Guillaume Gass, Jon Gordon, Danny Hirschel Burns, Angie Lederach, and Nicolás Torres-Echeverry, who have shared feedback, friendship, and insights from their research. I am particularly fortunate to be accepted as the sociologist interloper in the Laboratory for Anthropology of the State in Colombia. Its members— Charles Beach, Gwen Burnyeat, Felipe Fernández, Ana María Forero, Roxani Krystalli, Erin McFee, María Fernanda Olarte-Sierra, Valentina Pellegrino, and Sebastián Ramírez—have made invaluable comments on chapters of this book, and have inspired me with their own writing.

In 2020 an extended conversation about fieldwork experiences with Sneha Annavarapu over WhatsApp voice notes became *Ethnographic Marginalia*, a website and podcast that discuss the experiences behind ethnographic research that are often relegated to the margins. This collaborative project has greatly influenced my thinking about how to conduct ethnographic research, and Sneha has generously and generatively commented on sections of this book. I cannot imagine a better coeditor and cohost.

I am also grateful to Mollie McFee and the anonymous reviewers at the University of Chicago Press. I was recently asked by graduate students about my journey in getting this book accepted for publication; I raved about what a supportive and painless process it has been before realizing that I should probably point out that the support I received was unusual. Mollie, who has enthusiastically advocated for this project as its editor for more than two years, deserves all the credit.

During fieldwork in Colombia, Juan Pablo Blanco offered friendship, invaluable logistic help in maintaining the motorcycle I used for fieldwork, an escape to Medellín for needed fieldwork breaks, and the promise of commandeering a helicopter to save me if my research ever got out of hand (it didn't). Diana Bernal inspired me with her dedication to social justice and her repeated willingness to make personal sacrifices to attack corruption and injustice. Luis Alberto Rojas has been for years my favorite person with whom to discuss Briceño, combining deep political commitment with intellectual curiosity; imagine my surprise at being drawn into a discussion of Foucault in the village's main square! Yesid Zapata does the thankless work of defending Antioquia's beleaguered social leaders, and during my research intervened many times to protect threatened communities and publicize campesino mobilizations.

A special thanks goes to my parents, Norm Diamond and Patricia Kullberg, who supported me immeasurably throughout this process as sounding boards, emotional support, and in my mother's case, the country's best line editor. Their example, of denouncing injustice and struggling for a better world, inspires the values and politics at the heart of this project.

Finally, Dideison Espinosa was for six years a friend, collaborator, occasional roommate, and central figure of my research. It breaks my heart that I will not be able to give him a copy of this book. It is dedicated to his memory.

Portland, Oregon
December 2024

Notes

Introduction

1. I use the word "campesino" here and throughout the book to refer to landowning and landless agricultural workers because this is how they self-identify (with pride), and because translations like "peasant" fail to capture the depth of meaning behind the term.

2. David Beetham's classic text *The Legitimation of Power* suggests two ways social action can help construct state legitimacy, which is necessary for the establishment of authority. The first is that these actions have a "subjectively binding force" for those who engage in them, creating a normative commitment to a given authority (Beetham 1991:18). Second, they provide public evidence of consent to power, demonstrating recognition of the state's authority for all to see.

3. For the sake of simplicity for an international audience, throughout this book I convert Colombian pesos into dollar amounts. As the Colombian peso has been significantly devalued, rather than using a standard conversion rate, I take the average exchange rate for the year I am describing—in this case, 2000.

4. Throughout my research, paramilitary groups made several limited attempts to enter the territory, leading to violent confrontations with both the guerrillas and the army. With coca mostly gone, however, the region's attractiveness to the paramilitaries has lessened.

5. Briceño is neither Colombia's only nor first peace laboratory. This designation for areas where specific peacebuilding initiatives are launched and evaluated was first used for a European Union–funded program in the early 2000s (Rudqvist and Van Sluys 2005).

6. A notable exception came when Eduardo asked me to post about his community's roads, as I describe in chapter six.

7. While ethnographers have long defaulted to anonymity, I have decided to respect the wishes of those who wanted me to use their real names: Suso and Eugenia (and their children Adrián, Sebastián, Susana, and Dubian), Fabio, Angélica, and Dideison (whose family wanted me to use his real name). All other names in the text are pseudonyms, with the exception of those of national state officials and the two men who served as mayor during my fieldwork.

Chapter One

1. While Eduardo's community, as described in the introduction, was mostly subject to FARC control, other parts of the village were historically dominated by paramilitaries—though the boundaries between the groups shifted over time.

2. It should be noted that in following years the brothel reopened, farmers began replanting smaller amounts of coca (chapter 3), and the security situation worsened (chapter 5).

3. The fact that there were more victims than inhabitants is explained by two factors: first, that many people have been victims of multiple acts, and second, that thousands of locals—whether through forced displacement or by seeking better opportunities for their families—have left the territory, most for Medellín.

4. The ex-guerrilla commander's statement mirrors statements by national FARC leadership, which denies direct participation in drug trafficking and insists that the FARC accepted and taxed coca only because had become essential to the livelihoods of its campesino base (Brittain 2010). However, the Colombian military and many politicians have long denounced the FARC as narcoterrorists, and a common narrative in both academic and political circles is that involvement in the coca trade shifted the group's energy away from revolution and toward the violent control of drug economies (Collier 1999; Weinstein 2007).

5. The same dynamics played out with paramilitary groups, though in slightly more complex terms: paramilitaries had a shorter and more limited history of local governance and often collaborated with state forces rather than challenging them.

6. Around the turn of the twentieth century and until the 1930s, the Dutch also cultivated coca in their Indonesian colonies, and the Japanese grew it in both Japan and Taiwan (Gootenberg 2008).

7. I am hesitant to speculate about why the FARC was invested in removing military eradicators, but as time went on it increasingly called on communities to remove soldiers from rural areas as a means of maintaining territorial control.

Chapter Two

1. From internal UNODC figures.

2. Briceño has a hospital, but it is in notoriously poor condition and usually has only one doctor, a recent graduate fulfilling the requirement of a year of rural service before beginning their "real" medical career.

3. The onset of Covid-19, which stalled nearly all state projects, was likely also a factor in the delays.

Chapter Three

1. Eric Wolf's (1955) oft-cited definition describes peasants as (1) agricultural producers who (2) control their land and (3) are oriented primarily to subsistence rather than reinvestment to grow their farms.

2. The video for "Coca por copa" can be seen at https://www.youtube.com/watch?v=Q8Mbn3VXJgY.

3. The FARC were historically relatively unique in having 20 to 30 percent female combatants (Gutiérrez Sanín 2008). Still, the paramilitary groups were almost all male, and the rearmed guerrillas also seem to have a much higher proportion of male combatants.

Chapter Four

1. Shots of aguardiente, a traditional cane liquor.

2. Since the NGO Frontline Defenders began keeping track of the killing of human rights defenders in 2014, Colombia has led the list every year, usually by wide margins. In 2022, 186 of the 401 documented killings worldwide were in Colombia (Front Line Defenders 2023).

3. An agricultural technician explained to me that coffee beans now fall to the ground unripe because their cell walls are weakened by larger temperature swings created by a warming greenhouse effect from the daytime clouds, combined with increased cooling at night from condensation.

4. The turn to extractivism in the 2000s was also continent-wide, and crossed political lines—driven not only by the political right in Colombia, Peru, and Paraguay, but also by left-wing governments in Argentina, Bolivia, Brazil, Ecuador, Uruguay, and Venezuela that used natural resource extraction to fund progressive policies like cash transfers, infrastructural development, and social welfare programs (Gudynas 2018).

Chapter Five

1. These costs were nearly halved in 2023 by the new Petro administration in an attempt to make legality a realistic possibility for poor motorcyclists.

Conclusion

1. Most notorious is the "false positives" scandal of the 2000s, in which at least 6,402 innocent young men were murdered in cold blood by the military and then dressed up as guerrilla combatants to inflate body counts.

References

Abrams, Philip. 1988. "Notes on the Difficulty of Studying the State (1977)." *Journal of Historical Sociology* 1, no. 1: 58–89. doi: 10.1111/j.1467-6443.1988.tb00004.x.

Abu-Lughod, Lila. 1990. "The Romance of Resistance: Tracing Transformations of Power Through Bedouin Women." *American Ethnologist* 17, no. 1: 41–55.

Acero, Camilo, and Frances Thomson. 2022. "'Everything Peasants Do Is Illegal': Colombian Coca Growers' Everyday Experiences of Law Enforcement and Its Impacts on State Legitimacy." *Third World Quarterly* 43, no. 11: 2674–92. doi: 10.1080/01436597.2021.1971517.

Agencia para la Reincorporación y la Normalización. 2022. *Informe de resultados audiencia pública de rendición de cuentas.*

Alexander, Michelle. 2012. *The New Jim Crow: Mass Incarceration in the Age of Colorblindness.* The New Press.

Álvarez-Rivadulla, María José. 2017. *Squatters and the Politics of Marginality in Uruguay.* Springer.

Anand, Nikhil. 2017. *Hydraulic City: Water and the Infrastructures of Citizenship in Mumbai.* Duke University Press.

Anand, Nikhil, Akhil Gupta, and Hannah Appel. 2018. "Introduction: Temporality, Politics, and the Promise of Infrastructure." In *The Promise of Infrastructure*, edited by N. Anand, A. Gupta, and H. Appel, 1–38. Duke University Press.

Araghi, Farshad. 2009. "The Invisible Hand and the Visible Foot: Peasants, Dispossession and Globalization." In *Peasants and Globalization: Political Economy, Rural Transformation and the Agrarian Guestion*, edited by A. H. Akram-Lodhi and C. Kay, 111–47. Routledge.

Aretxaga, Begoña. 2003. "Maddening States." *Annual Review of Anthropology* 32:393–410.

Aretxaga, Begoña. 2005. *States of Terror: Begoña Aretxaga's Essays.* Center for Basque Studies, University of Nevada, Reno.

Arjona, Ana. 2016. *Rebelocracy: Social Order in the Colombian Civil War.* Cambridge University Press.

Arjona, Ana, Nelson Kasfir, and Zachariah Mampilly, eds. 2015. *Rebel Governance in Civil War.* Cambridge University Press.

Arroyave, Jesús, and Martha Romero-Moreno. 2023. "Peace, Public Opinion and Disinformation in Colombia: Social Media and Its Role in the 2016 Plebiscite." In *The Palgrave*

Handbook of Media Misinformation, edited by K. Fowler-Watt and J. McDougall, 63–77. Springer International.

Associated Press. 2020. "Amazon Rainforest Continues to Burn in 2020, Despite Promises to Save It." *Los Angeles Times*, August 19.

Auty, Richard M. 1993. *Sustaining Development in Mineral Economies: The Resource Curse Thesis.* Routledge.

Auyero, Javier. 1999. "'From the Client's Point(s) of View': How Poor People Perceive and Evaluate Political Clientelism." *Theory and Society* 28, no. 2: 297–334.

Auyero, Javier. 2001. *Poor People's Politics: Peronist Survival Networks and the Legacy of Evita.* Duke University Press.

Auyero, Javier. 2012. *Patients of the State: The Politics of Waiting in Argentina.* Duke University Press.

Auyero, Javier, and Sofía Servián. 2025. *Squatter Life: Persistence at the Urban Margins of Buenos Aires.* Duke University Press.

Azoulay, Ariella. 2008. *The Civil Contract of Photography.* Zone Books.

Ballvé, Teo. 2020. *The Frontier Effect: State Formation and Violence in Colombia.* Cornell University Press.

Basedau, Matthias, and Jann Lay. 2009. "Resource Curse or Rentier Peace? The Ambiguous Effects of Oil Wealth and Oil Dependence on Violent Conflict." *Journal of Peace Research* 46, no. 6: 757–76. doi: 10.1177/0022343309340500.

Bauman, Zygmunt. 2003. *Wasted Lives: Modernity and Its Outcasts.* Wiley.

Bayat, Nikki. 2022. "As Amazon Deforestation Reaches Record Levels, Brazil's Indigenous Continue Preservation Fight." *El Tecolote.* Accessed January 9, 2023, at https://eltecolote.org /content/en/as-amazon-deforestation-reaches-record-levels-brazils-indigenous-continue -preservation-fight/.

Becker, Gary S. 1974. "Crime and Punishment: An Economic Approach." In *Essays in the Economics of Crime and Punishment, Human Behavior and Social Institutions*, edited by W. M. Landes and G. S. Becker, 1–54. National Bureau of Economic Research, distributed by Columbia University Press.

Beetham, David. 1991. *The Legitimation of Power.* Macmillan International Higher Education.

Birch, Kean, and Matti Siemiatycki. 2016. "Neoliberalism and the Geographies of Marketization: The Entangling of State and Markets." *Progress in Human Geography* 40, no. 2: 177–98. doi: 10.1177/0309132515570512.

Borras, Saturnino, Jennifer C. Franco, Sergio Gómez, Cristóbal Kay, and Max Spoor. 2012. "Land Grabbing in Latin America and the Caribbean." *Journal of Peasant Studies* 39, no. 3–4: 845–72. doi: 10.1080/03066150.2012.679931.

Bourdieu, Pierre. 1999. "Rethinking the State." In *State/Culture: State-Formation After the Cultural Turn*, edited by G. Steinmetz, 53–76. Cornell University Press.

Bourdieu, Pierre. 2014. *On the State: Lectures at the Collège de France, 1989–1992.* Edited by P. Champagne, R. Lenoir, F. Poupeau, and M.-C. Rivière. Polity.

Bourgois, Philippe. 2018. "Decolonising Drug Studies in an Era of Predatory Accumulation." *Third World Quarterly* 39, no. 2: 385–98. doi: 10.1080/01436597.2017.1411187.

Bourgois, Philippe I. 2003. *In Search of Respect: Selling Crack in El Barrio.* 2nd ed. Cambridge University Press.

Bradford, James Tharin. 2019. *Poppies, Politics, and Power: Afghanistan and the Global History of Drugs and Diplomacy.* Cornell University Press.

Brass, Jennifer N. 2016. *Allies or Adversaries*. Cambridge University Press.

Breman, Jan. 2004. *Working in the Mill No More*. Amsterdam University Press.

Breman, Jan. 2013. *Outcast Labour in Asia: Circulation and Informalization of the Workforce at the Bottom of the Economy*. Oxford University Press.

Breman, Jan. 2019. *Capitalism, Inequality and Labour in India*. 1st ed. Cambridge University Press.

Brittain, James J. 2005. "A Theory of Accelerating Rural Violence: Lauchlin Currie's Role in Underdeveloping Colombia." *Journal of Peasant Studies* 32, no. 2: 335–60. doi: 10.1080/030 66150500094535.

Brittain, James Jeremiah. 2010. *Revolutionary Social Change in Colombia: The Origin and Direction of the FARC-EP*. Pluto Press.

Britto, Lina. 2020. *Marijuana Boom: The Rise and Fall of Colombia's First Drug Paradise*. University of California Press.

Bunce, Steven. 2019. "Life After Wartime: Post-Conflict Governance in the Bogotá Metropolitan Area." PhD thesis, University of Sydney.

Burnyeat, Gwen. 2022. *The Face of Peace: Government Pedagogy amid Disinformation in Colombia*. University of Chicago Press.

Cairo, Heriberto, Ulrich Oslender, Carlo Emilio Piazzini Suárez, Jerónimo Ríos, Sara Koopman, Vladimir Montoya Arango, Flavio Bladimir Rodríguez Muñoz, and Liliana Zambrano Quintero. 2018. " 'Territorial Peace': The Emergence of a Concept in Colombia's Peace Negotiations." *Geopolitics* 23, no. 2: 464–88. doi: 10.1080/14650045.2018.1425110.

Camacho, Adriana, and Daniel Mejía. 2017. "The Health Consequences of Aerial Spraying Illicit Crops: The Case of Colombia." *Journal of Health Economics* 54:147–60. doi: 10.1016/j.jhealeco.2017.04.005.

Cammett, Melani Claire, and Lauren M. MacLean. 2011. "Introduction: The Political Consequences of Non-State Social Welfare in the Global South." *Studies in Comparative International Development* 46, no. 1: 1–21. doi: 10.1007/s12116-010-9083-7.

Cardona, César Alejandro, Marcela Pinilla, and Aida Gálvez. 2016. "¡A un lado, que viene el progreso! Construcción del proyecto Hidroituango en el cañón del Cauca medio antioqueño." In *Extractivismos y posconflicto en Colombia: Retos para la paz territorial, Biblioteca abierta. Colección general. Perspectivas ambientales*, edited by A. Ulloa and S. Coronado, 303–29. CINEP / Programa por la Paz: Universidad Nacional de Colombia.

Casey, Nicholas. 2019. "Colombia's Peace Deal Promised a New Era: So Why Are These Rebels Rearming?" *New York Times*, May 20.

Centeno, Miguel Angel. 2002. *Blood and Debt: War and the Nation-State in Latin America*. Pennsylvania State University Press.

CEVCR. 2022. *Hallazgos y Recomendaciones*. Comisión para el Esclarecimiento de la Verdad, la Convivencia y la No Repetición.

Chakravarty, Anuradha, ed. 2015. "A History of Clientelism in Rwanda." In *Investing in Authoritarian Rule: Punishment and Patronage in Rwanda's Gacaca Courts for Genocide Crimes*, 47–70. Cambridge University Press.

Chatterjee, Partha. 2004. *The Politics of the Governed: Reflections on Popular Politics in Most of the World*. New York: Columbia University Press.

Chatterjee, Partha. 2008. "Democracy and Economic Transformation in India." *Economic and Political Weekly* 43, no. 16: 53–62.

Ciro Rodríguez, Estefanía. 2019. *Levantados de la selva: Vidas y legitimidades en los territorios cocaleros del Caquetá*. Ediciones Uniandes.

Civico, Aldo. 2016. *Para-State: An Ethnography of Colombia's Death Squads*. University of California Press.

CNMH. 2013. *¡Basta ya! Colombia, memorias de guerra y dignidad: Informe general*. Segunda edición corregida. Centro Nacional de Memoria Histórica.

Collier, Paul. 1999. "Doing Well out of War." In *Conference on Economic Agendas in Civil Wars, London*, vol. 26, p. 27.

Collier, Paul. 2008. *The Bottom Billion: Why the Poorest Countries Are Failing and What Can Be Done About It*. Oxford University Press.

Collier, Paul. 2009. "Post-Conflict Recovery: How Should Strategies Be Distinctive?" *Journal of African Economies* 18, suppl. 1: 199–131. doi: 10.1093/jae/ejp006.

Collier, Paul, and Anke Hoeffler. 2004. "Greed and Grievance in Civil War." *Oxford Economic Papers* 56, no. 4: 563–95.

Collier, Stephen J., James Christopher Mizes, and Antina Von Schnitzler. 2016. "Preface: Public Infrastructures / Infrastructural Publics." *Limn* 7 (July).

CORE. 2021. *Las caras de las disidencias: Cinco años de incertidumbre y evolución*. Fundación Conflict Responses.

Corrigan, Philip, and Derek Sayer. 1985. *The Great Arch: English State Formation as Cultural Revolution*. Blackwell.

Cowan, Tom, Stephen Campbell, and Don Kalb. 2023. "Theorizing Peripheral Labor: Rethinking 'Surplus Populations.'" *Focaal* 2023, no. 97: 7–21. doi: 10.3167/fcl.2023.970102.

Cuéllar Sarmiento, Sebastián. 2009. "Entre la hacienda y la sociedad civil: Lógicas culturales de la guerra en Colombia / Between the Hacienda and Civil Society: Cultural Logics of War in Colombia." Master's thesis, Universidad Nacional de Colombia.

Currie, Lauchlin. 1971. "The Exchange Constraint on Development: A Partial Solution to the Problem." *Economic Journal* 81, no. 324: 886–903. doi: 10.2307/2230323.

Dangl, Benjamin. 2010. *Dancing with Dynamite: Social Movements and States in Latin America*. AK Press.

Das, Veena. 1996. *Critical Events: An Anthropological Perspective on Contemporary India*. Oxford University Press.

Das, Veena, and Deborah Poole, eds. 2004. *Anthropology in the Margins of the State*. First edition. School for Advanced Research Press.

Dávila Ladrón de Guevara, Andrés. 1999. "Clientelismo, Intermediación y Representación Política En Colombia:?' Qué Ha Pasado En Los Noventa?" *Estudios Políticos* 15:61–78.

Davis, Mike. 2006. *Planet of Slums*. Verso.

Denning, Michael. 2010. "Wageless Life." *New Left Review* 66:79–97.

DeSilver, Drew. 2019. "Despite Global Concerns About Democracy, More than Half of Countries Are Democratic." *Pew Research Center*. Accessed October 12, 2024, at https://www.pewresearch.org/short-reads/2019/05/14/more-than-half-of-countries-are-democratic/.

Dest, Anthony. 2021. "The Coca Enclosure: Autonomy Against Accumulation in Colombia." *World Development* 137:105166. doi: 10.1016/j.worlddev.2020.105166.

Dewey, John. 1927. *The Public and Its Problems: An Essay in Political Inquiry*. Penn State Press.

Diamond, Alex. 2018. "Murder in Colombia's Peace Laboratory / Homicidio en el Laboratorio de Paz Colombiano." *NACLA*. Accessed September 27, 2019, https://nacla.org/news/2018/07/24/murder-colombia%E2%80%99s-peace-laboratory-homicidio-en-el-laboratorio-de-paz-colombiano.

Diamond, Alex. 2022. "'The State Is Coming': The Emotional Content of State Formation through a Colombian Coca Substitution Program." *Social Problems* 1–19. doi: 10.1093/socpro/spac042.

Diamond, Alex. 2023. "The Narrative Construction of State (Il)Legitimacy in Colombia's Peace Laboratory." *Sociological Forum* n/a(n/a):1311–33. doi: 10.1111/socf.12971.

Diamond, Alex, and Tomás Gold. Forthcoming. "How Colombian Farmers and Free-Market Think Tank Elites Across Latin America Mobilize Corruption Narratives." In *A Comparative Historical Sociology of Corruption*, edited by M. Garrido, N. Wilson, and M. Zaloznaya. Cambridge University Press.

Dreyfus, Hubert L., and Paul Rabinow. 1983. *Michel Foucault: Beyond Structuralism and Hermeneutics*. University of Chicago Press.

Dube, Oeindrila, Omar García-Ponce, and Kevin Thom. 2016. "From Maize to Haze: Agricultural Shocks and the Growth of the Mexican Drug Sector." *Journal of the European Economic Association* 14, no. 5: 1181–1224. doi: 10.1111/jeea.12172.

Durán-Martínez, Angélica. 2021. "South America: From Acquiescence to Rebellion." In *Transforming the War on Drugs: Warriors, Victims and Vulnerable Regions*, edited by A. Idler and J. C. G. Vergara, 133–60. Hurst Publishers.

Edelman, Marc. 1999. *Peasants Against Globalization: Rural Social Movements in Costa Rica*. Stanford University Press.

Escobar, Arturo. 2011. *Encountering Development: The Making and Unmaking of the Third World*. Princeton University Press.

Escobar, Cristina. 1994. "Clientelism and Social Protest: Peasant Politics in Northern Colombia." In *Democracy, Clientelism, and Civil Society*, edited by L. Roniger and A. Güneş-Ayata, 65–85. Lynne Rienner Publishers.

Espinosa, Nicolás. 2007. "Política de vida y muerte: Apuntes para una gramática del sufrimiento de la guerra en la Sierra de la Macarena." *AIBR: Revista de antropología Iberoamericana* 2(1):43–66. doi: 10.11156/aibr.020105.

FAO, IFAD, Unicef, WFP, and WHO. 2022. *The State of Food Security and Nutrition in the World (SOFI) Report: 2022*. World Food Programme.

Farrell, Maureen. 2023. "Years After Monsanto Deal, Bayer's Roundup Bills Keep Piling Up." *New York Times*, December 6.

Fattal, Alexander L. 2018. *Guerrilla Marketing: Counterinsurgency and Capitalism in Colombia*. University of Chicago Press.

Federico, Giovanni. 2010. *Feeding the World: An Economic History of Agriculture, 1800–2000*. Princeton University Press.

Felbab-Brown, Vanda. 2017. "Organized Crime, Illicit Economies, Civil Violence & International Order: More Complex Than You Think." *Daedalus* 146, no. 4: 98–111. doi: 10.1162/DAED_a_00462.

Ferguson, James. 1990. *The Anti-Politics Machine*. Cambridge University Press.

Ferguson, James. 2015. *Give a Man a Fish: Reflections on the New Politics of Distribution*. Duke University Press.

Ferguson, James, and Akhil Gupta. 2002. "Spatializing States: Toward an Ethnography of Neoliberal Governmentality." *American Ethnologist* 29, no. 4: 981–1002. doi: 10.1525/ae.2002.29.4.981.

Forero Rueda, Sebastián, and Terumoto Fukuda. 2023. "La Crisis de la coca: Areglia agoniza por la caída de los precios." *El Espectador*, April 30.

Foucault, M. 2007. *Security, Territory, Population: Lectures at the College De France, 1977—78.* Springer.

Fox, Jonathan. 1993. *The Politics of Food in Mexico: State Power and Social Mobilization.* Cornell University Press.

Frankel, Jeffrey. 2011. "The Natural Resource Curse: A Survey." In *Beyond the Resource Curse,* edited by B. Shaffer and T. Ziyadov, 17–57. University of Pennsylvania Press.

Friedmann, Harriet, and Philip McMichael. 1989. "Agriculture and the State System: The Rise and Decline of National Agricultural Systems, 1870 to the Present." *Agriculture et systéme étatique: Croissance et déclin de l'agriculture de 1870 à aujourd'hui* 29, no. 2: 93. doi: 10.1111/j.1467–9523.1989.tb00360.x.

Front Line Defenders. 2023. *Global Analysis 2022.* Front Line Defenders.

Gaventa, John. 1982. *Power and Powerlessness: Quiescence and Rebellion in an Appalachian Valley.* University of Illinois Press.

Gay, Robert. 1994. *Popular Organization and Democracy in Rio de Janeiro: A Tale of Two Favelas.* Temple University Press.

Ghiabi, Maziyar. 2022. "Critique of Everyday Narco-Capitalism." *Third World Quarterly* 43, no. 11: 2557–76. doi: 10.1080/01436597.2022.2053776.

Gill, Lesley. 2016. *A Century of Violence in a Red City: Popular Struggle, Counterinsurgency, and Human Rights in Colombia.* Duke University Press.

Gliessman, Steve. 2018. "Defining Agroecology." *Agroecology and Sustainable Food Systems* 42, no. 6: 599–600. doi: 10.1080/21683565.2018.1432329.

Goldstein, Joshua S. 2012. *Winning the War on War: The Decline of Armed Conflict Worldwide.* Reprint edition. Plume.

Gomez-Suarez, Andrei. 2017. "Peace Process Pedagogy: Lessons from the No-Vote Victory in the Colombian Peace Referendum." *Comparative Education* 53, no. 3: 462–82. doi: 10.1080/03050068.2017.1334425.

González Perafán, Leonardo, Juana Valentina Cabezas Palacios, and Paco Zimmermann. 2021. *Los focos del conflicto en Colombia: Informe sobre presencia de grupos armados.* Indepaz.

González, Ximena. 2019. "Comunidades votaron en 10 consultas populares mineras desde el 2013." *La República,* March 20.

Goodhand, Jonathan, Patrick Meehan, Jasmine Bhatia, Maziyar Ghiabi, and Francisco Gutierrez Sanin. 2021. "Critical Policy Frontiers: The Drugs-Development-Peacebuilding Trilemma." *International Journal of Drug Policy* 89, no. 103115.

Gootenberg, Paul. 2008. *Andean Cocaine: The Making of a Global Drug.* University of North Carolina Press.

Gootenberg, Paul. 2017. "Cocaine Histories and Diverging Drug War Politics in Bolivia, Colombia, and Peru." *A Contracorriente* 15, no. 1: 1–35.

Gootenberg, Paul. 2021. "Shifting South: Cocaine's Historical Present and the Changing Politics of Drug War, 1975–2015." In *Cocaine: From Coca Fields to the Streets,* edited by E. D. Arias and T. Grisaffi, 287–316. Duke University Press.

Grajales, Jacobo. 2013. "State Involvement, Land Grabbing and Counter-Insurgency in Colombia." *Development and Change* 44, no. 2: 211–32. doi: 10.1111/dech.12019.

Grajales, Jacobo. 2021. *Agrarian Capitalism, War and Peace in Colombia: Beyond Dispossession.* Routledge.

Gramsci, Antonio. 1991. *Prison Notebooks.* Columbia University Press.

Grisaffi, Thomas. 2018. *Coca Yes, Cocaine No: How Bolivia's Coca Growers Reshaped Democracy.* Duke University Press.

Gudynas, Eduardo. 2018. "Extractivisms: Tendencies and Consequences." In *Reframing Latin American Development*. Routledge.

Guldi, Jo. 2012. *Roads to Power: Britain Invents the Infrastructure State.* Harvard University Press.

Gupta, Akhil. 1995. "Blurred Boundaries: The Discourse of Corruption, the Culture of Politics, and the Imagined State." *American Ethnologist* 22, no. 2: 375–402.

Gupta, Akhil. 1998. *Postcolonial Developments: Agriculture in the Making of Modern India.* Duke University Press.

Gupta, Akhil. 2018. "The Future in Ruins: Thoughts on the Temporality of Infrastructure." In *The Promise of Infrastructure*, edited by N. Anand, A. Gupta, and H. Appel, 62–79. Duke University Press.

Gutiérrez Sanín, Francisco. 1998. "La Ciudad Representada: Política y Conflicto En Bogotá." *IEPRI-Tercer Mundo*.

Gutiérrez Sanín, Francisco. 2004. "Criminal Rebels? A Discussion of Civil War and Criminality from the Colombian Experience." *Politics & Society* 32, no. 2: 257–85. doi: 10.1177/0032329204263074.

Gutiérrez Sanín, Francisco. 2008. "Telling the Difference: Guerrillas and Paramilitaries in the Colombian War." *Politics & Society* 36, no. 1: 3–34. doi: 10.1177/0032329207312181.

Gutiérrez Sanín, Francisco. 2019a. *Clientelistic Warfare: Paramilitaries and the State in Colombia (1982–2007).* Peter Lang.

Gutiérrez Sanín, Francisco. 2019b. "The Politics of Peace: Competing Agendas in the Colombian Agrarian Agreement and Implementation." *Peacebuilding* 7, no. 3: 1–15.

Gutiérrez Sanín, Francisco. 2020. *¿Un nuevo ciclo de la guerra en Colombia?* First edition. Debate.

Habermas, Jürgen. 1991. *The Structural Transformation of the Public Sphere: An Inquiry into a Category of Bourgeois Society.* MIT Press.

Hagene, Turid. 2015. "Political Clientelism in Mexico: Bridging the Gap Between Citizens and the State." *Latin American Politics and Society* 57, no. 1: 139–62.

Hanlon, Joseph. 1991. *Mozambique: Who Calls the Shots?* James Currey Publishers.

Hansen, Thomas Blom, and Finn Stepputat. 2001. "Introduction: States of Imagination." In *States of Imagination: Ethnographic Explorations of the Postcolonial State, Politics, History, and Culture*, edited by T. B. Hansen and F. Stepputat, 1–40. Duke University Press.

Harvey, David. 2003. *The New Imperialism.* Oxford University Press.

Harvey, Penny. 2005. "The Materiality of State-Effects: An Ethnography of a Road in the Peruvian Andes." In *State Formation: Anthropological Perspectives, Anthropology, Culture, and Society*, edited by C. Krohn-Hansen and K. G. Nustad, 123–42. Pluto Press.

Havel, Vaclav. 2009. *The Power of the Powerless.* Routledge.

Hintjens, Helen, and Dubravka Zarkov. 2014. *Conflict, Peace, Security and Development: Theories and Methodologies.* Routledge.

Hobbes, Thomas. 1998 [1651]. *Leviathan.* Edited by J. C. A. Gaskin. Oxford University Press.

Högbladh, Stina. 2012. "Peace Agreements 1975–2011: Updating the UCDP Peace Agreement Dataset." In *States in Armed Conflict 2011: Department of Peace and Conflict Research Report*, edited by T. Petterson and L. Themner, 39–56. Uppsala University.

Hough, Phillip A. 2011. "Guerrilla Insurgency as Organized Crime: Explaining the So-Called 'Political Involution' of the Revolutionary Armed Forces of Colombia." *Politics & Society* 39, no. 3: 379–414. doi: 10.1177/0032329211415505.

Hough, Phillip A. 2022. *At the Margins of the Global Market: Making Commodities, Workers, and Crisis in Rural Colombia*. Cambridge University Press.

Human Rights Watch. 2000. *Colombia: The Ties That Bind: Colombia and Military-Paramilitary Links*. Human Rights Watch.

Huntington, Samuel P. 1993. *The Third Wave: Democratization in the Late Twentieth Century*. University of Oklahoma Press.

Hylton, Forrest. 2006. *Evil Hour in Colombia*. London ; New York: Verso.

Hylton, Forrest, and Aaron Tauss. 2016. "Peace in Colombia: A New Growth Strategy: Colombia's Peace Deal Is a Remarkable Achievement, but Its Economic Implications Are Troubling." *NACLA Report on the Americas* 48, no. 3: 253–59. doi: 10.1080/10714839.2016.1228174.

Idler, Annette, and Juan Carlos Garzón Vergara. 2021. "Introduction: Fifty Years of the War on Drugs: A Moment of Uncertainty." In *Transforming the War on Drugs: Warriors, Victims and Vulnerable Regions*, edited by A. Idler and J. C. Garzón Vergara, 1–17. Hurst Publishers.

International Crisis Group. 2021a. *A Broken Canopy: Deforestation and Conflict in Colombia*. International Crisis Group.

International Crisis Group. 2021b. *Deeply Rooted: Coca Eradication and Violence in Colombia*.

IPC, Agencia de Prensa. 2023. "Las AGC habrían infiltrado el paro minero en el Bajo Cauca." *Agencia de Prensa IPC*. Accessed December 14, 2024, at https://www.ipc.org.co/agenciadeprensa/las-agc-habrian-infiltrado-el-paro-minero-en-el-bajo-cauca/.

Isacson, Adam. 2021. *A Long Way to Go: Implementing Colombia's Peace Accord After Five Years*. Washington Office on Latin America.

Isacson, Adam. 2023. *Crisis and Opportunity: Unraveling Colombia's Collapsing Coca Markets*. Washington Office on Latin America.

Jaramillo, Carlos Felipe. 2001. "Liberalization, Crisis, and Change: Colombian Agriculture in the 1990s." *Economic Development and Cultural Change* 49, no. 4: 821–46. doi: 10.1086/452526.

Jaramillo, Juan Camilo. 2019. "Half of All Destroyed Coca Crops Replanted in Colombia." *InSight Crime*. Accessed July 8, 2022, at https://insightcrime.org/news/brief/half-coca-crops-replanted-colombia/.

Jaramillo, Sergio. 2014. "La Paz Territorial," paper presented March 13 at Harvard University and subsequently published by Alto Comisionado para la Paz, Bogotá. Accessed at https://interaktive-demokratie.org/files/downloads/La-Paz-Territorial.pdf.

Kalyvas, Stathis N. 2006. *The Logic of Violence in Civil War*. Cambridge University Press.

Kamola, Isaac A. 2008. "Coffee and Genocide: A Political Economy of Violence in Rwanda." *Transition: An International Review* 99:54–72. doi: 10.2979/TRS.2008.-.99.54.

Karl, Robert A. 2017. *Forgotten Peace: Reform, Violence, and the Making of Contemporary Colombia*. University of California Press.

Kasmir, Sharryn, and August Carbonella, eds. 2014. *Blood and Fire: Toward a Global Anthropology of Labor*. Berghahn Books.

Keane, Conor. 2016. "The Impact of Bureaucratic Conflict on US Counternarcotics Efforts in Afghanistan." *Foreign Policy Analysis* 12, no. 3: 295–314.

Kearney, Michael. 1996. *Reconceptualizing the Peasantry: Anthropology in Global Perspective*. Avalon Publishing.

Keen, David. 2000. "Incentives and Disincentives for Violence." In *Greed and Grievance: Economic Agendas in Civil Wars*, edited by M. Berdal and D. M. Malone, 19–42. Lynne Reinner Publishers, International Development Research Centre.

Kernaghan, Richard. 2009. *Coca's Gone: Of Might and Right in the Huallaga Post-Boom.* Stanford University Press.

Kingsbury, Benedict, and Nahuel Maisley. 2021. "Infrastructures and Laws: Publics and Publicness." *Annual Review of Law and Social Science* 17, no. 1: 353–73. doi: 10.1146/annurev-lawsocsci-011521-082856.

Kitschelt, Herbert, and Steven Wilkinson, eds. 2007. *Patrons, Clients, and Policies: Patterns of Democratic Accountability and Political Competition.* Cambridge University Press.

Klein Goldewijk, Kees, Arthur Beusen, and Peter Janssen. 2010. "Long-Term Dynamic Modeling of Global Population and Built-Up Area in a Spatially Explicit Way: HYDE 3.1." *The Holocene* 20, no. 4: 565–73. doi: 10.1177/0959683609356587.

Koram, Kojo. 2022. "Phantasmal Commodities: Law, Violence and the Juris-Diction of Drugs." *Third World Quarterly* 43, no. 11: 2731–46. doi: 10.1080/01436597.2022.2079486.

Kröger, Markus. 2020. "Deforestation, Cattle Capitalism and Neodevelopmentalism in the Chico Mendes Extractive Reserve, Brazil." *Journal of Peasant Studies* 47, no. 3: 464–82. doi: 10.1080/03066150.2019.1604510.

Krohn-Hansen, Christian. 2022. *Jobless Growth in the Dominican Republic Disorganization, Precarity, and Livelihoods.* Stanford University Press.

Lachmann, Richard. 2010. *States and Power.* Polity.

Lapegna, Pablo. 2016. *Soybeans and Power: Genetically Modified Crops, Environmental Politics, and Social Movements in Argentina.* Oxford University Press.

Latouche, Serge. 1993. *In the Wake of the Affluent Society: An Exploration of Post-Development.* Zed Books.

Lederach, Angela Jill. 2023. *Feel the Grass Grow: Ecologies of Slow Peace in Colombia.* First edition. Stanford University Press.

Leech, Garry M. 2011. *FARC: The Longest Insurgency.* Zed Books.

Lemaitre Ripoli, Julieta. 2018. *El estado siempre llega tarde: La reconstrucción de la vida cotidiana después de la guerra.* Siglo XXI-Argentina.

Lemay-Hébert, Nicolas. 2014. "The Political Sociology of Statebuilding: Looking Beyond Weber." In *Conflict, Peace, Security and Development: Theories and Methodologies*, edited by H. Hintjens and D. Zarkov, 52–65. Routledge.

Levenson, Zachary. 2022. *Delivery as Dispossession: Land Occupation and Eviction in the Post-apartheid City.* First edition. Oxford University Press.

Levi, Margaret, Audrey Sacks, and Tom Tyler. 2009. "Conceptualizing Legitimacy, Measuring Legitimating Beliefs." *American Behavioral Scientist* 53, no. 3: 354–75. doi: 10.1177/0002764209338797.

Levien, Michael. 2013. "Regimes of Dispossession: From Steel Towns to Special Economic Zones." *Development and Change* 44, no. 2: 381–407.

Li, Tania. 2007. *The Will to Improve: Governmentality, Development, and the Practice of Politics.* Duke University Press.

Li, Tania Murray. 2010. "To Make Live or Let Die? Rural Dispossession and the Protection of Surplus Populations." *Antipode* 41, s1: 66–93. doi: 10.1111/j.1467–8330.2009.00717.x.

Li, Tania Murray. 2014. *Land's End: Capitalist Relations on an Indigenous Frontier.* Duke University Press.

Lobo, Gregory J. 2017. "Charisma and Nation in the Hegemony of Uribismo in Colombia." In *Territories of Conflict: Traversing Colombia Through Cultural Studies*, edited by A. F. Castro, A. Herrero-Olaizola, and C. Rutter-Jensen, 80–94. Boydell & Brewer.

Loveman, Mara. 2005. "The Modern State and the Primitive Accumulation of Symbolic Power." *American Journal of Sociology* 110, no. 6: 1651–83. doi: 10.1086/428688.

Lujala, Päivi, Siri Aas Rustad, and Sarah Kettenmann. 2016. "Engines for Peace? Extractive Industries, Host Countries, and the International Community in Post-Conflict Peacebuilding." *Natural Resources* 07, no. 05: 239–50. doi: 10.4236/nr.2016.75021.

Lund, Christian. 2017. "Rule and Rupture: State Formation Through the Production of Property and Citizenship." In *Rule and Rupture: State Formation Through the Production of Property and Citizenship*, edited by M. Eilenberg and C. Lund. John Wiley & Sons.

Lyons, Kristina M. 2020. *Vital Decomposition: Soil Practitioners and Life Politics*. Duke University Press.

Mac Ginty, Roger, and Oliver P. Richmond. 2013. "The Local Turn in Peace Building: A Critical Agenda for Peace." *Third World Quarterly* 34, no. 5: 763–83. doi: 10.1080/01436597.2013.800750.

Machado C., Absalón. 1986. *Políticas agrarias en Colombia, 1900–1960*. First edition. Centro de Investigaciones para el Desarrollo.

Macrotrends. 2024. "Coffee Prices: 45-Year Historical Chart." Accessed January 8, 2024, at https://www.macrotrends.net/2535/coffee-prices-historical-chart-data.

Maldonado Aranda, Salvador. 2013. "Stories of Drug Trafficking in Rural Mexico: Territories, Drugs and Cartels in Michoacán." *Revista Europea de estudios Latinoamericanos y del Caribe / European Review of Latin American and Caribbean Studies* 94:43–66.

Mann, Michael. 1984. "The Autonomous Power of the State: Its Origins, Mechanisms and Results." *European Journal of Sociology* 25, no. 2: 185–213.

Mansfield, David. 2016. *A State Built on Sand: How Opium Undermined Afghanistan*. Oxford University Press.

Marres, N. 2012. *Material Participation: Technology, the Environment and Everyday Publics*. 2012 edition. Palgrave Macmillan.

Marx, Karl. 1942. *Capital*. J. M. Dent & Sons, E. P. Dutton.

Massé, Frédéric, and Philippe Le Billon. 2017. "Gold Mining in Colombia, Post-War Crime and the Peace Agreement with the FARC." *Third World Thematics: A TWQ Journal* 3, no. 1: 1–19. doi: 10.1080/23802014.2017.1362322.

Matsuzaki, Reo. 2019. *Statebuilding by Imposition: Resistance and Control in Colonial Taiwan and the Philippines*. Cornell University Press.

McMichael, Philip. 2005. "Global Development and The Corporate Food Regime." In *New Directions in the Sociology of Global Development*, vol. 11, *Research in Rural Sociology and Development*, edited by F. H. Buttel and P. McMichael, 265–99. Emerald Group Publishing.

McMichael, Philip. 2009. "A Food Regime Genealogy." *Journal of Peasant Studies* 36, no. 1: 139–69. doi: 10.1080/03066150902820354.

Meehan, Patrick. 2021. "Precarity, Poverty and Poppy: Encountering Development in the Uplands of Shan State, Myanmar." *International Journal of Drug Policy* 89:103064. doi: 10.1016/j.drugpo.2020.103064.

Mejía, Daniel, and Daniel M. Rico. 2010. *La microeconomía de la producción y tráfico de cocaína en Colombia*. Universidad de los Andes: CEDE.

Mercille, Julien. 2011. "Violent Narco-Cartels or US Hegemony? The Political Economy of the 'War on Drugs' in Mexico." *Third World Quarterly* 32, no. 9: 1637–53. doi: 10.1080/01436597.2011.619881.

Meyer, Peter J. 2023. *U.S. Foreign Assistance to Latin America and the Caribbean: FY2024 Appropriations*. Congressional Research Service.

Mezzadra, Sandro, and Brett Neilson. 2019. *The Politics of Operations: Excavating Contemporary Capitalism*. Duke University Press.

Migdal, Joel S. 1988. *Strong Societies and Weak States: State-Society Relations and State Capabilities in the Third World*. Princeton University Press.

Migdal, Joel S. 2001. *State in Society: Studying How States and Societies Transform and Constitute One Another*. Cambridge University Press.

Millar, Kathleen M. 2014. "The Precarious Present: Wageless Labor and Disrupted Life in Rio de Janeiro, Brazil." *Cultural Anthropology* 29, no. 1: 32–53. doi: 10.14506/ca29.1.04.

Miller, Peter, and Nikolas Rose. 1990. "Governing Economic Life." *Economy and Society* 19, no. 1: 1–31.

Mitchell, Lisa. 2023. *Hailing the State: Indian Democracy Between Elections*. Duke University Press.

Mitchell, Timothy. 2002. *Rule of Experts: Egypt, Techno-Politics, Modernity*. University of California Press.

Monsalve Gaviria, Ricardo. 2018. "Disidencias y Su Crecimiento Alarmante En Antioquia." *El Colombiano*, July 12.

Morgan, Kimberly J., and Ann Shola Orloff, eds. 2017. *The Many Hands of the State: Theorizing Political Authority and Social Control*. New York, NY: Cambridge University Press.

Morris, Nathaniel. 2020. "Serrano Communities and Subaltern Negotiation Strategies: The Local Politics of Opium Production in Mexico, 1940–2020." *Social History of Alcohol and Drugs* 34, no. 1: 48–81. doi: 10.1086/707589.

Mosse, David. 2010. *Cultivating Development: An Ethnography of Aid Policy and Practice*. Sage Publications India.

Munck, Ronaldo. 2013. "The Precariat: A View from the South." *Third World Quarterly* 34, no. 5: 747–62. doi: 10.1080/01436597.2013.800751.

Nadal, Paco Gómez. 2016. "Jesucristo contra la paz con 'ideología de género.'" *Colombia Plural*. Accessed December 26, 2022, at https://colombiaplural.com/jesucristo-la-paz-ideologia-genero/.

Negretto, Gabriel L., ed. 2013. "Constitutional Change as a Response to State Failure: Colombia 1991." In *Making Constitutions: Presidents, Parties, and Institutional Choice in Latin America*, 166–94. Cambridge University Press.

Nixon, Rob. 2011. *Slow Violence and the Environmentalism of the Poor*. Harvard University Press.

Nordland, Rod. 2010. "U.S. Turns a Blind Eye to Opium in Afghan Town." *New York Times*, March 20.

Nordstrom, Carolyn. 1997. *A Different Kind of War Story*. Philadelphia: University of Pennsylvania Press.

OECD. 2011. *Supporting Statebuilding in Situations of Conflict and Fragility: Policy Guidance*. OECD.

Olarte-Olarte, María Carolina. 2019. "From Territorial Peace to Territorial Pacification: Anti-Riot Police Powers and Socio-Environmental Dissent in the Implementation of Colombia's Peace Agreement." *Revista de Estudios Sociales* 67:26–39. doi: 10.7440/res67.2019.03.

Organization of American States. 2013. *The Drug Problem in the Americas*. Organization of American States.

Ortner, Sherry B. 1995. "Resistance and the Problem of Ethnographic Refusal." *Comparative Studies in Society and History* 37, no. 1: 173–93. doi: 10.1017/S0010417500019587.

Oslender, Ulrich. 2008. "Another History of Violence: The Production of 'Geographies of Terror' in Colombia's Pacific Coast Region." *Latin American Perspectives* 35, no. 5: 77–102. doi: 10.1177/0094582X08321961.

Paarlberg-Kvam, Kate. 2021. "Open-Pit Peace: The Power of Extractive Industries in Post-Conflict Transitions." *Peacebuilding* 9, no. 3: 1–22. doi: 10.1080/21647259.2021.1897218.

Paffenholz, Thania. 2015. "Unpacking the Local Turn in Peacebuilding: A Critical Assessment Towards an Agenda for Future Research." *Third World Quarterly* 36, no. 5: 857–74. doi: 10.1080/01436597.2015.1029908.

Paley, Dawn. 2014. *Drug War Capitalism*. AK Press.

Pardo Pedraza, Diana. 2022. "Landscapes of Suspicion: Minefields and Cleared-Lands in Rural Colombia." *Society for Cultural Anthropology*. Accessed November 7, 2023, at https://culanth .org/fieldsights/landscapes-of-suspicion-minefields-and-cleared-lands-in-rural-colombia.

Paris, Roland. 2002. "International Peacebuilding and the 'Mission Civilisatrice.'" *Review of International Studies* 28, no. 4: 637–56. doi: 10.1017/S026021050200637X.

Pellegrino, Valentina. 2021. "Cifras de papel: La rendición de cuentas del gobierno Colombiano ante la justicia como una manera de incumplir cumpliendo." *Cifras de papel: A prestação de contas do governo Colombiano ante a justiça como forma de "não cumprir cumprindo."* 42:3–27. doi: 10.7440/antipoda42.2021.01.

Peñaranda Currie, Isabel. 2020. "Failure, Politics, and Regional Development: What Developmentalism and Infrastructure Reveal About Present 'Post-Conflict' Programs." *PoLAR: Political and Legal Anthropology Review*. Accessed December 13, 2020, at https://polarjournal .org/2020/11/24/failure-politics-and-regional-development-what-developmentalism-and -infrastructure-reveal-about-present-post-conflict-programs/.

Peñaranda Currie, Isabel, Silvia Otero-Bahamon, and Simón Uribe. 2021. "What Is the State Made of? Coca, Roads, and the Materiality of State Formation in the Frontier." *World Development* 141:105395. doi: 10.1016/j.worlddev.2021.105395.

Phillips, Kristin. 2018. *An Ethnography of Hunger: Politics, Subsistence, and the Unpredictable Grace of the Sun*. Indiana University Press.

Polletta, Francesca. 2006. *It Was Like a Fever: Storytelling in Protest and Politics*. University of Chicago Press.

Polson, Michael. 2013. "Land and Law in Marijuana Country: Clean Capital, Dirty Money, and the Drug War's Rentier Nexus." *PoLAR: Political and Legal Anthropology Review* 36, no. 2: 215–30. doi: 10.1111/plar.12023.

Porter, Roy. 1996. "The History of the 'Drugs Problem.'" *Criminal Justice Matters* 24, no. 1: 3–5. doi: 10.1080/09627259608552771.

Presidencia de la República de Colombia, and FARC-EP. 2016. *Acuerdo final para la terminación del conflicto y la construcción de una paz estable y duradera.*

Przeworski, Adam. 1985. "Material Bases of Consent." In *Capitalism and Social Democracy: Studies in Marxism and Social Theory*, 133–70. Cambridge University Press.

Ramírez, Astríd Torres. 2018. *Colombia nunca más: Extractivismo—graves violaciones a los derechos humanos; Caso Hidroituango una lucha por la memoria y contra la impunidad*. Corporación Jurídica Libertad.

Ramírez Cuellar, Francisco. 2005. *The Profits of Extermination: How U.S. Corporate Power Is Destroying Colombia*. Common Courage Press.

Ramírez, María Clemencia. 2011. *Between the Guerrillas and the State: The Cocalero Movement, Citizenship, and Identity in the Colombian Amazon*. Duke University Press.

Ramírez, María Clemencia. 2015. "The Idea of the State in Colombia: An Analysis from the Periphery." In *State Theory and Andean Politics: New Approaches to the Study of Rule*, edited by C. Krupa and D. Nugent, 35–55. University of Pennsylvania Press.

Redacción Cambio. 2023. "¿Cuántos integrantes tienen los grupos armados ilegales en Colombia?" *Cambio Colombia*, April 13.

Redacción Economía, El. 2022. "Minagricultura anuncia subsidios para 120.000 campesinos." *El Espectador*, October 18.

Redacción Judicial. 2019a. "Hay una resiembra del 50%: Indepaz sobre erradicación forzada de cultivos ilícitos." *El Espectador*, August 4.

Redacción Judicial. 2019b. "Proyectos mineros podrán hacerse sin consultas populares previas." *El Espectador*, February 13.

Redacción Semana. 2023. "La apuesta de Petro que hace aguas: Este es el caos que viven los erradicadores de coca. Dicen que no les pagan y trabajan de manera indigna." *Semana.com: Últimas Noticias de Colombia y el Mundo*, November 15.

Restrepo-Ruiz, María Teresa, and Samuel Martinez. 2009. "The Impact of Plan Colombia on Forced Displacement." *International Migration and Human Rights: The Global Repercussions of U.S. Policy*, edited by S. Martinez, 199–215. University of California Press.

Richani, Nazih. 2013. *Systems of Violence*. State University of New York Press.

Rico Reyes, Guillermo. 2019. *Hidroituango: Las masacres que taparon con el agua*.

Roa-Clavijo, Felipe. 2021. *The Politics of Food Provisioning in Colombia: Agrarian Movements and Negotiations with the State*. Routledge.

Robinson, William I. 1999. "Latin America in the Age of Inequality: Confronting the New 'Utopia.'" *International Studies Review* 1, no. 3: 41–67.

Román, Martín Humberto, Alfonso Insuasty Rodríguez, José Fernando Valencia Grajales Valencia Grajales, and Hector Alejandro Zuluaga Cometa Zuluaga Cometa. 2020. *Proyecto Hidroituango: La historia de una tragedia*. Editorial Kavilando.

Romero, César. 2016. "Los cambios en el acuerdo de paz." *Centro Nacional de Memoria Histórica*. Accessed December 26, 2022, at https://centrodememoriahistorica.gov.co/los-cambios-en -el-acuerdo-de-paz/.

Rose, Nikolas S., and Peter Miller. 2008. *Governing the Present: Administering Economic, Social and Personal Life*. Polity.

Roseberry, William. 1994. "Hegemony and the Language of Contention." In *Everyday Forms of State Formation*, edited by G. M. Joseph and D. Nugent, 355–66. Duke University Press.

Rostow, W. W. 1971. *The Stages of Economic Growth: A Non-Communist Manifesto*. Second edition. University Press.

Rudqvist, Anders, and Fred Van Sluys. 2005. *Informe final de evaluación de medio término Laboratorio de Paz del Magdalena Medio*. European Consultants Organization.

RUV. 2023. *Registro único de víctimas*. Accessed at https://www.unidadvictimas.gov.co/es/registro -unico-de-victimas-ruv/37394.

Sánchez-Moreno, Maria McFarland. 2005. "Smoke and Mirrors." Human Rights Watch.

Sankey, Kyla. 2020. "The Political Economy of Mining in Colombia: The New Face of Globalization?" In *Latin American Extractivism: Dependency, Resource Nationalism, and Resistance in Broad Perspective*, edited by S. Ellner, 33–54. Rowman & Littlefield.

Sanyal, Kalyan K. 2007. *Rethinking Capitalist Development: Primitive Accumulation, Governmentality and Post-Colonial Capitalism*. Routledge.

Sayer, Derek. 1994. "Everyday Forms of State Formation: Some Dissident Remarks on Hege-mony." In *Everyday Forms of State Formation: Revolution and the Negotiation of Rule in Modern Mexico*, edited by G. M. Joseph and D. Nugent. Duke University Press.

Scott, James C. 1977. *The Moral Economy of the Peasant: Rebellion and Subsistence in Southeast Asia*. Yale University Press.

Scott, James C. 1985. *Weapons of the Weak: Everyday Forms of Peasant Resistance*. Yale University Press.

Scott, James C. 1998. *Seeing Like a State: How Certain Schemes to Improve the Human Condition Have Failed*. Yale University Press.

Scott, James C. 2009. *The Art of Not Being Governed: An Anarchist History of Upland Southeast Asia*. Yale University Press.

Segura, Renata, and Delphine Mechoulan. 2017. *Historical Background and Past Peace Processes*. International Peace Institute.

Selby, Jan. 2008. "The Political Economy of Peace Processes." Pp. 11–29 in *Whose Peace? Critical Perspectives on the Political Economy of Peacebuilding, New Security Challenges Series*, edited by M. Pugh, N. Cooper, and M. Turner, 11–29. Palgrave Macmillan UK.

Serje, Margarita. 2005. *El revés de la nación: Territorios salvajes, fronteras y tierras de nadie*. First edition. Universidad de los Andes, Colombia.

Serje, Margarita. 2012. "El mito de la ausencia del Estado: La incorporación económica de las 'zonas de frontera' en Colombia." *Cahiers des Amériques latines* 71:95–117. doi: 10.4000/cal.2679.

Shah, Alpa. 2019. *Nightmarch: Among India's Revolutionary Guerrillas*. University of Chicago Press.

Shams, Tahseen. 2020. *Here, There, and Elsewhere: The Making of Immigrant Identities in a Glo-balized World*. Stanford University Press.

Simpson, Audra. 2014. *Mohawk Interruptus: Political Life Across the Borders of Settler States*. Duke University Press.

Smith, Gavin. 1989. *Livelihood and Resistance: Peasants and the Politics of Land in Peru*. University of California Press.

Soifer, Hillel. 2008. "State Infrastructural Power: Approaches to Conceptualization and Mea-surement." *Studies in Comparative International Development* 43, no. 3-4: 231–51. doi: 10.1007/s12116-008-9028-6.

Sojo, Giordana García. 2023. "Un año del gobierno de Gustavo Petro y Francia Márquez." *CELAG*. Accessed January 4, 2024, at https://www.celag.org/un-ano-del-gobierno-de-gustavo-petro-y-francia-marquez/.

Staniland, Paul. 2012. "States, Insurgents, and Wartime Political Orders." *Perspectives on Politics* 10, no. 2: 243–64.

Star, Susan Leigh, and Karen Ruhleder. 1996. "Steps Toward an Ecology of Infrastructure: Design and Access for Large Information Spaces." *Information Systems Research* 7, no. 1: 111–34. doi: 10.1287/isre.7.1.111.

Stepputat, Finn. 1999. "Repatriation and Everyday Forms of State Formation in Guatemala." In *The End of the Refugee Cycle? Refugee Repatriation and Reconstruction*, edited by R. Black and K. Koser, 210–26. Berghahn Books.

Stoll, David. 1993. *Between Two Armies in the Ixil Towns of Guatemala*. Columbia University Press.

Stuart, Forrest. 2018. "Introspection, Positionality, and the Self as Research Instrument Toward a Model of Abductive Reflexivity." In *Approaches to Ethnography: Analysis and Representation in Participant Observations*, edited by C. Jerolmack and S. Khan, 211–37. Oxford University Press.

Sullivan, Zoe. 2019. "The Real Reason the Amazon Is On Fire." *Time*, August 26.

Tate, Winifred. 2015. *Drugs, Thugs, and Diplomats: U.S. Policymaking in Colombia*. Stanford University Press.

Taussig, Michael T. 1986. *Shamanism, Colonialism, and the Wild Man: A Study in Terror and Healing*. University of Chicago Press.

Taussig, Michael T. 1999. *Defacement: Public Secrecy and the Labor of the Negative*. Stanford University Press.

Thomas, Deborah A. 2019. *Political Life in the Wake of the Plantation: Sovereignty, Witnessing, Repair*. Duke University Press.

Thomson, Frances. 2023. "Escaping Capitalist Market Imperatives: Commercial Coca Cultivation in the Colombian Amazon." *Journal of Peasant Studies* 51, no. 4: 1–35. doi: 10.1080/03066150.2023.2224772.

Tilly, Charles. 1990. *Coercion, Capital, and European States, AD 990–1990*. B. Blackwell.

Tubb, Daniel. 2020. *Shifting Livelihoods: Gold Mining and Subsistence in the Chocó, Colombia*. University of Washington Press.

Unidad para la atención y reparación integral a las víctimas. 2022. *Registro Único de Víctimas (RUV)*.

UNODC. 2010. *World Drug Report, 2010*.

UNODC. 2021. *Monitoreo de territorios afectados por cultivos ilícitos 2020*. UNODC-SIMCI.

Urbanik, Marta-Marika, Robby Roks, Michelle Lyttle Storrod, and James Densley. 2020. "Ethical and Methodological Issues in Gang Ethnography in the Digital Age: Lessons from Four Studies in an Emerging Field." In *Gangs in the Era of Internet and Social Media*, edited by C. Melde and F. Weerman, 21–41. Springer International Publishing.

Urbanik, Marta-Marika, and Robert A. Roks. 2020. "GangstaLife: Fusing Urban Ethnography with Netnography in Gang Studies." *Qualitative Sociology* 43, no. 2: 213–33. doi: 10.1007/s11133-020-09445-0.

Uribe, Simón. 2019. "Illegible Infrastructures: Road Building and the Making of State-Spaces in the Colombian Amazon." *Environment and Planning D: Society and Space* 37, no. 5: 886–904. doi: 10.1177/0263775818788358.

Van de Walle, Steven, and Zoe Scott. 2011. "The Political Role of Service Delivery in State-Building: Exploring the Relevance of European History for Developing Countries." *Development Policy Review* 29, no. 1: 5–21. doi: https://doi.org/10.1111/j.1467-7679.2011.00511.x.

Verdad Abierta. 2011. "Investigarán si 'paras' favorecieron proyecto Hidroituango." *Verdad Abierta*. Accessed January 14, 2023, at https://verdadabierta.com/investigaran-si-paras-favorecieron-proyecto-hidroituango/.

Wainwright, Tom. 2016. *Narconomics: How to Run a Drug Cartel*. Ebury.

Weber, Eugen. 1976. *Peasants into Frenchmen: The Modernization of Rural France, 1870–1914*. Stanford University Press.

Weber, Max. 1947. *The Theory of Social and Economic Organization*. Edited by A. M. Henderson and T. Parsons. Martino Fine Books.

Weinstein, Jeremy M. 2007. *Inside Rebellion: The Politics of Insurgent Violence*. Cambridge ; New York: Cambridge University Press.

Welker, Marina. 2014. *Enacting the Corporation: An American Mining Firm in Post-Authoritarian Indonesia*. University of California Press.

Wolf, Eric R. 1955. "Types of Latin American Peasantry: A Preliminary Discussion." *American Anthropologist* 57, no. 3: 452–71.

Zarazaga, Rodrigo. 2014. "Brokers Beyond Clientelism: A New Perspective Through the Argentine Case." *Latin American Politics and Society* 56, no. 3: 23–45. doi: 10.1111/j.1548–2456.2014.00238.x.

Index